MW00359218

What the Bible Really Says

Breaking the Apocalypse Code

What the Bible Really Says

Breaking the Apocalypse Code

Find Out What Hank Hanegraaff REALLY Says
about the End Times
. . . and Why It Matters to You

THOMAS A. HOWE

WIPF & STOCK · Eugene, Oregon

WHAT THE BIBLE REALLY SAYS
Breaking the Apocalypse Code

Wipf & Stock
A Division of Wipf and Stock Publishers
199 W. 8th Ave., Suite 3
Eugene, OR 97401

www.wipfandstock.com

ISBN 13: 978-1-55635-858-6

Manufactured in the U.S.A.

Contents

Tables

Acknowledgments

I WOULD ESPECIALLY LIKE to thank Mr. Doug Beaumont and Dr. Richard Howe who read the manuscript and made many helpful suggestions, observations, and corrections. I would also like to thank Dr. Norman L. Geisler for encouraging me to pursue the publication of this critique. For the many years of guidance, instruction, and correction that I have had the great privilege of experiencing under Dr. Geisler's tutelage I will be eternally grateful.

Introduction

IT IS CUSTOMARY AT the outset of a critical examination to recount the points of agreement between the reviewer and the book reviewed. Rather than work through a list of these, this examination will comment on points of agreement as they arise. Hanegraaff's book, *The Apocalypse Code*, is reported to be able to equip the reader to "Find out what the Bible REALLY says about the end times."[1] This examination will follow the chapter structure of Hanegraaff's book labeling each chapter with the chapter titles of Hanegraaff's book.

This critique will not primarily be an attempt to assert my views as over against Hanegraaff's views. That has been done. My aim is to examine what Hanegraaff claims he is doing to discover whether or not he has accomplished his task. It will be necessary in such a study to critique his views in terms of the accuracy of handling the text, the history, the claims that he makes about the views of others, the validity of his arguments, and other kinds of critiques. Hanegraaff claims to provide his readers with the tools to be able to make judgments about questions of eschatology, and he claims that he will not persuade his reader toward a particular perspective.[2] The question considered here will be, Does he do what he says he is going to do, and does he refrain from doing what he says he will not do?

It must be made clear at the outset of this critique, that I do not necessarily advocate any of the beliefs or positions espoused by those with whom Hanegraaff interacts. Although I am a dispensational-premillennialist, this does not necessarily mean I espouse the beliefs that Tim LaHaye espouses, nor do I necessarily disagree with those views. Even though I may defend the claims of LaHaye against the criticisms of Hanegraaff, the

1. Hank Hanegraaff, *The Apocalypse Code: Find Out What the Bible REALLY Says About the End Times . . . and Why It Matters Today* (Nashville: Thomas Nelson, 2007). Hereinafter referred to as TAC. This acronym is not designed to belittle Hanegraaff's book or its title. It is simply a convenient way of referring to the title without having to re-type it each time.

2. Ibid., 3.

reader should not see this as an agreement with LaHaye's view. Although it may be necessary to assert my own view at times, I will want to keep that at a minimum. It is very difficult to set aside one's own assumptions in these kinds of circumstances, but I will endeavor to do this as much as I am able.

One final observation. Let me adapt to the current task an observation made in another context by Michael J. Buckley.[3] There is no thinker whose conclusions cannot be made to seem absurd by the reduction of his assertions and claims to a few pages in a popular level book where his conclusions are listed as if they were a series of idiosyncratic convictions and his name placed under hopelessly misleading characterizations. This danger is as relevant to my critique of Hanegraaff as it is to Hanegraaff's critiques of Tim LaHaye and others. I hope I can be more successful at avoiding this pitfall than Hanegraaff has.

---

3. Michael J. Buckley, *At the Origins of Modern Atheism* (New Haven: Yale University Press, 1987), 19.

1

Exegetical Eschatology e²

Method vs. Model

Hank Hanegraaff begins his section on Exegetical Eschatology by briefly discussing the book by Hal Lindsey which was published in 1997 by the title, *Apocalypse Code*. It should not escape the reader's notice that, in contrast to Lindsey's book, Hanegraaff's book employs the definite article—*The Apocalypse Code*. This corresponds to the subtitle that promises to give the reader what the Bible "REALLY" says. It should also not escape the reader's notice that interpreters have been making similar claims for at least two thousand years, that is, that so-and-such is going to tell you what the Bible "REALLY" says. Everyone from orthodox Christians to cultists have made the same claim, and it has done them no more honor than it does Hanegraaff. It would have been more in line with the humility of a servant of God to claim that he will endeavor to understand the Bible correctly and make his claims accordingly. Usually, those who claim to tell you what the Bible "REALLY" says are no more successful at it than Hanegraaff. Nevertheless, Hanegraaff declares that he will help the reader learn "to read the Bible for all it's worth!"[1] Hanegraaff says that the "backbone" of his book is a principle which he calls "Exegetical Eschatology."[2] He explains the term 'exegesis'[3] as "the method by which

---

1. TAC, 1.

2. Ibid.

3. I will employ a convention that finds its origin in the discipline of philosophy of language and semantics. When mentioning a word, that is, when I am talking about a word, I will put the word in single quotes, ' '. When I am using a word to refer to something, if I need to set it off from the surrounding text, I will put it in double quotes, " ". Because I am referring to the term 'exegesis' in the text, that is, I am mentioning the word, it is in single quotes.

a student seeks to uncover what an author intended his or her original audience to understand."[4]

EXEGESIS AND ESCHATOLOGY—DEFINING TERMS

Immediately we run into a problem. Hanegraaff tells his reader that "exegesis" is the method by which a student uncovers what an author intended his original audience to understand. The problem with this statement is that Hanegraaff does not tell the reader how to know if the meaning that is found in the text is what the author *intended* his original audience to understand. In fact, Hanegraaff never tells his reader how to discover who the original audience was. With reference to many books of the Bible, the identification of the original audience is a thorny debate, and most scholars are not agreed on who in fact the original audience was of many books of the Bible. For example, was the original audience of Ephesians the Ephesian Christians, the Galatian Christians or both? Which "Hebrews" constituted the original audience of the letter to the Hebrews?

Hanegraaff's claim that exegesis is the effort to discover what the author intended his original audience to understand is not dissimilar to the claim of Functional or Dynamic Equivalence translation theorists about the goal of translation. Eugene Nida and Charles Taber give the following definition of dynamic equivalence translation theory: "Dynamic equivalence is therefore to be defined in terms of the degree to which the receptors of the message in the receptor language respond to it in substantially the same manner as the receptors in the source language."[5] Rainer Schulte and John Biguenet point out that Matthew Arnold denounced the very idea of attempting to produce in a contemporary audience the same response that may have occurred in the original audience: "He [Arnold] elaborates on his own translation theories by discussing various translations of Homer's work. The nature of the impact of Homer's work cannot be reconstructed by the contemporary reader/translator. Thus, to expect the contemporary reader to react to Homer's work the way Homer's audience did in his time would be futile. Translators have to interact with Homer from their own frame of mind."[6] In Arnold's own words, "No one

---

4. TAC, 1.

5. Eugene A. Nida, and Charles A. Taber, *The Theory and Practice of Translating* (Leiden: E. J. Brill, 1969), 24.

6. Rainer Schulte and John Biguenet, ed. *Theories of Translation: An Anthology of*

can tell him [the translator] how Homer affected the Greeks; but there are those who can tell him how Homer affects *them*."[7] Likewise, if "exegesis" is supposed to be the method of uncovering what the author intended his original audience to understand, doesn't it matter who the original was? And how are we to know if the meaning we get from the text is the one the author intended his original audience to understand. And if Hanegraaff cannot tell his readers how to uncover this information, then he has failed even to get his exegetical eschatology off the ground.

Besides this, how can a reader know what an author "intended"? Haven't you had the experience of writing yourself a note, and then, some time later, reading the note and not being able to know what you intended? You can read the words of your note, and you know what the words mean, but you can't for the life of you remember what you intended. AND YOU ARE THE AUTHOR. If sometimes you cannot tell what you intended with your own writing, how can Hanegraaff promise to help you know what the authors of the Bible intended for their original audiences to understand?

The fact is, the term 'exegesis' does not mean what Hanegraaff says it means. The term 'exegesis' is from the Greek word ἐξήγησις (siseḡexe). According to the standard New Testament Greek lexicon, the word means to set forth something in great detail: "explanation, interpretation."[8] In the words of Grant Osborne, "Exegesis means to 'draw out of' a text what it means, in contrast to eisegesis, to 'read into' a text what one wants it to mean."[9] Exegesis is not about uncovering the author's intent. It is about uncovering the meaning of the text. Of course some will say, "That's what he meant!" which is not much different from saying, "That's what he intended!" But, of course, we don't know what he intended. All we know is what he said. Nevertheless, I am willing to give him the benefit of the doubt that what he intended to mean was that exegesis is the effort to uncover the meaning of the text. However, even though we may give him the benefit of the doubt that this is what he intended, it still remains that

Essays from Dryden to Derrida (Chicago: The University of Chicago Press, 1992), 4.

7. Matthew Arnold, *On Translating Homer: Three Lectures Given at Oxford* (London: Longman, Green, Longman, and Roberts, 1861), 3–4 (emphasis in original).

8. *A Greek-English Lexicon of the New Testament and Other Early Christian Literature* 3d ed. s.v. "ἐξήγησις." Hereinafter referred to as BDAG.

9. Grant R. Osborne, *The Hermeneutical Spiral* (Downers Grove, Illinois: InterVarsity Press, 1991), 41.

this is not what he said, and if he cannot more accurately communicate his intent than this, then any reader is going to have a difficult time knowing whether the meaning he gets from the text is what Hanegraaff actually meant.

But, it's not just that he got the definition of 'exegesis' wrong, he also got the definition of 'eschatology' wrong too. Hanegraaff says, "the word *eschatology* is an intimidating word with a simple meaning—the study of end times."[10] Although eschatology certainly does include the study of the end times, that is not what the term means. The term 'eschatology' comes from two Greek words. The first is ἔσχατος (sotahcse), which means "farthest" or "last," and the word λόγος (sogol), which means "word" or "matter."[11] Eschatology is the study of last things. Eschatology includes much more than simply a study of the end times.

These criticisms may sound trivial to some. Why is it even important whether Hanegraaff gets the definitions of these words precisely right. Isn't it close enough? Well, the fact is, he simply got the definitions wrong. One wonders that if Hanegraaff cannot even exegete his own terms, what does this say about his exegesis of the many and varied terms used in the Bible? And these terms aren't even English. Perhaps it says nothing. But, the reader ought to begin to be a bit critical of the kinds of claims that are made in the pages of this "Exegetical Eschatology e²," whatever that means, if the author can't even get some basic definitions correct.

EXEGETICAL ESCHATOLOGY— DEFINING A METHODOLOGY

An exegetical eschatology, according to Hanegraaff, is an exegesis of the relevant biblical passages that are usually associated with the study of eschatology. Hanegraaff says, "I coined the phrase Exegetical Eschatology to underscore that above all else I am deeply committed to a proper method of biblical interpretation rather than to any particular model of eschatology."[12] According to Hanegraaff, the proper methodology includes the notion that, "The plain and proper meaning of a biblical passage must always take precedence over a particular eschatological presupposition

---

10. TAC, 2.

11. BDAG, s.v. "ἔσχατος." BDAG, s.v. "λόγος."

12. TAC, 2 (emphasis in original).

or paradigm."[13] The reader is not told exactly what "the plain and proper meaning" means. It is assumed that the elucidation of the several principles, organized into the acronym "LIGHTS," will make this plain and proper.

It is particularly important to note that Hanegraaff, by his own admission, wants to put tools into the hand of his reader "so that you can draw from Scripture what God intends you to understand rather than uncritically accepting end-time models that may well be foreign to the text."[14] Of course, as the story progresses the reader discovers that Hanegraaff does not necessarily mean that the reader should not accept his end-time model. Hanegraaff assumes that his own musings about the end times are precisely coincident with "what God intends you to understand." So, it is not exactly correct to claim that his goal is to put hermeneutical tools into your hands so that "you can understand" for yourself. Rather, he wants to put tools into your hands and a particular end-time model into your head, namely, his. In fact, Hanegraaff declares, "In the final analysis, my purpose is not to entice you to embrace a particular model of eschatology but to employ a proper method of biblical interpretation."[15] But what if the reader discovers that these tools prove that Hanegraaff's interpretations are wrong—like his definitions? Apparently there is no fear of this since, when Hanegraaff invites the reader to be the judge of Dr. Tim LaHaye's eschatology model, he does not at the same time invite the reader to be the judge of Hanegraaff's eschatology model. In fact, this claim is totally disingenuous. It is obviously the case that Hanegraaff wants to entice the reader to his particular model of eschatology. He believes he can do this by discussing the various hermeneutic tools, but he none the less wants to do this. His criticisms of the claims of Dispensationalists and Premillennialists are calculated to convince the reader that their eschatological systems are wrong and his is right. Now there is certainly nothing wrong with writing a book to claim that your views are correct and your opponents' view are incorrect. The problem is that Hanegraaff attempts to disguise this aim of his book in the guise of a non-partisan effort to "instruct" the reader in proper methods. No doubt he wants to do this, but

13. Ibid.
14. Ibid., 3.
15. Ibid.

he also wants to convince his reader that he is right and they are wrong about eschatology.

LIGHTS

Hanegraaff organizes the hermeneutical principles he will discuss around the acronym LIGHTS. This stands for, the Literal principle, the Illumination principle, the Grammatical principle, the Historical principle, the Typology principle, and the Scriptural Synergy principle (LIGHTS, or perhaps LIGHTSS, or maybe LIGHTSs?).

Literal Principle

Hanegraaff defines his Literal principle as, "to interpret the Word of God just as we interpret other forms of communication—in the most obvious and natural sense."[16] Unfortunately for his reader, Hanegraaff fails to point out that what is "obvious and natural" for one reader may not be obvious or natural for another. After all, how "obvious" is apocalyptic literature? And what counts as "natural" when it comes to the bizarre descriptions of Daniel chapter 7 or the book of Revelation? The problem is not that Hanegraaff's definition is incorrect or that it is unexplained. At this point, one can only hope that he will explain this in his chapter on the literal principle. The problem is, however, he presents this definition as if it is self-evidently plain and proper. He says, "And when Scripture uses a metaphor or a figure of speech, we should interpret it accordingly."[17] But he says this like it is simply a matter of course to identify these things in the text. In fact, this is one of the principle difficulties when dealing with passages like those found in the book of Revelation. What one interpreter calls a metaphor, the next calls literal speech. But Hanegraaff makes this claim like it is so easy "a caveman could do it."

Additionally, the obvious interpretation is not consistently taken by Hanegraaff. Why is it any more obvious that the mark of the Father on the foreheads of the 144,000 is symbolic than real? The description is very precise. The text specifically points out that the mark is "written on their foreheads" (Rev 14:2).[18] The earlier passage, Rev 13:16, stated that the mark of the beast would be placed upon the right hand or forehead, and it

16. Ibid.
17. Ibid.
18. γεγραμμένον ἐπὶ τῶν μετώπων αὐτῶν (Rev 14:2).

would be very difficult to maintain that this was only a symbolic and not a real mark. It seems to be more obvious that one should be consistent in the application of one's hermeneutical principles and take the statement in Rev 14:2 as a literal mark also. If it is literal in 13:16 why not 14:2? And if one is literal and one is symbolic, then the interpreter needs to explain why he thinks this is the right way to take these two references, something Hanegraaff does not bother to do. It would be much more obvious to take them both literally than taking the second one as merely symbolic the way Hanegraaff does. In other words, Hanegraaff advocates taking Rev 14:2 in a most *un*-obvious way.

Also, the obvious interpretation is not always the correct interpretation or even the best interpretation. When Jesus says, "Destroy this temple, and in three days I will raise it up," the obvious interpretation is that Jesus is talking about the temple building. This is, of course, exactly what the Jews thought He meant. In fact, this interpretation is *so* obvious, that it was necessary for John to make sure that the reader understood what Jesus meant: "But He was speaking of the temple of His body" (Jn 2:21).[19] The problem with Hanegraaff's principle is, he does not instruct the reader on how to tell when one should take the obvious meaning or some other meaning. One can only hope that when he gets to the chapter where he explains his principle, that he will instruct the reader on how to do this.

The reader's hope for some instruction is raised by the anticipation of an example that will illustrate what he means. But wait a minute! Didn't Hanegraaff say that he was going to put hermeneutical tools into our hands so that we could be the judge? And didn't he say that ultimately his purpose was not to entice us to embrace a particular eschatology model? Then why now, before he explains the tools, is he telling us what the text means? His example is apparently designed to illustrate the literal principle, but how can the reader be expected to be the judge of whether his understanding of this passage is correct since he hasn't given us the tools yet? He's already telling us what his eschatology model says without letting us be the judge?

But give the man a chance! Let's consider his example:

> For example, the Bible says that at Armageddon the blood of
> Christ's enemies will rise "as high as the horses' bridles for a dis-

---

19. ἐκεῖνος δὲ ἔλεγεν περὶ τοῦ ναοῦ τοῦ σώματος αὐτοῦ (Jn 2:21).

tance of 1,600 stadia" (Revelation 14:20). Does Scripture intend to convey, as LaHaye contends, that Palestine will literally be submerged in a five-foot-deep river of blood that stretches the length of Palestine from north to south—or is the apostle John simply using a common apocalyptic motif to convey massive wartime death and slaughter?[20]

Hanegraaff quotes a portion of Rev 14:20, and he then poses the question, "Does Scripture intend to convey that Palestine will literally be submerged in a five-foot-deep river of blood that stretches the length of Palestine from north to south . . . ?"[21] It is not so much what is said, but how it is said. After depicting LaHaye's claim in the worst possible light, Hanegraaff contrasts this with the other part of the question, "or is the apostle John simply . . ." Well of course the reader, who has yet to be given Hanegraaff's tools, is going to go for the "simply" option! But didn't Hanegraaff say that he was not going to "entice" the reader? But his use of language is calculated to do precisely that.

Also, since we haven't got to Hanegraaff's chapter in which he explains his literal principle, one can only hope that he will include a section on logic—particularly informal fallacies. If so, then the reader will be equipped to see that Hanegraaff has actually committed the fallacy of poisoning the well. He depicts LaHaye's claim in such a way as to poison the reader against LaHaye before he even gets into explaining the principles. If he truly did not want to entice the reader to a particular eschatology principle, he should have presented this dichotomy in a more neutral light. Instead, he attempts to persuade the reader by the way he presents the case: "Is this meant to actually indicate that the blood will literally rise to horses' bridles, or is this a metaphor depicting massive wartime death and slaughter."[22]

But, let's give him the benefit of the doubt and consider his next example:

> Conversely, when Daniel was instructed to seal up prophecy because the time of fulfillment was in the far future (Daniel 8:26; 12:4, 9; cf. 9:24), and John was told not to seal up his prophecy because its fulfillment was near (Revelation 22:10), are we to accept LaHaye's interpretation that by "near" John really intends to

20. TAC, 3–4.

21. Ibid., 4.

22. This is a paraphrase of Hanegraaff's statement on pages 3–4.

communicate "far"? Or, for that matter, might we rightly suppose that the word "far" in Daniel really means "near"? Likewise, could John's repeated use of such words and phrases as "soon" or "the time is near," in reality indicate that he had the twenty-first century in mind? Armed with the principles embodied in Exegetical Eschatology, you will be the judge.[23]

A consideration of Hanegraaff's second example seems to confirm our suspicions. He poses the question, "are we to accept LaHaye's interpretation that by 'near' John really intends to communicate 'far'?" Of course, that depends on what LaHaye actually said. Since Hanegraaff does not bother to give the context in which LaHaye supposedly made these claims—in fact, he does not even bother to give us the name of the book in which he supposedly said it—it is hard to decide whether we should accept his interpretation or not. But also, why is Hanegraaff asking the reader whether we should accept LaHaye's interpretation before he has given us the tools by which to make these decisions? Once again the way Hanegraaff presents the situation is designed to poison the reader against anything LaHaye says. The question is asked in such a way as to elicit a particular response from the reader: "Of course we won't accept this interpretation. How in the world could anyone think that 'near' means 'far'!" And would not *any* reader "rightly suppose" that one should "rightly suppose"? But how can we know what is rightly "supposed" if we don't have the tools that Hanegraaff promised to give us to enable us to rightly suppose?

The word to which Hanegraaff is referring in his example is ἐγγύς (pronounced *engoos*). According to BDAG, the word can have a spatial or a temporal significance. The temporal significance is usually indicated by the English word "near." BDAG says, "pert. to being close in point of time, *near.*"[24] Hanegraaff is certainly correct that the word 'near' means "near." However, when you look at the text of Rev 22:10, you discover something quite curious. The text reads, "And he said to me, 'Do not seal the words of the prophecy of this book, for the time is at hand.'"[25] Notice that the text does not say "its fulfillment is near" as Hanegraaff wants his reader to think. In fact, the word 'fulfillment' does not appear in the text or

23. TAC, 4.

24. BDAG, s.v. "ἐγγύς."

25. Καὶ λέγει μοι· μὴ σφραγίσῃς τοὺς λόγους τῆς προφητητείας τοῦ βιβλίου τούτου, ὁ χαιρὸς γὰρ ἐγγύς ἐστιν (Rev 22:10).

even in the context. But didn't Hanegraaff warn the reader not to engage in *eisegesis*, the "reading into the biblical text something that simply isn't there"?[26] But the word 'fulfillment' "simply isn't there." What Jesus says is, "the time is near" (ὁ χαιρὸς γὰρ ἐγγύς ἐστιν, sugge rag soriahc oh nitse). The question is, to what "time" is Jesus referring? In the context, it seems that Jesus is referring to the prophecy of the book. However, this cannot be assumed. This must be proven. And, if by "time" Jesus means something else, then the term 'near' may in fact indicate something that is far by our standards, but near by God's. But, since Hanegraaff did not see fit to give us the context in which LaHaye makes his claim, nor did he explain what Jesus meant by the word "time," nor did he explain why he thought it necessary to add the word 'fulfillment,' we cannot be expected, as his readers who have not been given the tools, to make such a choice. But of course, as we said, Hanegraaff is not actually expecting his reader to make the choice. What he is expecting is for the reader to agree with him that LaHaye cannot be right, and his tactics bear witness to the fact that this is precisely what he wants.

There is an interesting use of the word 'near' in Matt 24:32–33. The text reads, "Now learn the parable from the fig tree: when its branch has already become tender and puts forth its leaves, you know that summer is near [ἐγγὺς, sugge]; So, you too, when you see all these things, recognize that He is near [ἐγγὺς, sugge], at the door."[27] In the first comparison, Jesus refers to the leaves of the fig tree and the fact that this indicates that summer is near. Here the word 'near' probably refers to a few days. In the second comparison, Jesus refers to those who see the signs He described in the context and that seeing them they should know that He is near. Let us take this as the Preterists do, as a reference to the destruction of the Temple in 70 AD. Knowing that Jesus is near by seeing the signs also probably indicates a very short time, perhaps a matter of hours or minutes. But, the event to which Jesus is referring, according to the Preterists, would not take place for about 40 years from the time that Jesus is speak-

---

26. TAC, 1.

27. Ἀπὸ δὲ τῆς συκῆς μάθετε τὴν παραβολήν· ὅταν ἤδη ὁ κλάδος αὐτῆς γέ νηται ἁπαλὸς καὶ τὰ φύλλα ἐκφύῃ, γινώσκετε ὅτι ἐγγὺς τὸ θέρος· οὕτως καὶ ὑμεῖς, ὅταν ἴδητε πάντα ταῦτα, γινώσετε ὅτι ἐγγὺς ἐστιν ἐπὶ θύραις (Matt 24:32–33).

Figure 1: Time Is Near

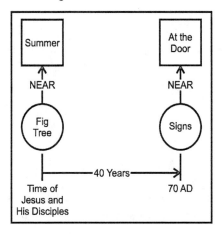

ing. Here, Jesus is referring to an event yet 40 years away as *near*. He does not mean that it is near to the time He is speaking to His disciples, but near to the time when they see "these things." In other words, the word 'near' can be used relative to some point in the present, or some point in the distant future. The event itself was at least 40 years away, but it was near relative to the time of seeing the signs (see Figure 1).

So, seeing the fig tree bring forth leaves would indicate, to the one who sees it, that summer is near for him. So also, seeing the signs yet forty years in the future, Jesus' coming would be near to that person who, forty years from the time of Jesus' statement, would see these signs. So, from the perspective of the one to whom Jesus was speaking, His coming would be far in the future for them, but it would be near for the person who sees those signs at that time. It is possible, then, that this is the way these terms are being used in the passages that LaHaye is interpreting. Of course, we don't know this, but Hanegraaff has misrepresented the case as if it were a straightforward matter of near and far. Maybe it is, but the reader is not given this information by Hanegraaff, and yet Hanegraaff presents LaHaye's view as if it is self-evidently absurd. Maybe LaHaye is wrong, but that's no excuse for Hanegraaff misrepresenting the situation. It may be more complicated than he lets the reader know. Remember what Michael Buckley said: There is no thinker whose conclusions cannot be made to seem absurd by the reduction of his assertions and claims to a few pages in a popular level book where his conclusions are listed as if they were a series of idiosyncratic convictions and his name placed under hopelessly misleading characterizations. This is exactly what Hanegraaff is doing.

What this shows is that the word 'near' is sometimes a relative term. Something is near relative to some given point. Yet Hanegraaff treats the word as if it is necessarily absolute. But that is just not how the word is used. In fact, Hanegraaff has failed to see the difference between sense and reference. The word 'sense' is roughly equivalent to meaning. And the word 'reference' indicates that to which a word refers. A word can have the same meaning, "near," but have a different reference. In the Revelation passage, Jesus could be using the expression "the time is near" to refer to some point in the distant future, that is, it is near relative to some point, for example, relative to some viewer at that time. Another aspect is that some point can be near relative to some measuring standard. That is, according to God's standard of measure, the event is near. According to ours, it may be far. If something is going to happen in 2,000 years, it is near in comparison to the thousands of years of past history. To Abraham the events of the year 2000 would be far away. But, in comparison to Abraham's time, for the disciples in this passage, the events of the year 2000 would be considered near. Now this may not convince anyone, but that is not the point. The point is that Hanegraaff has simply ignored these factors, and he has presented the case as if his point of view is necessarily the correct one. But, this isn't exegesis, and it certainly isn't letting the reader be the judge. He hasn't given the reader the tools, and he is enticing the reader to accept his understanding of these words and to reject LaHaye's. Hanegraaff is not doing what he said he would do, and he is doing what he said he would not do.

Exegesis is the process of bringing out of the text its meaning, and it includes arguing for one's position to try to show why one's interpretation is likely to be correct. Hanegraaff has not done that, nor has he given his reader the tools to do this. You will say, "But he is only in the introduction to the exegetical eschatology. Give him a chance!" But, that's the problem. He is only in the introduction to his exegetical eschatology, and he is already trying to entice the reader to embrace his point of view and his interpretation. Perhaps we should hold our criticisms until we see what he has to say in the chapters on these topics. But, likewise he should have held his attempts to sway the reader until he gave the reader the tools by which the reader could make his own judgment. In fact, that's what he promised to do.

Illumination Principle

The illumination principle of the LIGHTS scheme involves the Spirit. "The Spirit of truth not only provides insights that permeate the mind, but also provides illumination that penetrates the heart."[28] The notion that the Holy Spirit illuminates the mind of the interpreter is a traditional position of evangelical theology and hermeneutics. Hanegraaff goes on to claim, "Clearly, however, the Holy Spirit does not supplant the scrupulous study of Scripture."[29] Exactly how this relationship is explained has been a problem for evangelicals by whomever this doctrine is espoused. Hanegraaff attempts to explain this: "Rather, he provides us with insights that can only be spiritually discerned. Put another way, the Holy Spirit illuminates what is *in* the text; illumination does not *go beyond* the text."[30] Of course this does not really explain anything. What does it mean to "go beyond" the text? If the Holy Spirit gives insights, then how is the interpreter to know which "insights" are from the Spirit and which are not? To say they are "spiritually discerned" doesn't explain it. How does one "spiritually discern" something? And, does spiritual discernment assume an already present amount of Bible knowledge? If so, was that Bible knowledge spiritually discerned? It seems as though one would need to have spiritual discernment before he even studies the Bible in order to assure that his studying does not yield incorrect "insights." But, if an interpreter must have spiritual discernment first, from where does this come, and how can the interpreter know that what seems to be spiritual discernment isn't actually the activity of the deceiver? Many interpreters claim to have spiritual discernment and that their insights have been given to them by the Holy Spirit. Benny Hinn claimed that he had spiritual discernment. But, if he actually believed that his "insights" were given to him by the Spirit, but it turned out that these insights were wrong, how can the average interpreter expect to guard against being deceived? Perhaps these issues will be ironed out in Hanegraaff's chapter on the Illumination principle.

It is particularly interesting that to "underscore the significance of the illumination principle of Exegetical Eschatology," Hanegraaff will "shine this principle on beliefs . . ." However, in the first paragraph of this sec-

28. TAC, 4.
29. Ibid.
30. Ibid.

tion, Hanegraaff indicated that "illumination" or "shining" was the work of the Holy Spirit. On what basis does Hanegraaff assume the responsibility of the Holy Spirit in illuminating the text? What he seems to mean is that, because *he* has been illuminated by the Holy Spirit and has spiritual discernment, *he* will use this to help the rest of us see. But, how do we know that his insights really are from the Holy Spirit? Of course, the basis of his action is obviously his superior eschatology method. He is going to illuminate his reader about the truth, or falsehood, of dispensational eschatology. Once again Hanegraaff is feeding the reader with his eschatological perspective before he has given the reader the tools by which to be the judge. Once again he is poisoning the well.

And, there is nothing like misrepresentation to make your view look good and the other guy's view look bad. Hanegraaff says the "pretribulation rapture" is "dispensational eschatology's cardinal doctrine."[31] This simply is not true. There are a myriad of dispensationalists who hold to a midtribulation rapture view, or a posttribulation rapture view, or a pre-wrath rapture view. Pretribulation rapture is not a "cardinal doctrine" of Dispensationalism. Also, there is nothing like chronological snobbery—that's a term to identify a certain logical fallacy of making a view look false on the basis of when it was believed or when it was first articulated—to make an opponent's view seem false. Hanegraaff says, "As we will see, prior to the nineteenth century, all Christians—including all premillennialists—believed the rapture or the resurrection of believers and the visible bodily return of Christ were simultaneous events."[32] What "all Christians" believed in the past, or even in the present, does not determine whether a belief is true or false. The only thing anyone can prove from the fact that all Christians believed something is that they all believed it. But, to "go beyond" that, it is very unlikely that Hanegraaff, or any historian of theology, can say for certain what "all Christians" believed in the past. Most of the lives of most of the Christians are not recorded in the annals of history. How do we know this? Well, we have historical records of the fact that large numbers of Christians existed at various times in history, but we have no records of their individual lives or what they individually believed. So, Hanegraaff has not only committed the fallacy of chronological snobbery, he has also committed the fallacy of hasty generalization. There

31. Ibid., 5.
32. Ibid.

14

is no way he can know what "all Christians" believed with reference to a controversial doctrine prior to the nineteenth century. As Don O'Leary points out, "Until the late twentieth century there were no opinion polls providing a mass of information about religious beliefs and practices."[33] The kind of statement Hanegraaff uses is calculated to make the view criticized look as bad as possible.

Besides, it is absurd to disregard a view because it was not thought of in the past. The claims of relativity physics were not thought of in the past, but that hardly disqualifies Einstein's assertions. The beliefs of later generations may be discovered as latent in older members of a tradition. The wisdom of analysis is not to reject that which is new, but to discover the development of thought that has issued in the new and that connects the new with the old. The task is to overcome the distance and bring the old and the new together so they can be related in analysis to discover their differences and similarities so each can be critiqued. Hanegraaff has not attempted this more difficult task of analysis, but has opted for the easy rejection of that with which he disagrees on the basis that it does not fit into a period which he prefers. It is one thing to insist that truth is the same in all ages; it is quite another to claim that truth is static, that the understanding of one age exhausts the content of truth or that new truth cannot be discovered. As Buckley puts it, "Philosophy and theology contain events of inner development in which the initial principles of a system are allowed time for the maturation and emergence of their organic consequence."[34] The challenge, of course, is to know the difference between what is true and what merely purports to be true.

Coupled with the fact that Hanegraaff simply has his facts wrong, it is simply unfair to prejudice the reader against the notion of a "pretribulation rapture" just because it may be a newly developed doctrine and to do this before Hanegraaff has given the reader the tools by which he can "be the judge." Even if we grant that Hanegraaff is right, he promised earlier that his purpose "is not to entice you to embrace a particular model of eschatology but to employ a proper method of biblical interpretation."[35] But before he gives the reader the tools by which to employ a proper method,

33. Don O'Leary, *Roman Catholicism and Modern Science: A History* (New York: The Continuum International Publishing Group, 2006), xix.

34. Buckley, *Modern Atheism*, 26. The basic flow of thought of this paragraph is adapted from Buckley's observations.

35. TAC, 3.

he has prejudiced the reader not to accept the notion of a pretribulation rapture. Since he promised that his purpose was not to entice the reader toward a particular eschatology, shouldn't he have waited to give his criticism until his reader was equipped to "judge for himself"? Once again this is poisoning the well.

In the closing paragraph Hanegraaff says, "In chapter 2 you will be equipped to determine whether the pretribulational rapture is the product of faithful illumination or the by-product of a fertile imagination."[36] But, he has already set the reader up to make the decision he wants the reader to make by the way he has presented the case. Of course the Christian reader who does not have the tools will think that it is better to believe something that has always been believed than to accept something that supposedly arose only recently. In fact, many pastors will certainly recognize this tendency of Christians in the popular expression, "We've never done it that way before!" Hanegraaff could have posed this conflict of beliefs in a much more neutral manner, actually giving his reader the opportunity to "be the judge."

Grammatical Principle

The "G" in LIGHTS represents the Grammatical Principle. Hanegraaff explains: "As with any literature, a thorough understanding of the Bible cannot be attained without a grasp of the basic rules that govern the relationships and usages of words."[37] Unfortunately, Hanegraaff seems to forget that the basic rules of the original languages of the Bible may not precisely overlap the basic rules of a translation. So, for a "REALLY" thorough understanding of the Bible, the interpreter needs to have a grasp of the basic rules of the languages in which the Bible was originally written, that is, Hebrew, Aramaic, and Greek. Nowhere is this more evident than in Hanegraaff's own examples.

Hanegraaff claims that "all scholars agree that in Matthew 23 Jesus is pronouncing judgment on the Jewish leaders . . ." Hanegraaff then gives a quote from the chapter that includes verses 29 and 33–36. He italicizes each occurrence of the pronoun "you" or "your." Having done this, he then declares, "Grammatically, scholars see no option. 'You' could not possibly refer to a future generation. And when Jesus says all this will come upon

36. Ibid.
37. Ibid.

'this generation,' he could not possibly have a future generation in mind."[38] Of course, it is simply not true that scholars see "no option." In fact, that scholars do see options is the very reason Hanegraaff has written his book. Scholars from different eschatological camps disagree on the reference of some of the uses of the pronoun 'you.'

But the fact that Hanegraaff does not understand the basic rules of grammar is seen in the fact that, although he quotes verse 35, he completely misses its significance for his argument. The text of Matt 23:35 states: "so that upon you may fall *the guilt of* all the righteous blood shed on earth, from the blood of righteous Abel to the blood of Zechariah, the son of Berechiah, whom you murdered between the temple and the altar."[39] The curious part of this statement is that Jesus accuses the scribes and Pharisees of murdering Zechariah between the temple and the altar. The exact accusation is found in the latter part of the verse: "whom *you* murdered." This is a translation of the relative clause, "ὅν ἐφονεύσατε [noh etasuenohpe]." The verb 'murdered' (ἐφονεύσατε, etasuenohpe) is a second person, plural verb translated "you murdered." Now on the surface, it does not seem that the scribes and Pharisees to whom Jesus was talking actually murdered Zechariah. Many scholars argue that this event is referred to in 2 Chron 24:21: "So they conspired against him [Zechariah] and at the command of the king they stoned him to death in the court of the house of the Lord."[40] The murder of Zechariah took place during the reign of Amaziah, king of Judah, who reigned between 796–767 BC. The question is, why does Jesus seem to say these scribes and Pharisees murdered Zechariah? Jesus had already pointed out how they claimed to be different from their fathers who murdered the prophets (23:30), but by killing the ones Jesus would send to them, and ultimately killing Jesus, they demonstrated that they were of the same spirit as those who killed the prophets. In other words, they were the same kind of people as their fathers—evil and unbelieving.

38. Ibid., 6.

39. ὅπως ἔλθῃ ἐφ᾽ ὑμᾶς πᾶν αἷμα δίκαιον ἐκχυννόμενον ἐπὶ τῆς γῆς αἵματος Ἀβελ τοῦ δικαίου ἕως τοῦ αἵματος Ζαχαρίου υἱοῦ Βαραχίου, ὅν ἐφονεύσατε μεταξὺ τοῦ ναοῦ καὶ τοῦ θυσιαστηρίου (Matt 23:35). The words *'the guilt of'* are italicized in the translation because they do not actually occur in this verse.

40. וַיִּקְשְׁרוּ עָלָיו וַיִּרְגְּמֻהוּ אֶבֶן בְּמִצְוַת הַמֶּלֶךְ בַּחֲצַר בֵּית יְהוָה: (2 Chron 24:21).

Now, assuming for the sake of argument that this presentation is valid, the relevance of this observation is that even though Jesus is using the second person form of the verb, 'you murdered,' He is not claiming that they actually murdered Zechariah, but that they were just as guilty as those who did. But the 'you' both does and does not refer to the scribes and Pharisees to whom Jesus is speaking. It *does* refer to them in the sense that they are the one's Jesus is directly condemning, but it *does not* refer to them in the sense that they were not the ones who actually murdered Zechariah, but they were the same kind of people as those who did. So, even though the meaning of the 2nd person pronoun is the same throughout this passage Hanegraaff quotes, the referent may be different in this verse.

Now, not all scholars accept this argument (and we deal with this in more detail in chapter 4), but what this shows is that Hanegraaff is simply wrong that scholars see "no option." And this also shows that a word can have the same meaning, but a different referent, and that figures of speech allow terms to have a broader referent than they would normally have in strictly literal expressions. This is important since Hanegraaff ignores this feature of the basic rules of grammar. So, when Jesus uses the pronoun "you," it is not a simple matter of claiming that the word "could not possible refer to a future generation." If it doesn't, this must be proven, not simply asserted. But, once again Hanegraaff has made the judgment for the reader instead of waiting until he has given his reader the grammatical principle so that, as he promised he would do, the reader could "be the judge."

Concerning his example from Matthew 24, Hanegraaff quotes a claim from D. A. Carson, but he fails to quote from other scholars with a different perspective. In fact, Carson just happens to be wrong. It is not "with the greatest difficulty" that one can see that it is entirely possible that the expression "this generation" can refer to some other generation than the one to whom Jesus is talking. It is simply a matter of making a distinction between sense and reference, as we discussed above. The problem here, however, is not a matter of simple grammar or syntax. There are no grammatical or syntactical rules that necessarily determine the reference of a word in a given context. The reference is determined by the context of the statement, not necessarily its grammar or syntax. Now, both Hanegraaff and Carson may be right that this isn't talking about a future generation, but Carson is simply wrong that it is "with the greatest difficulty" that an interpreter can make it refer to a future generation. And, as a matter of fact, neither Hanegraaff nor Carson has bothered to try to prove their respective claims. They merely assert them as if they are obviously true. But, exegesis isn't just making assertions. Exegesis is about supporting your assertions with evidence and argument.

We have already seen from Matt 23:35 that it is not necessarily the case that the use of the 2nd person personal pronoun 'you' confines a reference to the immediate audience only. If that is the case here, then we must look for other indicators in the text that might point us to who might be the referent in Matt 24:34–35. One of these likely indicators is the prior statement of Jesus: "when you see all these *things*, recognize that He is near, *right* at the door" (Matt 24:33).[41] This statement seems to indicate that the referent of the word 'generation' is the ones who see all these things. This, of course, raises the question, "To what 'things' is Jesus referring?" Before we pursue this question, we must point out that we are not claiming that the word 'generation' has a different meaning in this context. Just like the word 'you' in chapter 23 did not have a different meaning although it had a different referent, so also the word 'generation' here has the same meaning as all the other instances in Matthew's Gospel, but it may have a different referent. In this instance, if there is a difference in referent, this does not make a difference in the meaning.

Now, to what is Jesus referring when he says, "all these *things*" (πά ντα ταῦτα, atuat atnap). At the very least "these things" seem to refer to the immediately previous "things" Jesus has described:

- sign of the Son of Man will appear in the sky

- all the tribes of the earth will mourn

- they will see the Son of Man coming on the clouds of the sky with power and great glory

- He will send forth His angels with a great trumpet

- they will gather together His elect from the four winds, from one end of the sky to the other

So, the referent of the term 'generation' seems to be the generation that sees these things. But, not just "these things"—literally, "*all* [πάντα,

---

41. οὕτως καὶ ὑμεῖς, ὅταν ἴδητε πάντα ταῦτα, γινώσκετε ὅτι ἐγγύς ἐστιν ἐπὶ θύραις (Matt 24:33).

atnap] these *things* [ταῦτα, atuat]."[42] Jesus actually seems to be saying that the generation that sees *all* of these things will not pass away. This may imply that the *things* to which Jesus is referring is more than just these few that immediately precede our statement. In fact, verse 30 begins with the connector, 'and then' (καὶ τότε, etot iak). This seems chronologically to connect the sign of the Son of Man with the events previously described. This would seem at least to include the events referred to in verse 29: "But immediately after the tribulation of those days the sun will be darkened, and the moon will not give its light, and the stars will fall from the sky, and the powers of the heavens will be shaken."[43] So, the list of "these *things*" seems to include the following:

- the sun will be darkened

- the moon will not give its light

- the stars will fall from the sky

- the powers of the heavens will be shaken

- sign of the Son of Man will appear in the sky

- all the tribes of the earth will mourn

- they will see the Son of Man coming on the clouds of the sky with power and great glory

- He will send forth His angels with a great trumpet

- they will gather together His elect from the four winds, from one end of the sky to the other

The list of "things" to which Jesus seems to be referring may ultimately include more, but it does not seem to include less than these. The point here is that to understand the terms 'you' or 'this generation' to be referring only to the disciples is not as certain a case as Hanegraaff or Carson want to make it. The term 'generation' could be referring to who-

---

42. The word 'things' is in italics because there is no individual Greek word that corresponds to this word in the English translation. However, this is the significance of the word ταῦτα. It is a neuter plural demonstrative adjective and is literally translated "these." The English word 'things' is added in most translations to make smoother sounding English (see for example William D. Mounce, *Basics of Biblical Greek*, 2d ed. (Grand Rapids: Zondervan Publishing House, 2003), 84–85.

43. Εὐθέως δὲ μετὰ τὴν θλῖψιν τῶν ἡμερῶν ἐκείνων ὁ ἥλιος σκοτισθήσεται, καὶ ἡ σελήνη οὐ δώσει τὸ φέγγος αὐτῆς, καὶ οἱ ἀστέρες πεσοῦνται ἀπὸ οὐρανοῦ, καὶ αἱ δυνάμεις τῶν οὐρανῶν σαλευθήσονται (Matt 24:29).

ever sees all these things. If these things occurred on or before 70 AD, then the disciples would certainly be included in this referent. If, however, it can be shown that these things have not yet occurred, then the referent to the word 'you' and the expression "this generation" would be a yet future group, and this without changing the meaning of the term, without taking the expression out of context, without distorting the text, without the "greatest of difficulty," and without doing the myriad of other less than flattering charges that are often made against Futurists. In other words, it is not a difficult a matter to show that "this generation" may not be referring to the people to whom Jesus was speaking.

Whether or not this convinces anyone is not the point. What it does show is that, once again, rather than allowing the reader to be the judge, Hanegraaff is enticing his reader to reject a dispensational or futurist eschatology for Hanegraaff's own eschatology, which he promised not to do, and he is doing this without yet giving the reader the tools to "be the judge." And notice how Hanegraaff again attempts to poison the well against LaHaye. He refers to Carson as a "scholar" while using the derogatory appellation "prophecy expert" of LaHaye. Even if LaHaye is not a scholar, Hanegraaff could have been more gracious—Christian?—in the way he contrasts these two interpreters. In fact, what Hanegraaff has done is to oversimplify a very complex group of factors in failing to recognize the role of such factors as sense/meaning and reference in the interpretation of this passage. Not only does this involve a grasp of the grammar and syntax of the original language, but it also involves a basic grasp of how language works—what is known as philosophy of language.

Historical Principle

The Historical principle is the principle indicated by the "H" in LIGHTS. According to Hanegraaff, "the biblical text is best understood when one is familiar with the customs, culture, and historical context of biblical times."[44] Hanegraaff discusses the dating of the book of Revelation as an example of the need for having a knowledge of the history. He particularly focuses on LaHaye's claim that the beast of Revelation could not refer to Nero. Hanegraaff says, "Placing the Beast in the twenty-first century, however, may well pose insurmountable historical difficulties. For example, the apostle John tells his first-century audience that with 'wisdom' and

44. TAC, 7.

'insight' they can 'calculate the number of the beast, for it is man's number. His number is 666 (Revelation 13:18).'"[45]

Unfortunately for his readers, Hanegraaff has actually misrepresented and misquoted the verse. The text actually reads, "Here is wisdom. Let him who has understanding calculate the number of the beast, for the number is that of a man; and his number is six hundred and sixty-six" (Rev 13:18).[46] First of all, Jesus does not say that *with wisdom* they can calculate the number of the beast. He simply says, "Here is wisdom." Apparently, the statement, "let him who has understanding calculate . . ." is a wise saying. It has nothing to do with claiming that with wisdom anyone can calculate the number of the beast. Second, Jesus does not say that these first-century Christians should or would be able to do this. He says, "Let him who has understanding calculate . . ." Whether Jesus expected these first-century Christians to have this understanding is at best unclear. In other words, if you have understanding, then you can calculate. You may not have this understanding, and those who have this understanding may not actually appear for several years. But this is left open. Third, Hanegraaff claims, "Obviously no amount of wisdom would have enabled a first-century audience to figure out the number of a twenty-first century Beast."[47] My response to that statement is, Why not? How does Hanegraaff know that they could not have done this? He doesn't present any arguments to support his claim. He merely states that it is "obvious." But the fact is, it is not obvious. Why couldn't a first-century audience figure out the number of a twenty-first-century beast? Nowhere in Scripture is such a possibility outlawed. And, given the fact that God can do whatever is logically possible, couldn't God have helped this first-century audience to figure this out? In fact, couldn't God have given the first-century audience the understanding necessary to figure this out? Why is this so obviously impossible? So, the way Hanegraaff presents the statement of the verse is simply misleading and false. Hanegraaff says, "you will be equipped to make a right judgment."[48] And obviously, a "right judgment" is a judgment that agrees with Hanegraaff.

45. Ibid., 8.

46. Ὧδε ἡ σοφία ἐστίν. ὁ ἔχων νοῦν ψηφισάτω τὸν ἀριθμὸν τοῦ θηρίου, ἀριθμὸς γὰρ ἀνθρώπου ἐστίν, καὶ ὁ ἀριθμὸς αὐτοῦ ἑξακόσιοι ἑξήκοντα ἕξ (Rev 13:18).

47. TAC, 8.

48. Ibid.

Typology Principle

The "T" in LIGHTS stands for typology. Hanegraaff says this principle is "of paramount importance."[49] He defines typology as, "Persons, places, events, or things in redemptive history serve as types of Christ or spiritual realities pertaining to Christ."[50] Once again he uses LaHaye as his whipping-boy: "In LaHaye's theology, the physical land is of paramount importance. Thus, we ask, should we fixate on Palestine regained? Or should we, like our Lord, focus on Paradise restored?"[51] There are several problems with Hanegraaff's questions. First, to define a term by using another form of the term in the definition is not a definition at all. To say that typology is the use of types doesn't say anything instructive. It can only be hoped that Hanegraaff will provide a better definition and explanation in his chapter on this topic.

Second, Hanegraaff may have constructed a false dilemma. Hanegraaff assumes that restored Palestine and restored Paradise are not referring to the same thing. Now it certainly may be the case they these two are not the same thing, but that has not been proven to be the case by any argument from Hanegraaff. He just assumes that his understanding is the correct one, and he assumes that his reader agrees with his understanding and does not need any argument to demonstrate this. But this isn't exegesis. This is argument by presupposition, and it just goes to show that Hanegraaff is as guilty of assuming his eschatological scheme as anyone he criticizes. If this is what an Exegetical Eschatology is, then the reader ought to close his book and go somewhere else to learn how actually to do exegesis that is not based on an already assumed eschatological scheme.

Third, just because LaHaye says Palestine is of paramount importance does not mean that he proposes that anyone "fixate" on it. The same could be said for Hanegraaff's statement about typology. Should we "fixate" on typology as if this is the most important aspect of biblical hermeneutics? Of course that's not what Hanegraaff is saying, and it's not what LaHaye is saying either. For Hanegraaff to present the case in this manner is prejudicial to the reader. Nobody wants to "fixate" on something, and the derogatory term 'fixate' serves to poison the well.

49. Ibid., 9.
50. Ibid.
51. Ibid.

Fourth, if there was any question in the reader's mind up to this point whether Hanegraaff is poisoning the well against LaHaye, there should be none after this statement. It is completely unfair for Hanegraaff to present the dichotomy in the form of whether the reader is going to choose LaHaye or "our Lord." What kind of options are these? Without the least justification, Hanegraaff has painted a picture of LaHaye as somehow being against "our Lord." In fact, in the same way Hanegraaff indicates that LaHaye is fixated on Palestine, we could say that Hanegraaff is fixated on typology. But Jesus did not "fixate" on typology! Does that mean we have to choose between "our Lord" and Hanegraaff? In fact, since Hanegraaff has not bothered to present his case by any argumentation, this is an artificial choice, and it begs the question. Why does Hanegraaff assume that LaHaye and Jesus are not in total agreement? If they aren't then Hanegraaff needs to demonstrate this by argumentation, not by accusation.

Of course Hanegraaff has not actually gotten to the section where he wants to present his argumentation. That is supposed to come in the chapter dedicated to this topic. But again, that is the very problem. Since Hanegraaff has not argued his point, he should not be couching his presentation here as if he has already demonstrated his position to be the correct one. And, Hanegraaff claims that once the reader has been armed with the typology principle, "you will make a right judgment." But the way Hanegraaff has unfairly presented the case, he has predisposed the reader to make only one judgment—the one he wants.

Scriptural Synergy Principle

The final "S" (or "SS" or perhaps "Ss"), is what Hanegraaff calls "the principle of *scriptural synergy*."[52] Hanegraaff defines this principle as follows: "Simply stated, this means that the whole of Scripture is greater than the sum of its individual passages. You cannot comprehend the Bible as a whole without comprehending its individual parts, and you cannot comprehend its individual parts without comprehending the Bible as a whole."[53] By way of explanation, Hanegraaff goes on to add:

> Scriptural synergy demands that individual Bible passages may never be interpreted in such a way as to conflict with the whole of Scripture. Nor may we assign arbitrary meanings to words or

52. Ibid. (emphasis in original).
53. Ibid.

phrases that have their referent in biblical history. The biblical interpreter must keep in mind that all Scripture, though communicated through various human instruments, has one single Author. And that Author does not contradict himself, nor does he confuse his servants.[54]

What Hanegraaff calls "scriptural synergy" seems to be what the Reformers called the analogy of faith. However, just because God does not deliberately seek to confuse his servants does not mean that some of those who read the Bible do not become confused. Just because I may be confused when reading the Bible does not mean that God is the cause of my confusion. However, consider the opening verses of Proverbs:

2　To know wisdom and instruction, to discern the sayings of understanding,

3　To receive instruction in wise behavior, righteousness, justice and equity;

4　To give prudence to the naive, to the youth knowledge and discretion,

5　A wise man will hear and increase in learning, and a man of understanding will acquire wise counsel,

6　To understand a proverb and a figure, the words of the wise and their riddles.

לָדַעַת חָכְמָה וּמוּסָר לְהָבִין אִמְרֵי בִינָה:	2
לָקַחַת מוּסַר הַשְׂכֵּל צֶדֶק וּמִשְׁפָּט וּמֵישָׁרִים:	3
לָתֵת לִפְתָאיִם עָרְמָה לְנַעַר דַּעַת וּמְזִמָּה:	4
יִשְׁמַע חָכָם וְיוֹסֶף לֶקַח וְנָבוֹן תַּחְבֻּלוֹת יִקְנֶה:	5
לְהָבִין מָשָׁל וּמְלִיצָה דִּבְרֵי חֲכָמִים וְחִידֹתָם:	6

(Prov 1:2–6)

The interesting part is the last phrase of verse 6: "the words of the wise and their riddles." The word translated "riddles" (חִידֹתָם, m̄odyh) is from חִידָה (ḥadyh) and means "ambiguous saying," or "designation

54. Ibid., 9–10.

of something by enigmatic allusions."[55] The opening verses of this book of wisdom tells the reader that these are the proverbs of Solomon that are designed to give wisdom, instruction, prudence, knowledge, and discretion. Yet verse 6 tells us that the words of the wise are expressed in riddles—ambiguous sayings expressed in enigmatic allusions. Why, if God wanted to give us wisdom, instruction, prudence, knowledge, and discretion does He do this in ambiguous sayings expressed in enigmatic allusion? Wouldn't this promote confusion? We don't have time to go into what this text is saying, but it shows that cliché Christian expressions like the one Hanegraaff uses—"nor does he confuse his servants"—are not as accurate as they sound. The situation is more complex than this. God is not the author of confusion, but sometimes He says things that require more than a simple reading of the text. Sometimes He says things that are designed to be ambiguous so that we will have to stop and meditate and think about and wrestle with the text in order gradually to come to understand what it is saying, and it is this process of wrestling with the text—working hard to discover what it means—that changes us. If someone simply tells you what the text means, you may remember, and you may not. But, if you have to struggle with the text in order to come to understand what it means, then you will never forget it. That struggle will change you, just as Jacob's struggle with the man in Gen 32:24ff changed him (Look at the text again. The text does not say Jacob struggled with an angel. It says he struggled with a man.) Perhaps exegesis involves more than the simple acronym LIGHTS.

FINAL NOTES

In his concluding material on this chapter, Hanegraaff gives a brief recap of each of his principles. What is particularly interesting is that he gives no argument why anyone should accept his acronym "LIGHTS" as either accurate or desirable. Why should anyone think that this is either complete or sufficient to do exegesis? What about the original languages of the Bible? Isn't it important to know them? Where do they fit in LIGHTS? We have already seen that Hanegraaff's own deficiency in the languages of the original text has led him to the wrong conclusions. And what about the question of the presuppositions of the interpreter—his world view

55. *The Hebrew and Aramaic Lexicon of the Old Testament* (2001), s.v. "חִידָה." Hereinafter referred to as KBH.

and assumptions? Isn't that an important part of doing good exegesis? There is no place for this principle in LIGHTS either, and yet we have already seen how Hanegraaff's presuppositions about eschatology have led him to make assumptions that he does not bother either to acknowledge or justify.

The point is not that LIGHTS is either good or bad. The point is that Hanegraaff doesn't make any attempt to justify his choice of these and not other or additional principles. He just assumes that this is correct or sufficient to prepare the reader to do good exegesis—to be the judge. Also, we have seen that Hanegraaff has failed to do what he said he was going to do. He said he wasn't going to entice the reader to a certain eschatological position. But that is precisely what he has been doing all along, and this becomes even more overt in these final notes.

The Literal Principle

In the concluding remarks on this principle, Hanegraaff says, "*The literal principle* demands that this text [Rev 13:16] be interpreted in the sense in which it is intended rather than in a literalistic sense."[56] The obvious question here is, How does Hanegraaff know that it was not intended to be taken in a literalistic sense? Where would an interpreter go to discover whether or not this text was intended to be taken in a literalistic sense? You can't go to the text itself, because that's the very thing that is in question. But if you can't go to the text to decide whether it was intended to be taken in a literalistic sense, where did Hanegraaff go to discover this? He went to his own prior eschatological commitment. Because he assumes a certain eschatology, he looks at this passage a certain way.

He uses the example, "If I tell you that it is raining cats and dogs, my intent is to convey that it is raining hard—not that cats and dogs are literally falling from the sky."[57] But just because that may be what Hanegraaff intended does not mean that what every other person in history always meant by this expression. How does Hanegraaff know that his intentions are necessarily the intentions of every speaker throughout history, and yet that is exactly what he is implying. He is implying that every time this expression is used the author necessarily intends the same thing. But, besides the fact that this can never be proven, it just does not follow. It sounds

56. TAC, 10 (emphasis in original).
57. Ibid.

convincing at first, but it is simply a hasty generalization. Since there is no way for Hanegraaff to know what other authors intended when they used this expression just because he had his own intent, it likewise follows that just because Hanegraaff understands his own intent does not mean he necessarily understands the intended meaning of the text of Revelation.

In fact, the literal principle does not lead "to the inevitable conclusion that the mark of the Beast is symbolic language intended to convey identification with the Beast."[58] In fact, the literal principle and the principle of scriptural synergy require that there should be some kind of literal mark. Rev 13:16 says, "He causes all, both small and great, rich and poor, free and slave, to receive a mark on their right hand or on their foreheads."[59] But, verse 17 says, "and that no one may buy or sell except one who has the mark or the name of the beast, or the number of his name."[60] Now unless we are going to be inconsistent in the application of our principles, if we take the first part as a symbol, shouldn't we take the second part as a symbol? So, the buying and selling is not literal buying and selling—it's only symbolic buying and selling. But that is absurd. It certainly seems to be talking about literal buying and selling. But, if we take the second part literally, shouldn't we take the first part literally? So, it's not a symbolic mark. Also, if it is a symbolic mark, does this mean that these people were putting the mark on a symbolic right hand and a symbolic forehead? That sounds absurd also. It certainly seems that this passage is referring to an actual, literal mark of some kind. It may not be a social security number or a biochip, but it is some kind of physical mark that is able to distinguish those who have it from those who don't.

Once again the point is not to convince anyone of this interpretation. The point is to show that Hanegraaff's own principles do not necessarily lead to his conclusions. The reason he reaches these conclusions is because he has already made up his mind. And again, he is making these claims before he has given the reader the tools to be the judge, and in fact, he has not allowed the reader to be his own judge. Rather, he has already made the judgment for his reader. Just out of faithfulness to his own pro-

---

58. Ibid.

59. καὶ ποιεῖ πάντας, τοὺς μικροὺς καὶ τοὺς μεγάλους, καὶ τοὺς πλουσίους καὶ τοὺς πτωχούς, καὶ τοὺς ἐλευθέρους καὶ τοὺς δούλους, ἵνα δῶσιν αὐτοῖς χά ραγμα ἐπὶ τῆς χειρὸς αὐτῶν τῆς δεξιᾶς ἢ ἐπὶ τὸ μέτωπον αὐτῶν (Rev 13:16).

60. καὶ ἵνα μή τις δύνηται ἀγοράσαι ἢ πωλῆσαι εἰ μὴ ὁ ἔχων τὸ χάραγμα τὸ ὄνομα τοῦ θηρίου ἢ τὸν ἀριθμὸν τοῦ ὀνόματος αὐτοῦ (Rev 13:17).

fessed purpose he should wait until he explains these principles and how they should be applied before he tells the reader what he ought to think.

The Illumination Principle

In his final notes on the illumination principle, Hanegraaff claims it "adds clarity in that the Holy Spirit illumines what is in the text; illumination does not go beyond the text."[61] According to Hanegraaff it follows that "the notion that the mark of the Beast is Sunday worship, a social security number, or a silicon microchip is the product of a fertile imagination rather than faithful illumination."[62] But how does Hanegraaff know this? How does he know that the interpreters who made the claims he is criticizing were not "illumined" by the Holy Spirit? He can't appeal to the text to support his claim because it is the understanding of the text that is in question. If Hanegraaff claims that these statements "go beyond" the text, that is only his interpretation, and it may not be "illumined" by the Holy Spirit. How does he know that these claims are not the clarifying by the Holy Spirit? In fact, he cannot know this, and the only reason he thinks these are the product of a "fertile imagination" is because he disagrees with them. Claiming that he is illumined by the Holy Spirit doesn't work either, because he has no way of proving this. Many people claim to be illumined by the Holy Spirit, but many of these interpreters claim things that contradict what other interpreters claim the Holy Spirit has clarified for them. As it turns out, unless he can give some additional evidence and explanation in the chapter on this topic, Hanegraaff's Illumination principle doesn't seem to clarify anything—it brings no light.

The Grammatical Principle

According to Hanegraaff, "*The grammatical principle* precludes LaHaye's interpretation that the mark is a biochip physically *in* the body."[63] Why is this the case? "By LaHaye's own standard, a grammatically accurate interpretation would require that the mark is specifically placed *on* the right hand and forehead rather than being scientifically implanted *in* the body (see Revelation 13:16)."[64] This passage reads, "He causes all, both small

---

61. TAC, 10.
62. Ibid., 10–11.
63. Ibid., 11 (emphasis in original).
64. Ibid. (emphasis in original).

and great, rich and poor, free and slave, to receive a mark on their right hand or on their foreheads." The word in question is in the last phrase: ἵνα δῶσιν αὐτοῖς χάραγμα ἐπὶ τῆς χειρὸς αὐτῶν τῆς δελιᾶς ἢ ἐπὶ τὸ μέτωπον αὐτῶν. The word translated "on" is the Greek preposition ἐπὶ, and according to BDAG it has several possible meanings depending on the context. One interesting instance of the use of this preposition is found in Matt 9:9: "As Jesus went on from there, He saw a man called Matthew, sitting in the tax collector's booth; and He said to him, 'Follow Me!' And he got up and followed Him."[65] The significant part is the statement that Jesus saw Matthew "sitting *in* the tax collector's booth": ἐπὶ τὸ τελώνιον. Here the preposition ἐπὶ is translated "in" and is used to indicate where Matthew was sitting. It is unlikely that he was sitting "upon" or "on" the tax collector's booth. Another important instance is Matt 18:5: "And whoever receives one such child in My name receives Me."[66] Here the preposition ἐπὶ is translated "in," but in this instance it probably does not mean physically inside. In this instance it probably indicates "with reference to." What this shows is that the Revelation passage does not have to be taken in a physical sense either. It could be saying "with reference to their right hand or their foreheads" specifically avoiding any indication of whether it would be in or on.

This demonstrates again that Hanegraaff does not have a command of the original language of the New Testament and is making his claims based on the English text. This accentuates the inadequacy of Hanegraaff's acronym LIGHTS. It has omitted an important and necessary aspect of exegesis, that is, a good working knowledge of the original languages of the Bible. Hanegraaff's grammatical principle in fact does not preclude LaHaye's interpretation. What it does is preclude Hanegraaff's criticism.

The Historical Principle

Again Hanegraaff attempts to entice his reader to accept his eschatology. He says, "*The historical principle* similarly precludes LaHaye's notion that the mark of the Beast is the physical implantation of a biochip."[67] How

---

65. Καὶ παράγων ὁ Ἰησοῦς ἐκεῖθεν εἶδεν ἄνθρωπον καθήμενον ἐπὶ τὸ τελώνιον, Ματθαῖον λεγόμενον, καὶ λέγει αὐτῷ· ἀκολούθει μοι. καὶ ἀναστὰς ἠκολούθησεν αὐτῷ (Matt 9:9).

66. καὶ ὃς ἐὰν δέξηται ἓν παιδίον τοιοῦτο ἐπὶ τῷ ὀνόματί μου, ἐμὲ δέχεται (Matt 18:5).

67. TAC, 11 (emphasis in original).

does he do it this time? By repeating the same argument he presented earlier in this chapter: "In context John tells first-century readers that with 'wisdom' and 'insight' they can 'calculate the number of the beast.' No amount of wisdom and insight would have allowed John's first-century audience to calculate the number of a twenty-first century Beast. Nor would a first-century Beast have been able to employ twenty-first century biochip technology."[68] We have already shown the fallacy of this argument.

The Typology Principle

Hanegraaff claims, "*The typology principle* adds to our understanding by underscoring that the mark of the Beast is simply a parody of the mark of the Lamb."[69] Of course nothing in this paragraph precludes the possibility that the mark is both physical and visible and also a parody. A physical thing can also function as a symbol for something else or for some concept or as a parody. Just because it is a parody does not mean it cannot be physical and visible. In fact, how effective a parody is it if nobody can see it? Of course, it is a parody for those who read the Bible, but is it meant to be a parody only for them? Also, since Jesus' mark was physical, doesn't it follow that the mark of the Beast would be physical also? Hanegraaff doesn't bother even to address these kinds of questions or demonstrate his point.

The Scriptural Synergy Principle

Hanegraaff counsels his reader that, "*the principle of scriptural synergy* warns us not to interpret the mark of the Beast in a way that conflicts with Scripture as a whole."[70] Of course, according to Hanegraaff, the dispensational interpreters have violated this principle too: "Thus, saying that the 144,000 have the Lamb's name written on their foreheads is a symbolic way of identifying them with Christ. Likewise, when Jesus says, 'I will write on him [the one who overcomes] the name of my God, and the name of the city of my God . . . and I will also write on him my new name' (Revelation 3:12), we intuitively realize that Jesus does not have a

68. Ibid.
69. Ibid. (emphasis in original).
70. Ibid. (emphasis in original).

Magic Marker in mind."[71] But ridiculing a fellow believer does not prove Hanegraaff's point. This is called the fallacy of *ad hominem abusive*. An *ad hominem abusive* fallacy involves attacking your opponent on a personal level when this personal level is not relevant to the issue. I doubt that any dispensationalist scholar has proposed that Jesus was referring to a Magic Marker. Whether Jesus had a Magic Marker in mind or not does not prove that He did not mean to refer to an actual mark on the person. In no way does the notion of an actual mark conflict with Scripture as a whole.

IN SHORT

Finally, Hanegraaff claims, "the principles of Exegetical Eschatology taken as a whole preclude the possibility that followers of the Beast are twenty-first-century characters with biochip technology implanted in their bodies."[72] On the contrary, what we have seen is that the Exegetical Eschatology is totally inadequate to make such determinations, particularly if the person who is using it does not have some of the basic skills necessary to do exegesis—basic skills like a working understanding of the original languages and basic principles of logic. Hanegraaff concludes this chapter by promising the reader that, "armed with Exegetical Eschatology, you will be empowered to make a right judgment."[73] And, of course, a right judgment is a judgment that agrees with the judgment Hanegraaff has already predisposed his reader to make.

71. Ibid., 11–12.
72. Ibid., 12.
73. Ibid.

2

Literal Principle

Reading the Bible as Literature

THIS CHAPTER OF HANEGRAAFF's book is dedicated to explaining and illustrating the literal principle. Hanegraaff gives the following definition: "Simply put, this [interpreting the Bible as literature] means that we are to interpret the Word of God just as we interpret other forms of communication—in its most obvious and natural sense."[1] So, we should interpret figures of speech as figures of speech, allegory as allegory, and so on. And after briefly critiquing Bill Maher's characterizations of the Bible, Hanegraaff turns his attention to Tim LaHaye.

THE GOLDEN RULE OF BIBLE INTERPRETATION

Hanegraaff declares that LaHaye's definition of literalism is "meaningless." Hanegraaff quotes a statement from Tim LaHaye: "When the plain sense of Scripture makes common sense, seek no other sense, but take every word at its primary, literal meaning unless the facts of the immediate context clearly indicate otherwise."[2] It is significant that Hanegraaff characterizes LaHaye's definition as a "definition of literalism."[3] It is unfortunate that Hanegraaff feels the necessity constantly to engage in *ad hominem abusive* tactics when discussing LaHaye. There is no reason to characterize this definition as a definition of literalism except to attempt to disparage the view before analyzing it.

1. TAC, 14.
2. Ibid., 16.
3. Ibid., 15.

Of this definition Hanegraaff says, "Not only is there nothing distinctive about this definition, but it is so vague as to be utterly useless."[4] However, it is not substantively different from the definition that Sproul gives in the book from which Hanegraaff himself quotes: "That is, the natural meaning of a passage is to be interpreted according to the normal rules of grammar, speech, syntax and context."[5] Sproul refers to the "natural meaning" while LaHaye refers to the "plain sense." Sproul refers to the normal rules while LaHaye refers to common sense. Granted, Sproul's definition is more precise when he enumerates the kinds of rules to which he is referring, but this is simply a matter of degree of precision, not difference of kind. Hanegraaff's antagonism toward LaHaye is evident in this kind of criticism.

Hanegraaff declares, "Plain sense to a first-century Jew is clearly not plain sense to LaHaye."[6] But how can Hanegraaff know this? Does he have some special access what a Jew of the first-century thought about "plane sense"? This term is not defined in the Bible, so Hanegraaff could not have gotten this information from the text of Scripture. And it is unlikely that there is any historical record setting forth what Jews thought about "plain sense." Once again this is simply an *ad hominem abusive* attack on another Christian. Disagreeing with what LaHaye teaches is one thing. But attacking the man because you don't agree with his eschatology is another. Perhaps LaHaye is guilty of the same kind of tactics, but that is all the more reason for Hanegraaff to abstain.

EXAMPLES OF GOLDEN RULE INTERPRETATION

Following his personal attacks on LaHaye, Hanegraaff turns to considering some of the passages he thinks LaHaye has misinterpreted.

John 14:1–3

Hanegraaff gives the following translation of this passage: "Do not let your hearts be troubled. Trust in God; trust also in me. In my Father's house are many rooms; if it were not so, I would have told you. I am going there to prepare a place for you. And if I go and prepare a place for you, I

---

4. Ibid., 16.

5. R. C. Sproul, *Knowing Scripture* (Downers Grove, Illinois: InterVarsity Press, 1977), 48–49.

6. TAC, 16.

will come back, and take you to be with me that you also may be where I am."[7] Hanegraaff then says, "According to the *Tim LaHaye Prophecy Study Bible*, this is 'the first teaching on the Rapture in Scripture.'"[8]

Hanegraaff's first criticism of LaHaye's claim is that this is not what most Christians believe, past or present. This is another logical fallacy called *consensus gentium*. This logical fallacy is an effort to persuade simply because a majority of people hold something to be true—in this case the majority hold something to be false. Whether everyone believes something or not does not indicate whether that thing is true or false. This is a popular persuasive tool, and Hanegraaff has already used it earlier in his book.

He says, "Prior to the nineteenth century, all Christians, futurists included, believed that a commonsense reading of Scripture inevitability [*sic*] led to the conclusion that the second coming/bodily return of Christ and the rapture/resurrection of believers are simultaneous events."[9] As we pointed out earlier, it is extremely unlikely that either Hanegraaff or Timothy P. Weber, the individual from whom Hanegraaff gets this information, is able to discover what "all Christians" believed throughout the history of the Christian church. This is certainly an exaggeration. But, even granting that this can be known, it still does not prove anything other than that this is what they believed. Hanegraaff claims, "Thus, a plain-sense or commonsense reading of passages like John 14:1–3 did not lead believers to believe in a pretribulational rapture."[10] But Hanegraaff's conclusion simply does not follow automatically. Even if it was true that this conclusion was the "plain-sense" or "commonsense" interpretation of "all Christians," that does not necessarily make it the correct view. Augustine believed that the plain-sense and commonsense interpretation of the statement in Gen 2:8, "The Lord God planted a garden toward the east, in Eden,"[11] could not possible mean that God actually planted a gar-

---

7. Ibid. Μὴ ταρασσέσθω ὑμῶν ἡ καρδία· πιστεύετε εἰς τὸν θεὸν καὶ εἰς ἐμὲ πιστεύετε. ἐν τῇ οἰκίᾳ τοῦ πατρός μου μοναὶ πολλαί εἰσιν· εἰ δὲ μή, εἶπον ἂν ὑμῖν ὅτι πορεύομαι ἑτοιμάσαι τόπον ὑμῖν; καὶ; ἐὰν πορευθῶ καὶ ἑτοιμάσω τόπον ὑμῖν, πάλιν ἔρχομαι καὶ παραλήμψομαι ὑμᾶς πρὸς ἐμαυτόν, ἵνα ὅπου εἰμὶ ἐγὼ καὶ; ὑμεῖς ἦτε (Jn 14:1–3).

8. TAC, 16.

9. Ibid., 17.

10. Ibid.

11. (Gen 2:8) וַיִּטַּע יהוה אֱלֹהִים גַּן־בְּעֵדֶן מִקֶּדֶם.

den, because God would not demean Himself to become a gardener.[12] As a result he rejected the historicity of the garden narrative. Sometimes the commonsense meaning is not necessarily correct. What Hanegraaff has to do is demonstrate from the text what the text means, not appeal to what "all Christians" may have believed.

Also, even if it was true that Darby was the first one to make an absolute distinction between Israel and the church, as Hanegraaff claims, this does not in any way mean that it is a false dichotomy. This fallacy is called *argumentum ad annis*, or *chronological snobbery*. This fallacy is committed when someone claims that a view is false simply because it is dated. People will disparage a view because it is too new, and others will disparage a view because it is too old. When a view was first developed says nothing about whether it is true.

The Time Is Near

Hanegraaff next criticizes LaHaye for not living up to "his own standard of taking 'every word at its primary, literal meaning unless the facts of the *immediate* context clearly indicate otherwise.'"[13] According to Hanegraaff, LaHaye commits this error because, "when our Lord says 'the time is near,' LaHaye says the time is far off; when our Lord says the apocalypse 'must *soon* take place,' LaHaye says the apocalypse is in the distant future; and when our Lord says to his disciples, 'I tell you the truth, some who are standing here will not taste death before they see the Son of Man coming in his kingdom' (Matt 16:28), LaHaye says our Lord is speaking of 'the second coming,' even though every one of the disciples would have long ago tasted death."[14] Unfortunately for his readers, Hanegraaff does not provide any references to where LaHaye said these things or the passages to which the comments were related. We can only trust Hanegraaff that he is not misrepresenting either LaHaye or the text, but given Hanegraaff's already evident antagonism toward LaHaye, the reader ought to be cautious about accepting these criticisms as more than just personal attacks.

12. See Augustine, *On Genesis: Two Books on Genesis Against the Manichees*, trans. Roland J. Teske (Washington, D.C.: The Catholic University of America Press, 1991), 2.2.3; 19.12.

13. TAC, 17.

14. Ibid.

Rhetoric

This next criticism of LaHaye is surprising. Hanegraaff says, "What is particularly disturbing is the rhetoric LaHaye reserves for those who do not subscribe to his understanding of what is and is not literal."[15] As we have seen already, Hanegraaff is no stranger to the use of rhetoric. It is unfortunate that LaHaye uses the terminology he does—although it is not clear from the quote given by Hanegraaff that LaHaye is talking about Christians or non-Christians. But, it is equally disturbing that Hanegraaff feels like he must respond in kind. The quote from LaHaye that Hanegraaff provides does not make it clear that he is "judging the motives of his critics,"[16] as Hanegraaff claims he is. All we have to go on that LaHaye is actually doing this is Hanegraaff's claim. We do not suppose that Hanegraaff would lie about something like this, but it would have been helpful for the reader actually to see what LaHaye was saying that would lead Hanegraaff to make this observation, and with Hanegraaff's track record of using his own rhetoric, the reader can only wonder if perhaps Hanegraaff may not be exaggerating or taking something out of context.

Allegorizing and Spiritualizing

Hanegraaff presents a lengthy quote from LaHaye and makes the following observations: "Ironically, by LaHaye's standards, our Lord and his disciples could easily be pawned off as false teachers who allegorize or spiritualize prophecy."[17] As support for this attack Hanegraaff refers to Jn 2:19: "Destroy this temple, and I will raise it again in three days."[18] Hanegraaff then says, "The Jews interpreted Jesus in a wooden, literal fashion. They understood the plain-sense or commonsense meaning of Jesus's words to refer directly and specifically to the destruction of their temple, which had taken 'forty-six years to build' (John 2:20). Jesus, however, spiritualized his prophecy."[19] But Hanegraaff's characterization of Jesus' words is completely inaccurate. The difference between the Jews' understanding and John's comment that Jesus was speaking of His body is not a case of literal verses spiritual meaning. Rather, it is a difference of the reference

15. Ibid., 18.
16. Ibid.
17. Ibid.
18. λύσατε τὸν ναὸν τοῦτον καὶ ἐν τρισὶν ἡμέραις ἐγερῶ αὐτόν (Jn 2:19b).
19. TAC, 18–19.

of the term 'temple.' The Jews understood Jesus to be literally referring to the actual Temple, whereas Jesus was literally referring to His actual body. This is not a question of a literal or a spiritualizing interpretation of prophecy. This is a matter of the distinction between sense and reference. Jesus' body was an actual, physical temple in which the fullness of the Godhead dwelt, and the Jews would actually destroy His body by sending Him to the cross. This is not spiritualizing, this is simply a matter that the Jews misunderstood to which temple Jesus was referring.

And this is not a "deeper" meaning. Rather it is the correct meaning. And it is the literal meaning. And notice the way Hanegraaff reads into the text what is not there. He says, "after our Lord's sacrifice and subsequent resurrection, the temple would no longer have substantial significance."[20] But the text says nothing about the Temple losing significance, and Hanegraaff himself has already pointed out that Jesus was referring to His body, not to the Jerusalem Temple. This is a classic example of eisegesis, which Hanegraaff warned against.

Hanegraaff goes so far as to endorse the claim by G. B. Caird that, "The death of Christ was no sacrifice . . ."[21] But Hanegraaff must have realized the problematic nature of Caird's claim, because he actually misquotes Caird's statement. Caird actually says, "Literally the death of Christ was no sacrifice . . ."[22] Hanegraaff strategically omits the term 'Literally' in Caird's statement. For Caird to claim that Christ's death was *literally* no sacrifice borders on heresy. And since Hanegraaff is by far no heretic, nor does he hold any doctrines that would be considered heresy, apparently he altered the quote in order to avoid any such appearance. To claim that Christ's death was only *regarded* as a sacrifice goes against the many statements of the New Testament that His death was indeed a sacrifice, not simply regarded as such:

> Therefore purge out the old leaven, that you may be a new lump, since you truly are unleavened. For indeed Christ, our Passover, was sacrificed for us. (1 Cor 5:7)[23]

20. Ibid., 19.

21. Ibid.

22. G. B. Caird, *The Language and Imagery of the Bible* (London: Gerald Duckworth & Company, 1980; reprint, Grand Rapids: William B. Eerdmans Publishing Company, 1997), 157.

23. ἐκκαθάρατε τὴν παλαιὰν ζύμην, ἵνα ἦτε νέον φύραμα, καθώς ἐστε ἄζυμοι· καὶ γὰρ τὸ πάσχα ἡμῶν ἐτύθη Χριστός (1 Cor 5:7).

... as Christ also has loved us and given Himself for us, an offering and a sacrifice to God for a sweet-smelling aroma. (Eph 5:2)[24]

He then would have had to suffer often since the foundation of the world; but now, once at the end of the ages, He has appeared to put away sin by the sacrifice of Himself. (Heb 9:26)[25]

But this Man, after He had offered one sacrifice for sins forever, sat down at the right hand of God. (Heb 10:12)[26]

When Caird said that Christ's death *literally* was no sacrifice, he was not treating it as a metaphor as Hanegraaff depicts it. What Caird is claiming is that the notion that Christ's death was a sacrifice is only metaphorical, but that His death was not literally a sacrifice. To claim that Christ's death was a "criminal execution" ignores the fact that no one took Christ's life from Him: "Therefore My Father loves Me, because I lay down My life that I may take it again. No one takes it from Me, but I lay it down of Myself. I have power to lay it down, and I have power to take it again" (Jn 10:17–18).[27] So, not only did Hanegraaff misrepresent Caird's statement, his point about shadows and metaphors fails.

That Caird has completely misrepresented the sacrifice of Christ is evident in his claim, which Hanegraaff also quotes approvingly: "But because Christ himself chose to regard his death as a sacrifice, and by his words at the Last Supper taught his disciples so to do, he transformed its tragedy into something he could offer to God to be used in the service of his purpose."[28] But it is simply not true that Christ had to "transform" the "tragedy" of His death into something God could use. This claim ignores the statement in Rev 13:8 that Jesus is "the Lamb slain from the founda-

24. καὶ περιπατεῖτε ἐν ἀγάπῃ, καθὼς καὶ ὁ Χριστὸς ἠγάπησεν ἡμᾶς καὶ παρέ δωκεν ἑαυτὸν ὑπὲρ ἡμῶν προσφορὰν καὶ θυσίαν τῷ εἰς ὀσμὴν εὐωδίας (Eph 5:2).

25. ἐπεὶ ἔδει αὐτὸν πολλάκις παθεῖν ἀπὸ καταβολῆς κόσμου· νυνὶ δὲ ἅπαξ ἐπὶ συντελείᾳ τῶν αἰώνων εἰς ἀθέτησιν τῆς ἁμαρτίας διὰ τῆς θυσίας αὐτοῦ πεφανέ ρωται (Heb 9:26).

26. οὗτος δὲ μίαν ὑπὲρ ἁμαρτιῶν προσενέγκας θυσίαν εἰς τὸ διηνεκὲς ἐκά θισεν ἐν δεξιᾷ τοῦ θεοῦ (Heb 10:12).

27. Διὰ τοῦτό με ὁ πατὴρ ἀγαπᾷ ὅτι ἐγὼ τίθημι τὴν ψυχήν μου, ἵνα πάλιν λάβω αὐτήν. οὐδεὶς αἴρε αὐτὴν ἀπ᾽ ἐμοῦ, ἀλλ᾽ ἐγὼ τίθημι αὐτὴν ἀπ᾽ ἐμαυτοῦ. ἐξουσίαν ἔχω θεῖναι αὐτήν, καὶ ἐξουσίαν ἔχω πάλιν λαβεῖν αὐτήν· ταύτην τὴν ἐντολὴν ἔλαβον παρὰ τοῦ πατρός μου (Jn 10:17–18).

28. TAC, 19.

tion of the world."[29] That Jesus' death would be a sacrifice was determined in the eternal will of God. It was not a fortuitous turn of events of which Jesus took advantage. I most emphatically do not believe that this is what Hanegraaff is proposing. Hanegraaff would be the first to defend the truth of the sacrifice of Christ and the sovereignty of God in planning our salvation by it. For many years Hanegraaff has been on the front lines of the defense of orthodoxy. Rather, it appears that Hanegraaff simply made a poor choice of authorities from whom to quote to try to make his point, and because of this his point falls flat.

LaHaye's Misunderstanding

Hanegraaff next accuses LaHaye of misunderstanding "the cardinal truth of Christ's sacrifice."[30] He argues, "The writer of Hebrews explicitly says that in Christ the old covenant order, including temple sacrifices, are 'obsolete' and 'will soon disappear' (Hebrews 8:13)."[31] The verse says, "When He said, 'A new *covenant*,' He has made the first obsolete. But whatever is becoming obsolete and growing old is ready to disappear."[32] But once again Hanegraaff has committed a logical fallacy—a different one this time. This time it is the fallacy of selective reporting. This fallacy is committed by reporting only those facts that tend to support your position and conveniently ignoring those facts that tend not to support your position. In this case, Hanegraaff fails to put this statement into its context:

> For if that first covenant had been faultless, then no place would have been sought for a second. Because finding fault with them, He says: Behold, the days are coming, says the Lord, when I will make a new covenant with the house of Israel and with the house of Judah not according to the covenant that I made with their fathers in the day when I took them by the hand to lead them out of the land of Egypt; because they did not continue in My covenant, and I disregarded them, says the Lord. For this is the covenant that I will make with the house of Israel after those days, says the Lord: I

29. ἀρνίου τοῦ ἐσφαγμένου ἀπὸ καταβολῆς κόσμου (Rev 13:8).

30. TAC, 19.

31. Ibid.

32. ἐν τῷ λέγειν καινὴν πεπαλαίωκεν τὴν πρώτην· τὸ δὲ παλαιούμενον καὶ γηράσκον ἐγγὺς ἀφανισμοῦ (Heb 8:13).

will put My laws in their mind and write them on their hearts; and
I will be their God, and they shall be My people. (Heb 8:7–10)[33]

Notice that the text actually says the new covenant is with the house
of Israel and the house of Judah. So, the statement of verse 13 is not as
plain and proper, to use Hanegraaff's own words, as he would have his
reader think. He criticizes LaHaye for teaching "that the temple must be
rebuilt and that the temple sacrifices must be reinstated."[34] But, if the New
Covenant is to be made with the house of Israel and the house of Judah,
and yet Israel has not turned back to God in faith even today, then it
seems to follow that the New Covenant with Israel and Judah has not
yet been established. So, as far as the people of Israel are concerned, they
are still operating under the Old Covenant. They do not know about the
New Covenant yet. That being the case, Israel as a nation would certainly
take steps to rebuild the temple and re-institute the sacrificial system.
Martin Goodman makes an interesting observation about the rebuilding of the Temple: "In fact, the detailed prescriptions for the sacrifices
to be found in the Mishnah, redacted around 200 CE, presuppose that
even at that date rabbis expected, or at least hoped, that the Temple could
and would be rebuilt. The hope was entirely reasonable. Jerusalem had
lost one Temple in 587 BCE only to see it restored. The more Josephus
pointed out the parallels between the two destructions, which had taken
place in both cases on the same day of the month of Ab (in late July), the
more plausible was a parallel rebuilding."[35] The fact that these sacrifices
are no longer of any value is beside the point, because the people of Israel
don't know that. They think the sacrificial system is still valid. And, since
they rebuilt the temple and re-instituted the sacrificial system after it was
destroyed by Nebuchadnezzar, there is no reason to think that the people

33. Εἰ γὰρ ἡ πρώτη ἐκείνη ἦν ἄμεμπτος, οὐκ ἂν δευτέρας ἐζητεῖτο τόπος.
μεμφόμενος γὰρ αὐτοὺς λέγει· ἰδοὺ ἡμέραι ἔρχονται, λέγει κύριος, καὶ συντελέ
σω ἐπὶ τὸν οὖκον Ἰσρὴλ καὶ ἐπὶ τὸν οἶκον Ἰούδα διαθήκην καινήν, οὐ κατὰ
τὴν διαθήκην, ἣν ἐποίησα τοῖς πατράσιν αὐτῶν ἐν ἡμέρᾳ ἐπιλαβομένου μου τῆς
χειρὸς αὐτῶν ἐξαγαγεῖν αὐτοὺς ἐκ γῆς Αἰγύπτου, ὅτι αὐτοὶ οὐκ ἐνέμειναν ἐν
τῇ διαθήκῃ μου, κἀγὼ ἠμέλησα αὐτῶν, λέγει κύριος· ὅτι αὕτη ἡ διαθήκη, ἣν
διαθήσομαι τῷ οἴκῳ Ἰσραὴλ μετὰ τὰς ἡμέρας ἐκείνας, λέγει κύριος· διδοὺς νό
μους μου εἰς τὴν διάνοιαν αὐτῶν καὶ ἐπὶ καρδίας αὐτῶν ἐπιγράψω αὐτούς, καὶ
ἔσωμαι αὐτοῖς εἰς θεόν, καὶ αὐτοὶ ἔσονταί μοι εἰς λαόν· (Heb 8:7–10).

34. TAC, 19.

35. Martin Goodman, *Rome and Jerusalem: The Clash of Ancient Civilizations* (New
York: Alfred A. Knopf, 2007), 427.

of Israel would not believe they can do it again. Neither LaHaye nor other dispensationalists are claiming that the rebuilding of the temple and the reestablishing of the sacrificial system will re-institute the Old Covenant. Rather, they are claiming that Israel, as a people who are still in rebellion and still think that the Old Covenant is in force and valid, will rebuild the temple and re-institute the sacrificial system because they think this is the right thing to do.

So, not only has Hanegraaff misrepresented Caird's statement about Christ's sacrifice, but he has also misrepresented LaHaye's and dispensationalists' claims about the rebuilding of the temple. Hanegraaff's criticism of the notion of Israel rebuilding the temple is like claiming that just because Jesus offers salvation by grace through faith, the Buddhists will not build another temple. But this doesn't follow. The Jews do not accept Jesus as their Messiah any more than the Buddhists accept the salvation He offers. And the Jews will do what they think is the right thing to do even though Christians believe differently. And the claim that LaHaye's "literalism forces him to conclude that such temple sacrifices are not merely memorial but absolutely necessary for the atonement of sins such as ceremonial uncleanness" is completely irrelevant. Whether LaHaye believes this or not does not prove Hanegraaff's point because this is not a part of dispensational belief. If LaHaye believes this, then he believes this as part of his own doctrine. But to claim that the temple will be rebuilt and the sacrificial system re-instituted does not force anyone to believe what Hanegraaff claims. The position Hanegraaff criticizes does not follow necessarily nor is it entailed by the prior belief.

Grabbing Everything

Hanegraaff warns his reader, "once you begin heading down that road, everything is up for grabs."[36] He even implies that LaHaye denies the sufficiency of Christ's atonement on the cross and his bodily resurrection. But this is simply a personal attack on a fellow believer. The denial of these doctrines does not logically or necessarily follow from a literal or even a literalistic hermeneutic. To support his point, Hanegraaff claims, "As noted in the introduction, LaHaye's literalism causes him to conclude that the Antichrist has the power to lay down his life and to take it up again,

36. TAC, 20.

thus demonstrating that he is God."[37] But, once again, if LaHaye believes this (interestingly Hanegraaff provides the reader with no indication as to where LaHaye's statement can be found) then this is his own doctrine, but it is not a standard dispensationalist position. Consequently, Hanegraaff's criticism has simply become a criticism of Tim LaHaye, not one of either premillennialism or dispensationalism. To argue against LaHaye's beliefs on this point is not to argue against the system, but to argue only against the person. It is certainly true, as Hanegraaff asserts, "the careful student of the Bible recognizes and accurately interprets *form, figurative language, and fantasy imagery*."[38] But, if Hanegraaff has demonstrated that LaHaye employs a "hyper-literalism," then this says nothing one way or the other about premillennialism or dispensationalism. I agree! The careful student *ought* to interpret the language according to the kind of language it is. This applies as much to Hanegraaff as anyone else. But, as we have seen, Hanegraaff is just as capable as anyone else of ignoring these principles when it serves his purpose.

FORM

Genre

Hanegraaff begins his section on "Form" by discussing genre. He says, "to interpret the Bible as literature, it is crucial to consider the kind of literature we are interpreting. Just as a legal brief differs in form from a prophetic oracle, so too there is a difference in genre between Leviticus and Revelation."[39] He illustrates the importance of genre by pointing out that one cannot treat Genesis as allegory since "the very foundation of Christianity would be destroyed."[40] Of course from Hanegraaff's point of view, a literalistic method "often does as much violence to the text as does a spiritualized interpretation that empties the text of objective meaning."[41] He warns, "A literal-at-all-costs method of interpretation is particularly troublesome when it comes to books of the Bible in which visionary imagery is the governing genre."[42] Once again, for Hanegraaff to criticize

37. Ibid.
38. Ibid.
39. Ibid.
40. Ibid., 21.
41. Ibid.
42. Ibid.

what he characterizes as a "literal-at-all-costs" method is not an argument against dispensationalism or pretribulationism, since such a method is not advocated by this eschatological system. Rather, his criticism boils down to a criticism of some particular interpreters.

However, Hanegraaff has placed more emphasis on genre than the concept can support. The book of Revelation does not come with a tag warning the interpreter that he is approaching apocalyptic literature, so how does Hanegraaff know that Revelation is an apocalyptic vision? Well, he would need to begin to read the text in order to discover the features of the text that might signal the kind of genre. But, if, as Hanegraaff declares, "To interpret the Bible literally, we must first pay special attention to what is known as *form* or *genre*," then we would need to know the genre before we began to interpret the text. But, in order to discover the genre we would need to read the text and understand at least some of it in order to decide which genre it is. But if we cannot interpret the text until we know which genre it is, and we can't discover the genre until we read the text and understand at least some of it, then we are at a loss to be able to read and understand the Bible at all. So, it seems that a certain amount of interpretation must occur before we know the genre in order to discover those characteristics of the text that alert us to the particular genre. But, if interpretation to some degree can occur before we know the genre, then genre is not as crucial as Hanegraaff makes it out to be.[43]

Of course, someone will say that we are told by other interpreters that Revelation is apocalyptic vision. But, this argument doesn't work since somewhere someone would have to discover the genre by his or her own interpretative efforts, and then the problem would arise. The fact of the matter is, genre does not determine meaning. We can and do understand some meaning before we know what the genre is. In fact, we must understand some meaning in order to discover the genre. So, Hanegraaff has made the mistake of listening to others who have made these kinds of statements about genre without realizing the contradictions these claims involve.

Additionally, genre classifications are not rigid straight jackets that force interpreters, or ever writers, to abide by predetermined categories and features. Whether Revelation is apocalyptic literature is an ongoing debate. And, even if we acknowledge that the book of Revelation is apoca-

---

43. For a fuller discussion of this issue, see Thomas A. Howe, "Does Genre Determine Meaning," *Christian Apologetics Journal* 6 (Spring 2007): 1–20.

lyptic literature, this does not guarantee that everything that is contained in the book is necessarily a vision, image, symbol, or whatever else this kind of literature might contain. The very nature of genre is fluid, and authors push the boundaries of a genre sometimes making it difficult to apply a single genre class or category. In fact, this is how genres like apocalyptic literature were developed. There was no such genre until some author developed it. So, the first author of an apocalyptic text was not confined by the existing literary classifications. Rather, he developed a new style which came to be known as apocalyptic literature. But, this genre is constantly undergoing change and development itself. So, by classifying Revelation as apocalyptic does not guarantee that its style will exactly coincide with other instances of the same genre. Rather, each aspect of the text must be taken in its own right. Hanegraaff is simply not acquainted with the technical aspects of or debates surrounding genre and genre criticism, so he ends up making uninformed assertions.

Revelation and Apocalyptic Literature

What this means is, just because Hanegraaff thinks that Revelation is apocalyptic, or whatever genre he chooses, this does not guarantee that some particular passage must be understood as an apocalyptic vision. That is just not how genre works. Genre does not force everything in a given book to conform to the characteristics of that genre. Genesis is primarily narrative history. However, it does contain features of other kinds of genre, like genealogical record, poetry, etc. Hanegraaff cannot claim that because Revelation is apocalyptic, or whatever, that its various parts must conform to what he thinks this genre entails.

And again, just because some particular interpreter employs a "woodenly literal sense" in his interpretation of various portions of Revelation is no argument against dispensationalism or pretribulationism. What Hanegraaff must show is that these systems necessarily require such a practice. But in fact they don't. So, Hanegraaff's criticism amounts to nothing more than objecting to the way a particular interpreter does his job.

An example Hanegraaff uses is "an apocalyptic vision in which an angel swinging a sharp sickle gathers grapes into 'the great winepress of the wrath of God.' The blood flowing out of the winepress rises as high as 'the horses' bridles for a distance of 1,600 stadia' (14:19–20)."[44] Notice how Hanegraaff has already decided for the reader that this must be an apocalyptic vision, and he does this without the least argument as to why anyone should think that it is. The fact that it occurs in the book of Revelation is no argument that this must be an apocalyptic vision. John often refers to Jesus in the book, but are we to think that this isn't really a reference to the literal Jesus? Perhaps this is an apocalyptic vision, but Hanegraaff needs to argue the case and make his case for the reader, not just assume that his classification is necessarily *the* correct one.

But, even granting that this is an apocalyptic vision, does this necessarily mean that everything referred to in the vision is not about that literal thing, but a symbol of something else? Is the reference to the wrath of God not a reference to the real, literal wrath of God? And, why does Hanegraaff think that the reference to 1,600 stadia, if taken literally, must mean that the reference to the horses' bridles must also be strictly literal? Could not that be an hyperbole, but still be literal? We find this very kind of thing in Matt 2:3: "When Herod the king heard this, he was troubled, and all Jerusalem [πᾶσα Ἱεροσόλυμα, pasa hIerosoluma] with him."[45] Now, it certainly seems to be the case that Matthew is referring to the real, literal Jerusalem, but it is very unlikely that literally all of Jerusalem was troubled with Herod. There were probably little children in Jerusalem who were not troubled with Herod. There were probably many people in Jerusalem who were not even privy to this information. And there were certainly hundreds of people who did not like Herod, and might even be glad that Herod was troubled. So, the word 'all' does not necessarily mean every single person in Jerusalem. Rather, this is an hyperbole, an exaggeration for the purpose of emphasis. So, even though the word 'all' is figurative, the word 'Jerusalem' refers to the real place, and the description as a whole is talking about a literal, actual event that actually literally occurred. Likewise, it is possible that the reference to the blood "to the horses' bridles" is an hyperbole even though the description as a whole refers to a literal, actual event in which there is a huge amount of blood that literally actually stretches 1,600 stadia.

Now, this may not convince anyone, but that's not the point. The point is, it is possible to understand this reference without being "wood-

44. TAC, 21.

45. ἀκούσας δὲ ὁ βασιλεὺς Ἡρῴδης ἐταράχθη καὶ πᾶσα Ἱεροσόλυμα μετ' αὐτοῦ (Matt 2:3).

enly literal" and yet at the same time not agreeing with Hanegraaff's interpretation. The fact that this reference can legitimately be taken another way, and is by competent scholars, requires Hanegraaff to make his case, not simply assume that he is right. And why does he assume he is right? Because he has a prior eschatological perspective through which he is interpreting the text.

Now interpreting the text through one's prior eschatological commitment is not necessarily bad or wrong. The bad thing is to do this and yet pretend as if you're not doing it by claiming that this is just a function of the genre. That is simply disingenuous and false. If Hanegraaff thinks he is right, then he owes it to his readers to demonstrate why his understanding is the correct one. In fact, such a demonstration is precisely what he must do if he is going to equip his reader to "be the judge." His readers need to see how and why he has come to the conclusion he has, and he needs to show the steps by which he has reached this conclusion. Simply using his assumptions to attack LaHaye does not equip anyone to do anything other than use their own assumptions to attack others. And appealing to genre doesn't cut it since that's not what genre does. Hanegraaff accuses LaHaye of a "failure to consider form and genre," but Hanegraaff has failed to understand form and genre. You simply cannot assume that because Revelation is apocalyptic, if it is, that everything that is described is necessarily an apocalyptic vision that contains only imagery and symbol. Sometimes even apocalyptic vision contains references to real, literal, actual things and events.

Destruction of Jerusalem

Also, Hanegraaff has failed to study history. He claims, "Far from merely communicating that twenty-first-century Israel would be submerged in a literal river of blood, John is using the apocalyptic language of Old Testament prophets to warn his hearers of the massive judgment and destruction of the land of Israel that 'must soon take place.'"[46] But apparently Hanegraaff has never actually studied the history of the destruction of Jerusalem and the Temple in 70 AD. As a matter of historical fact, the destruction was relatively localized and did not cover "the land of Israel" as Hanegraaff supposes. Historian S. Safari points out, "the Jewish people in the Land of Israel was [*sic*] not reduced to total devastation. Not only

46. TAC, 22.

WHAT THE BIBLE REALLY SAYS

was it able to wage a great war only one generation after the destruction, but the population had to a remarkable degree recovered its numeric and economic strength by the end of the first century."[47] Safrai goes on to note, "As a matter of fact, there is evidence to show that both during and after the war many Jewish farmers stayed on the land, cultivated it and even owned it."[48] In other words, there were farmers in the land of Israel who were totally unaffected by the events of 70 AD. So, Hanegraaff's characterization of the event as a "massive judgment and destruction of the land of Israel" is completely inaccurate. This kind of information should have been discovered by Hanegraaff in his "historical principle." If Hanegraaff is not adequately applying his own principles in this case, how can the reader be assured that he is adequately applying his own principles in other instances? This is a particularly acute problem since Hanegraaff does not provide any argumentation for most of what he claims.

Vesture Dipped in Blood

And notice how Hanegraaff reads into the text what is not there. He says, "the blood-spattered robe of Christ is not only emblematic of grapes of wrath but of blood that flowed from Immanuel's veins."[49] Yet nowhere in the text is there any reference to Immanuel's blood. Now, it may certainly be the case that this is the meaning of the picture, but Hanegraaff doesn't even bother to argue that this is the correct interpretation. He simply declares it as if this must be correct. But, simply assuming that his interpretation is correct doesn't equip the reader to be the judge. Rather, Hanegraaff's interpretation serves as the real judge without allowing the reader the opportunity of learning how and why his understanding should be accepted as correct. Unfortunately, this is one of Hanegraaff's consistent practices throughout his book. He simply does not follow through on his promise to equip the reader to be his own judge. Interpreters certainly need to "seriously consider form or genre in order to rightly interpret," but Hanegraaff has not demonstrated how this should be done. He presented several of his own conclusions, but he didn't show the reader how he got

47. S. Safari, "The Jews in the Land of Israel (70–335 CE)," in *A History of the Jewish People*, ed. H. H. Ben-Sasson (Cambridge: Harvard University Press, 1976), 314.

48. Ibid., 315.

49. TAC, 22.

to these conclusions other than to illustrate that he did this in part from his prior eschatological commitment.

FIGURATIVE LANGUAGE

The next topic in this chapter on the literal principle is figurative language. Hanegraaff says, "Such language differs from literal language, in which words mean exactly what they say. Figurative language requires readers to use their imagination to comprehend what the author is driving at. Such imaginative leaps are the rule rather than the exception in that virtually every genre of literature contains metaphorical language."[50] It is not clear what it means for an interpreter to use his imagination or to take "imaginative leaps." But it would seem to be much more important to attempt to discover what an original author meant by a particular figure of speech than to leap into one's imagination. An "imaginative leap" sounds dangerously like dreaming up a meaning.

Hanegraaff quotes from Gene Edward Veith to illustrate his point.

> Many people have *bouts of depression*, but when they learn to *reach out* to others they find that life looks *brighter* [emphasis added]. ... [While] the term *depression* literally means a low point in the ground; it has become a metaphor for a mental condition, of feeling "low" (another metaphor). Bout refers to a round of fighting. The gesture of "reaching out" and the optical image of something becoming "brighter" are more obvious metaphors. The point is (notice the metaphor involved in that phrase), dull prose (another metaphor) is actually alive with unconscious metaphors.[51]

It doesn't take a rocket scientist to realize that a good practice to follow in doing research is to look up words in an actual dictionary, not a metaphorical one. Veith says "the term *depression* literally means a low point in the ground," but this is in fact not accurate. According to *Webster's New Twentieth Century Dictionary, Unabridged, second edition*, the term 'depression' has the following literal meanings:

50. Ibid., 23.

51. Gene Edward Veith, Jr., *Reading Between the Lines: A Christian Guide to Literature* (Wheaton: Crossway, 1990), 84; quoted in TAC, 24.

1. A depressing or being depressed.

2. A depressed part of place; a hollow or low place on a surface.

3. Low spirits; gloominess; dejection; sadness.

4. A decrease in force, activity, amount, etc.[52]

There are seven more literal meanings. None of these is listed in the dictionary as figurative. They are all literal. This dictionary indicates that this English word came from the Latin, oisserped. According to the *Oxford Latin Dictionary*, the word "oisserped" did not even literally mean "a low point in the ground"; "The action of sinking down or lowering."[53] Perhaps Hanegraaff should have included another 'L' in his acronym to stand for "Lexicography," or another 'S' for "Semantics." In fact, the term 'depression' has not "become a metaphor for a mental condition." If the English word was initially a metaphor for this condition, it has long since become literal speech. But the development of a word over time is not an aspect of literal interpretation, or even of figurative language. It comes under the heading of Etymology, the study of the origins and history of words. Unfortunately for both Veith and Hanegraaff, the same is true of the word 'bout.' It is not a figure of speech. One of the possible, literal meanings of the word is "a contest; a match; as, a fencing *bout*."[54] This word is actually from the Anglo Saxon word *byht* which meant "a bend, from *bugan*, to bend."[55]

What this shows is that identifying a figure of speech it is not as easy and simple a matter as Hanegraaff would try to make us think. And, even if a word can be used as a figure of speech, it is not necessarily an easy and simple thing to identify when it is being used this way. So, for Hanegraaff to say, "we might well say that figurative language is the principle [*sic*] means by which God communicates spiritual realities to his children"[56] is a questionable claim at best. Even communicating spiritual realities "through means of earthly, empirically perceptible events, persons, or objects"[57] does not necessarily entail the use of metaphors. But again Hanegraaff does not bother to indicate how he arrived at this

---

52. *Webster's New Twentieth Century Dictionary* (1977), s.v. "depression."

53. *Oxford Latin Dictionary* (2005), s.v. "depressiō."

54. *Webster's New Twentieth Century Dictionary* (1977), s.v. "bout."

55. Ibid.

56. TAC, 24.

57. Ibid.

conclusion. He simply asserts it as if no one can question its accuracy. But seeing that Hanegraaff neglected to verify the accuracy of Veith's claims, the reader should be skeptical about any of Hanegraaff's claims that are not supported by demonstration or verification.

Metaphor

Definition

Hanegraaff defines metaphor as "an implied comparison that identifies a word or phrase with something that it does not literally represent."[58] The whole concept of metaphor is a hotly debated issue not only in disciplines that consider it in a literary sense, but also in philosophy, and philosophy of language. In fact, according to Richard Moran, "Aside from its obvious importance in poetics, rhetoric, and aesthetics, it also figures in such fields as philosophy of mind (as in the question of the metaphorical status of ordinary mental concepts), philosophy of science (as in the comparison of metaphors and explanatory models), in epistemology (as in analogical reasoning), and in cognitive studies (as in the theory of concept-formation)."[59] So the whole concept of metaphor, both defining it and identifying it, is not a simple matter, and Hanegraaff's definition is simplistic at best.

But for the purposes of this discussion we may provisionally accept Hanegraaff's definition, provided we can obtain from Hanegraaff's discussion an explanation of what he means by "imaginative leap." We can perhaps also supplement Hanegraaff's definition: "In metaphor we interpret an utterance as meaning something different from what the words would mean, taken literally. . . . The words, or the utterance, have one meaning when intended or taken literally, and another when spoken metaphorically."[60] As an example of an imaginative leap in grasping a metaphor, Hanegraaff refers the reader to Jn 6:48: "For example, when Jesus said, 'I am the bread of life,' he was obviously not saying that he was literally the 'staff of life' (i.e., physical bread). Rather, he was metaphorically communicating that he is the 'stuff of life' (i.e., the essence of true life)."[61]

---

58. Ibid.

59. Richard Moran, "Metaphor," in *A Companion to the Philosophy of Language*, ed. Bob Hale and Crispin Wright (London: Blackwell Publishers, 1997), 248.

60. Ibid., 249.

61. TAC, 25.

But, is this what this metaphor means? In the context of this statement in John 6, Jesus identifies Himself as the living bread that came down from heaven. He even challenges His readers to eat this bread. Is this about being the essence of life or being the source of life? Maybe these mean the same thing, but Hanegraaff doesn't bother to clear up these kinds of questions and issues. He doesn't even bother to justify his claim that this is about Jesus being the essence of true life.

Example from John 6:48

If a metaphor is a comparison that describes or refers to one thing using terms that describe or refer to something else, then there must be some point of comparison by which the two can be compared. For example, we could say that the terms of the metaphor are to the thing described as the terms of literal speech are to the thing to which the comparison is being made. So, in Jn 6:48 we could say, bread is to beings who need food in order to live physically as Jesus is to beings who need Him in order to live spiritually. However, bread is not the essence of physical life, nor is it the essence of food stuffs. Bread was a staple of the diet in the time Jesus made this statement, but there were other foods, and life is certainly more than bread: "Man shall not live on bread alone, but on every word that proceeds out of the mouth of God" (Matt 4:4).[62] So, the metaphor may not be a comparison between bread being the essence of food and Jesus being the essence of life. Rather, the metaphor may be a comparison between the fact that man needs bread to sustain his physical life, and so likewise man needs Jesus to sustain his spiritual life. It may not have anything to do with being the essence of anything.

And besides this, what does "true life" mean? Hanegraaff does not explain this expression, so the reader does not know what he means and how "true life" differs from "life." Now, if Hanegraaff cannot get this simple metaphor right, how can his reader trust that he is getting any other metaphors right?

Example from Matthew 26:63–64

Hanegraaff discusses another example from Matt 26:63–64. In discussing this passage, Hanegraaff says, "First, they [Caiaphas and the Sanhedrin] understood that in saying he was 'the Son of Man' who would come 'on

---

62. ὁ δὲ ἀποκριθεὶς εἶπεν· γέγραπται· οὐκ ἐπ' ἄρτῳ μόνῳ ζήσεται ὁ ἄνθρωπος, ἀλλ' ἐπὶ παντὶ ῥήματι ἐκπορευομένῳ διὰ στόματος θεοῦ (Matt 4:4).

the clouds of heaven,' Jesus was making reference to his coronation as the Son of Man in Daniel's vision (Daniel 7:13–14)."[63] It is important to quote these verses from Daniel: "I kept looking in the night visions, and behold, with the clouds of heaven one like a Son of Man was coming, and He came up to the Ancient of Days and was presented before Him. And to Him was given dominion, glory and a kingdom, that all the peoples, nations and men of every language might serve Him. His dominion is an everlasting dominion which will not pass away; and His kingdom is one which will not be destroyed."

חָזֵה הֲוֵית בְּחֶזְוֵי לֵילְיָא וַאֲרוּ עִם־ עֲנָנֵי שְׁמַיָּא

13   כְּבַר אֱנָשׁ אָתֵה הֲוָה וְעַד־עַתִּיק יוֹמַיָּא מְטָה

וּקְדָמוֹהִי הַקְרְבוּהִי:

וְלֵהּ יְהִיב שָׁלְטָן וִיקָר וּמַלְכוּ וְכֹל עַמְמַיָּא אֻמַיָּא

14   וְלִשָּׁנַיָּא לֵהּ יִפְלְחוּן שָׁלְטָנֵהּ שָׁלְטָן עָלַם דִּי־לָא

יֶעְדֵּה וּמַלְכוּתֵהּ דִּי־לָא תִתְחַבַּל:

(Dan 7:13–14)

The interesting thing here is that nowhere in these verses, or in the context for that matter, is anything said about this being a "coronation" of Jesus as the Son of Man. This may sound like splitting hairs, but it is this very kind of eisegesis that causes misinterpretation and misunderstanding. As much as is possible an interpreter must not "go beyond," Hanegraaff's own words, what the text actually says. Whole heretical doctrines have been built upon what the text did not say. Perhaps another letter should be added to LIGHTS, 'O' for Observation, that is, observing what is and what is not there.

Hanegraaff goes on to say, "It is crucial to note that in Daniel's prophecy the Son of Man is not *descending* to earth at the end of history but rather *ascending* to heaven."[64] Here Hanegraaff makes a confident assertion about something scholars have debated for hundreds of years, and he does this without the least bit of supporting argument or evidence. Once

---

63. TAC, 25.
64. Ibid., 26.

again we need to reproduce the text in order to consider Hanegraaff's statement.

> I kept looking until thrones were set up, and the Ancient of Days took His seat; His vesture was like white snow and the hair of His head like pure wool. His throne was ablaze with flames, its wheels were a burning fire. A river of fire was flowing and coming out from before Him; Thousands upon thousands were attending Him, and myriads upon myriads were standing before Him; The court sat, and the books were opened. (Dan 7:9–10)

וְיָדַעְתָּ כִּי־יהוה אֱלֹהֶיךָ הוּא הָאֱלֹהִים הָאֵל הַנֶּאֱמָן

שֹׁמֵר הַבְּרִית וְהַחֶסֶד לְאֹהֲבָיו וּלְשֹׁמְרֵי מִצְוֹתָו   9

לְאֶלֶף דּוֹר:

וּמְשַׁלֵּם לְשֹׂנְאָיו אֶל־פָּנָיו לְהַאֲבִידוֹ לֹא יְאַחֵר   10

לְשֹׂנְאוֹ אֶל־פָּנָיו יְשַׁלֶּם־לוֹ:

(Dan 7:9–10)

But the court will sit for judgment, and his dominion will be taken away, annihilated and destroyed forever. (Dan 7:26)

וְדִינָא יִתִּב וְשָׁלְטָנֵהּ יְהַעְדּוֹן לְהַשְׁמָדָה וּלְהוֹבָדָה   26

עַד־סוֹפָא

(Dan 7:26)

Notice that neither in the text that describes the setting up of the thrones in 7:9, nor in the interpretation of this in 7:26, nor in the passage quoted earlier, is there any statement about the Son of Man descending to earth or ascending to heaven. And, just because the Ancient of Days took a seat does not necessarily mean that these thrones were set up in heaven. Maybe they were, but that cannot simply be assumed, it must be demonstrated to be the case. Also, verse 13 does not say the Son of Man ascended or descended. It simply says Daniel saw Him coming with the clouds.[65] The word translated "coming" is the Aramaic word אָתֵה (hta'). It is a Pe'al participle that simply means "coming." It doesn't mean "coming down" or "coming up,"—just "coming." Verse 13 also says, "and He came

---

65. The Aramaic for Dan 7:13 is given in footnote 136 above.

up to the Ancient of Days [וְעַד־עַתִּיק יוֹמַיָּא]." The translation "came up
to" is a translation of the one Aramaic word עַד ('ad). According to KBH,
this word can have several possible meanings: "up to, even to, as much as,
until, during, within."[66] So, it is not necessary to translate this as "He came
up to." It could be translated "He came even to the Ancient of Days." So,
you cannot appeal to this verse to prove that the Son of Man is ascending
to heaven. In fact, there is nothing in the whole chapter that can prove
that the Son of Man is ascending to heaven. Again, Hanegraaff's lack of
understanding of the original languages, Aramaic in this case, leads him
to accept an interpretation that may not be correct. And notice that he
doesn't offer any support or argument for his claim—he just states it as if
it must be true.

When Hanegraaff talks about combining Daniel's prophecy and
Psalm 110, you should notice that he doesn't say who did this or where it
is done. In fact, this is not even hinted at in the passages in Matthew and
Mark to which Hanegraaff appeals. So, the combining must be something
that Hanegraaff does, but there is no reason to do this and there is no
Scriptural support for doing this. The Daniel passage is not necessarily
about ascending to the throne of God. When Hanegraaff says, "Like the
Old Testament prophets, Jesus employs the symbolism of clouds to warn
his hearers that as judgment fell on Egypt, so too, judgment would soon be-
fall Jerusalem,"[67] he doesn't bother to site a passage. So, the reader can only
conclude that he is referring either to Mark 14:63–64 or Matt 26:63–64.
However, in neither one of these passages is either Egypt or Jerusalem
mentioned. Hanegraaff is simply reading into the text what he wants to
find there, and he does this without offering any argument to show that
maybe he is correct. Why does he do this? Because he is interpreting these
passages from his prior eschatological commitment even though he attempts to present his claims as if they are actually in the text.

The Sign or the Son of Man?

Hanegraaff declares, "Gary DeMar rightly notes that 'Jesus was not telling
them to look for Himself in the sky. He told them that they would see a
sign that proved He was in heaven, sitting at His Father's right hand (Acts
2:30–36). Those who had witnessed Jerusalem's destruction would see the

66. KBH, s.v. "עַד."
67. TAC, 26.

sign of Jesus's enthronement when they saw Jerusalem's destruction.'"[68] Once again we need to quote the passage to see if the text actually says what Hanegraaff claims.

> For as the lightning comes from the east and flashes to the west, so also will the coming of the Son of Man be. For wherever the carcass is, there the eagles will be gathered together. Immediately after the tribulation of those days the sun will be darkened, and the moon will not give its light; the stars will fall from heaven, and the powers of the heavens will be shaken. Then the sign of the Son of Man will appear in heaven, and then all the tribes of the earth will mourn, and they will see the Son of Man coming on the clouds of heaven with power and great glory. And He will send His angels with a great sound of a trumpet, and they will gather together His elect from the four winds, from one end of heaven to the other. (Matt 24:27–31)[69]

Now DeMar and Hanegraaff claim that Jesus is not telling His hearers to look for Him in the sky. But, if that's not the case, then why in the world did Jesus compare this event to lightening coming from the east and flashing to the west, and why did He say this would be the "coming of the Son of Man"? Jesus said the sign would be the sign of the Son of Man coming on the clouds of heaven: "Then the sign of the Son of Man will appear in heaven . . . and they will see the Son of Man coming on the clouds of heaven [ἐρχόμενον ἐπὶ τῶν νεφελῶν τοῦ οὐρανοῦ]." If this isn't talking about looking for Him in the sky, then one has to wonder how such a event can be expressed? It is simply absurd to try to make this text refer to some sign that Jesus is on the throne rather than taking the "plain and commonsense" statement just for what it says. Please forgive my harsh language, but it stretches the credulity of the most faithful Preterist

68. Ibid., 26–27.

69. ὥσπερ γὰρ ἡ ἀστραπὴ ἐξέρχεται ἀπὸ ἀνατωλῶν καὶ φαίνεται ἕως δυσμῶν, οὕτως ἔσται ἡ παρουσία τοῦ βίου τοῦ ἀνθρώπου· ὅπου ἐὰν ᾖ τὸ πτῶμα, ἐκεῖ συναχθήσονται οἱ ἀετοί. Εὐθέως δὲ μετὰ τὴν θλῖψιν τῶν ἡμερῶν ἐκείνων ὁ ἥλιος σκοτισθήσεται, καὶ ἡ σελήνη οὐ δώσει τὸ φέγγος αὐτῆς, καὶ οἱ ἀστέρες πεσοῦνται ἀπὸ τοῦ οὐρανοῦ, καὶ αἱ δυνάμεις τῶν οὐρανῶν σαλευθήσονται. καὶ τότε φανήσεται τὸ σημεῖον τοῦ υἱοῦ τοῦ ἀνθρώπου ἐν οὐρανῷ, καὶ τότε κόψονται πᾶσαι αἱ φυλαὶ τῆς γῆς καὶ ὄψονται τὸν υἱὸν τοῦ ἀνθρώπου ἐρχόμενον ἐπὶ τῶν νεφελῶν τοῦ οὐρανοῦ μετὰ δυνάμεως καὶ δόξης πολλῆς· καὶ ἀποστελεῖ τοὺς ἀγγέλους αὐτοῦ μετὰ σάλπιγγος μεγάλης, καὶ ἐπισυνάξουσιν τοὺς ἐκλεκτοὺς αὐτοῦ ἐκ τῶν τεσσάρων ἀνέμων ἀπ' ἄκρων οὐρανῶν ἕως τῶν ἄκρων αὐτῶν (Matt 24:27–31).

to think that this could possibly be a serious suggestion. If Jesus is not talking about seeing Himself in the sky, but rather seeing some "sign," then what is the sign? Why doesn't Jesus tell His hearers what the sign is? And how could they seriously suggest that the sign is the destruction of Jerusalem? The text explicitly states that the sign will be in the sky: "Then the sign of the Son of Man will appear in heaven [ἐν οὐρανῷ]." Are we to believe that Jerusalem or the destruction of Jerusalem is somehow "in heaven" as a sign? And, if there is some other sign that is supposed to be a sign in heaven pointing to the destruction of Jerusalem, then what is that sign? And, is that sign now a sign of both the destruction of Jerusalem and the Son sitting on the throne?

Nowhere in the context of either one of these passages is there anything even mentioned about Jesus sitting at the Father's right hand. And to stick the reference to Acts 2:30–36 as if these verses are somehow connected is not sufficient to prove his point. DeMar and Hanegraaff need to do much more than simply stick up a reference to some verses. Why should anyone think these verses are connected? Also, not only is the destruction of Jerusalem not even mentioned in the whole of Matthew 24 or Mark 14, the name Jerusalem does not even occur in either one of these chapters. Now if the destruction of Jerusalem is what Jesus is talking about, then Hanegraaff is going to have to explain why it's not mentioned and why anyone should think that the destruction of Jerusalem is somehow a sign "in heaven." But, he doesn't bother to do that. Perhaps yet another letter ought to be added to LIGHTS: 'C' for Context. The context simply does not support these claims—at least not the kind of straightforward, plain and proper, commonsense reading of the context that Hanegraaff himself encourages. And if it can be demonstrated that this is what these texts are saying, then Hanegraaff is obligated to do much more than simply claim that it is. He is obligated because he promised to give the reader the tools to "be the judge."

No Clouds in the Twenty-First Century?

Hanegraaff declares, "Finally, the 'coming on clouds' judgment metaphor was clearly not directed to a twenty-first-century audience as LaHaye presumes. Rather, it was intended for Caiaphas and the first-century crowd that condemned Christ to death. In the words of our Lord, 'I say to all of *you*: In the future *you* will *see* the Son of Man sitting at the right hand of the Mighty One and coming on the clouds of heaven' (Matt 26:64). The generation that crucified Christ would *see* the day that he was exalted and enthroned at 'the right hand of the Mighty One' (another metaphor)."[70] We have already shown that the pronoun 'you' is not necessarily always restricted to those to whom Jesus was directly speaking. In fact, consider the uses of this pronoun by Jesus as found in Matt 24:4–9.

> Take heed that no one deceives *you*. For many will come in My name, saying, I am the Christ, and will deceive many. And *you* will hear of wars and rumors of wars. See that *you* are not troubled; for all these things must come to pass, but the end is not yet. For nation will rise against nation, and kingdom against kingdom. And there will be famines, pestilences, and earthquakes in various places. All these are the beginning of sorrows. Then they will deliver *you* up to tribulation and kill *you*, and *you* will be hated by all nations for My names sake. (Matt 24:4–9)[71]

Now, are we to think that in each one of these instances Jesus was talking only about the disciples to whom He was directly speaking? In fact, some of these disciples died before there were "famines, pestilence, and earthquakes in various places," and before they even went out so that they could be "hated by all nations." Most of the disciples did not even get to "all nations." Of course some will say, "Of course some of the disciples died before some of these things happened, but Jesus was talking to all the disciples and this didn't mean that everyone of them would see every one of these things." But, that argument does not help. Once you start modifying and changing the references of "you," then it's no longer the case that 'you' necessarily is restricted only to His immediate audience. Now it's restricted to His audience, with these modifications. But, if the reference of 'you' can be modified here, then why not in Matt 26:24, and why these modifications and not others?

But, someone will say, "But it was still a reference to His immediate audience even if not to every one in that audience." But, this argument

---

70. TAC, 27.

71. Καὶ ἀποκριθεὶς ὁ Ἰησοῦς εἶπεν αὐτοῖς· βλέπετε μή τις ὑμᾶς πλανήσῃ· πολλοὶ γὰρ ἐλεύσονται ἐπὶ τῷ ὀνόματί μου λέγοντες· ἐγώ εἰμι ὁ Χριστός, καὶ πολλοὺς πλανήσουσιν. μελλήσετε δὲ ἀκούειν πολέμους καὶ ἀκοὰς πολέμων· ὁρᾶτε μὴ θροεῖσθε· δεῖ γὰρ γενέσθαι, ἀλλ᾽ οὔπω ἐστὶν τὸ τέλλος. ἐγερθήσεται γὰρ ἔθνος ἐπὶ ἔθνος καὶ βασιλεία ἐπὶ βασιλείαν καὶ ἔσονται λιμοὶ καὶ σεισμοὶ κατὰ πόπους· πάντα δὲ ταῦτα ἀρχὴ ὠδίνων. Τότε παραδώσουσιν ὑμᾶς εἰς θλῖψιν καὶ ἀποκτενοῦσιν ὑμᾶς, καὶ ἔσεσθε μισούμενοι ὑπὸ πάντων τῶν ἐθνῶν διὰ τὸ ὄνομά μου (Matt 24:4–9).

doesn't work either. Are we to think that Jesus meant for only His immediate audience to be careful about being deceived? Was He saying that
only His immediate audience would hear of wars and rumors of wars?
Was He telling only His immediate audience not to be troubled? Was He
saying that only His immediate audience would be delivered up to tribulation, or that only those in His immediate audience would be killed, or
that only His immediate audience would be hated by all nations? And we
have already seen that 'you' can be used to refer to people in the past. This
was the case in Matt 23:35: "... Zechariah, the son of Berechiah, whom
you murdered between the temple and the altar" (We will discuss this
in more detail later). Another very telling use of the pronoun is found in
Matthew 3.

> But when he saw many of the Pharisees and Sadducees coming to
> his baptism, he said to them, "Brood of vipers! Who warned you to
> flee from the wrath to come. Therefore bear fruits worthy of repen-
> tance, and do not think to say to yourselves, We have Abraham as
> our father. For I say to you that God is able to raise up children to
> Abraham from these stones. And even now the ax is laid to the root
> of the trees. Therefore every tree which does not bear good fruit is
> cut down and thrown into the fire. I indeed baptize *you* with water
> unto repentance, but He who is coming after me is mightier than
> I, whose sandals I am not worthy to carry. He will baptize *you* with
> the Holy Spirit and fire." (Matt 3:7–11)[72]

Notice the two uses of the pronoun 'you' that appear in italics. John
the Baptist is talking to the Pharisees and Sadducees, and he says, "I indeed baptize *you* with water unto repentance ..." But, are we to think that
the Pharisees and Sadducees were being baptized with water unto repentance? Of course someone will say, "Well, John is telling them that if they
'bear fruits worthy of repentance,' then he will baptize them." But, this
argument doesn't work. In the next instance he says, "He will baptize *you*

72. Ἰδὼν δὲ πολλοὺς τῶν Φαρισαίων καὶ Σαδδουκαίων ἐρχομένους ἐπὶ βά
πτισμα αὐτοῦ εἶπεν αὐτοῖς· γεννήματα ἐχιδνῶν, τίς ὑπέδειξεν ὑμῖν φυγεῖν ἀπὸ
τῆς μελλούσης ὀργῆς; ποιήσατε οὖν καρπὸν ἄξιον τῆς μετανοίας καὶ μὴ δόξητε
λέγειν ἐν ἑαυτοῖς· πατέρα ἔχομεν τὸν Ἀβραάμ. λέγω γὰρ ὑμῖν ὅτι δύναται ὁ
θεὸς ἐκ τῶν λίθων τούτων ἐγεῖραι τέκνα τῷ Ἀβραάμ. ἤδη δὲ ἡ ἀξίνη πρὸς τὴν
ῥίζαν τῶν δένδρων κεῖται· πᾶν οὖν δένδρον μὴ ποιοῦν καρπὸν καλὸν ἐκκόπτεται
καὶ εἰς πῦρ βάλλεται. Ἐγὼ μὲν ὑμᾶς βαπτίζω ἐν ὕδατι εἰς μετάνοιαν, ὁ δὲ
ὀπίσω μου ἐρχόμενος ἰσχυρότερός μού ἐστιν, οὗ οὐκ εἰμὶ ἱκανὸς τὰ ὑποδήματα
βαστάσαι· αὐτὸς ὑμᾶς βαπτίσει ἐν πνεύματι ἁγίῳ καὶ πυρί· (Matt 3:7–11).

with the Holy Spirit and fire." Now are we to think that only the Pharisees and Sadducees would be baptized with the Holy Spirit and fire? But the Pharisees and Sadducees were not baptized with the Holy Spirit and fire, and it certainly isn't the case that they were the only people in history who could be baptized by the Holy Spirit and fire. The fact is, the pronoun 'you' cannot be restricted only to John's immediate audience. John is using a very common manner of expression which is very common even today—using 'you' as a generic reference to whomever. It is the indefinite use of the pronoun. John would baptize whomever would come in repentance, not just the Pharisees and Sadducees. Jesus will baptize whomever He chooses, not just the Pharisees and Sadducees. So also, Jesus is referring to whomever sees these things. Arbitrarily to restrict the reference to Jesus' immediate audience ignores the normal way language is used. 'You' means "you," but it doesn't always have a restricted reference.

When Is Seeing Actually Seeing?

In support of his assertion, Hanegraaff comments on Rev 1:7: "John makes this point explicit in Revelation 1:7: 'Look, he is *coming with the clouds*, and *every eye will see him* [yet another metaphor], *even those who pierced him*; and all the peoples of the earth will mourn because of him."[73] Hanegraaff quotes Chilton to make his point: "The crucifiers would see Him coming in judgment—that is, they would *experience* and *understand* that His Coming would mean wrath on the Land. . . . In the destruction of their city, their civilization, their Temple, their entire world-order, they would understand that Christ had ascended to His Throne as Lord of heaven and earth."[74] Notice how when Hanegraaff wants to avoid the problem of literal speech he classifies a word as a metaphor, but when he wants use a passage against an opponent, he requires it to be literal. So, here since the Jews in the time of Christ did not actually see Jesus, the word 'see' is now a metaphor. But earlier when he wanted to use the pronoun 'you' against his opponents, he restricted it to a literalistic sense. But what if the 'you' is a figure of speech for 'anyone'? And why is the 'see' in Rev 1:7 suddenly a metaphor? And notice how Hanegraaff conveniently ignores the text when it serves his purpose. The text says, "they would see Him *coming*." But, all of a sudden, seeing Him coming doesn't really mean "seeing Him

73. TAC, 27.
74. Ibid.

coming." Apparently, against the plain and proper, commonsense meaning, now it means "experiencing and understanding."

Granted, the word 'see' is often used as a metaphor for intellectual sight. But it is also often used for actual seeing. Earlier Hanegraaff assumed that 'seeing' necessarily meant actual seeing and did not even entertain the possibility that the word could be used as a metaphor in Matt 26:64: "The generation that crucified Christ would *see* the day that he was exalted and enthroned at 'the right hand of the Mighty One' (another metaphor)."[75] But, why must the reader accept Hanegraaff's assumption that seeing in the one place necessarily means an actual seeing, and seeing in the other place is necessarily a metaphor? And once again, Hanegraaff doesn't bother to try to prove that his interpretation is correct. He simply assumes it and assumes that his readers must agree. But apparently Hanegraaff is as capable of using rhetoric and manipulation as those whom he criticizes. I hate to do it, but maybe Hanegraaff should add yet another letter to his acronym—'C' for Consistency.

Simile

According to Hanegraaff, "a simile draws a comparison between two things, but whereas the comparison is *implicit* in a metaphor, it is *explicit* in a simile."[76] Hanegraaff has a good discussion of the uses of similes, and he presents some very good examples—that is, until he gets to his comment on Dan 2:31–45. Once again attacking what he believes to be "hyperliteral" interpretation, he refers to Jesus' use of the comparison between a mustard seed and the kingdom of God. He claims that Jesus uses this simile "to illustrate that while the kingdom of God began in obscurity in the end it would 'fill the earth' and 'endure forever' (Daniel 2:31–45)."[77] Now, as true at this may be with reference to Jesus' parable, this characterization certainly does not apply to Daniel. In Nebuchadnezzar's dream, reported and then interpreted by Daniel, the stone that is cut out of the mountain without hands strikes the statue on the feet and pulverizes the statue, completely destroying it so that "not a trace of them was found" (Dan. 2:35).[78] Now the sudden and utter annihilation of the kingdoms

75. Ibid.
76. Ibid.
77. Ibid., 29.
78. וּנְשָׂא הִמּוֹן רוּחָא וְכָל־אֲתַר לָא־הִשְׁתֲּכַח (Dan 2:35b).

of men is hardly a beginning "in obscurity." But notice that Hanegraaff simply cites the verses in Daniel. He doesn't try to give any reason why the reader should think that these verses relate to his claims about Jesus' use of the simile. Of course there is nothing contradictory about the two pictures. The kingdom of God as it is presented in the Gospel accounts does begin in relative obscurity, but when it comes to the Daniel passage, there is no way to take this as indicating a beginning in obscurity. This seems to indicate a different stage in the development of the kingdom of God. The point is, the way Hanegraaff presents the case, the reader is left with the impression that the Daniel passage has something to do with the "mustard seed" stage of the kingdom when in fact it does not. But, even if this brief explanation does not convince anyone, it shows that Hanegraaff needs to do more than simply cite verses. He needs to make his point with argumentation and demonstration.

Hyperbole

Hanegraaff says, "hyperbole employs exaggeration for effect or emphasis."[79] Hanegraaff gives some examples of obvious hyperbole, but then he ventures once again into unsubstantiated claims about Bible passages: "In prophesying Jerusalem's destruction, Jesus says, 'For then there will be great distress unequaled from the beginning of the world until now—and never to be equaled again' (Matthew 24:21)."[80] Of course whether this is talking about Jerusalem's destruction is a matter of debate. In fact, this is precisely why Hanegraaff has written his book. But, he doesn't try to convince the reader that this is talking about Jerusalem's destruction. He merely asserts it as if it were obviously true. But why should anyone think it is true if Hanegraaff is unwilling to make his case?

He goes on to say, "In doing so, he was not literally predicting that the destruction of Jerusalem would be more cataclysmic than the catastrophe caused by Noah's flood."[81] But why isn't He? Why should the reader think that this is an hyperbole? Hanegraaff has not proffered any argument or evidence to prove that this is the case. Why does he think that this is hyperbole? Because he has a prior eschatological perspective through which he is interpreting the statement, and he cannot allow that this is a literal

79. TAC, 30.
80. Ibid.
81. Ibid.

statement, because that would contradict what he wants the text to say. Why should anyone think that this is an "apocalyptic hyperbole" simply because that's what Hanegraaff claims it is. If Hanegraaff was actually trying to equip the reader to "be the judge," then why doesn't he present the reasons for his conclusion in order to show his reader how to judge for himself?

He continues, "Jesus goes on to predict that 'immediately after the distress of those days the sun will be darkened, and the moon will not give its light; the stars will fall from the sky, and the heavenly bodies will be shaken' (Matthew 24:29). Again, Jesus is not predicting the eradication of the cosmos."[82] Here Hanegraaff engages in a little hyperbole of his own, but this hyperbole also serves to misrepresent the text. Nowhere does the text claim that this is an "eradication of the cosmos," nor do dispensationalists make this claim. And, even if it may sound like that, if taken literally, the fact is, the text doesn't say that, and to make this inference requires some evidence that this is a valid inference. But, in his usual manner, Hanegraaff fails to give any evidence. But, someone will probably argue, "Well, if the stars are falling and the sun and moon go dark, that certainly sounds like the eradication of the cosmos." And it may indeed sound like that. But, that is not what the text says. And, the text says that the sun and moon go dark, not that they stop existing. Maybe they would have to stop existing in order to go dark, but that is not a necessary conclusion, and to draw this inference requires justification, not simple assertion.

And, again, Hanegraaff must classify this as hyperbole in order to make it fit his scenario. Now, we must point out once again that it is not necessarily wrong to interpret a text in order to make it fit one's assumptions—it is possible that it is wrong to do this, but it is not *necessarily* wrong. What is wrong is to do this while pretending that this is simply a matter of identifying the figure of speech. But, hyperboles are very often subject to the judgment of the interpreter, and interpreters should argue for their choices, not simply assert conclusions as if they are unquestioningly correct.

And Hanegraaff's appeal to Isaiah does not serve as proof since the Isaiah passage is just as subject to interpretation as the Matthew passage. Why should the reader think Hanegraaff has correctly understood the Isaiah passage? Now someone will say, "All this justification and demon-

82. Ibid., 30–31.

stration could go one indefinitely. If you have to justify and prove your interpretation for every verse you cite, then your book would be thousands of pages." And my response to that is, That's right! Regardless of how difficult the task is, if Hanegraaff is supposed to be equipping his reader to "be the judge," if he is supposed to be giving us the tools to do exegesis, then he needs to do the difficult task. He needs to show why any interpretation or appeal to any verses should be understood the way he does. If that is difficult, then that's just the way it is! But if he is going to argue by assumption, unjustified conclusion, and prior eschatological commitment then he ought not to chide others for doing the same.

Does this imply that in order to understand God's Word you must be competent in the biblical languages, in ancient culture and customs, in the history of nations and people who have interacted with Israel and the church; that the interpreter must be a competent philosopher of history, philosopher of language, philosopher of science, metaphysician as well as an accomplished theologian and hermeneutician? Vincent Brümmer has addressed this same question.

> One of the difficulties in doing theology, [sic] is that the theologian is required to master the basic tools of various other disciplines. Thus he should be a philologist and master the elements of Greek and Hebrew in order to do Biblical exegesis; he ought to be a historian and master the methods of historiography in order to study church history and the history of religions; he should be able to deal with the sort of questions asked by cultural anthropologists and social scientists in order to study comparative religions; and ... he should master some of the basic tools of conceptual inquiry as practiced by philosophers, in order to do systematic theology. ... Since these requirements are rather comprehensive, theologians often try to take short cuts, for example, by doing exegesis without an adequate knowledge of Greek and Hebrew, or systematic theology without an adequate ability to deal with conceptual issues.[83]

Does this imply that in order to understand God's Word one must be an accomplished linguist, theologian, and philosopher? The answer seems to be both "yes" and "no." If by "to understand the Bible" you mean the capacity to grasp and receive the message of salvation through Christ which is the aim of the Word of God, then the answer is emphatically, No!

---

83. Vincent Brümmer, *Theology and Philosophical Inquiry: An Introduction* (Philadelphia: The Westminster Press, 1982), "Preface."

The nature of man, having been created in the image of God as a rational creature, seems to be a sufficient prerequisite to hear, understand, and receive the message of salvation through Christ. As St. Thomas Aquinas explained:

> Since, therefore, there exists a twofold truth concerning the divine being, one to which the inquiry of the reason can reach, the other which surpasses the whole ability of the human reason, it is fitting that both of these truths be proposed to man divinely for belief.
>
> Yet, if this truth were left solely as a matter of inquiry for human reason, three awkward consequences would follow.
>
> The first is that few men would possess the knowledge of God.
>
> The second awkward effect is that those who would come to discover the above mentioned truth would barely reach it after a great deal of time.
>
> The third awkward effect is this. The investigation of the human reason for the most part has falsity present within it, and this is due partly to the weakness of our intellect in judgment, and partly to the admixture of images. The result is that many, remaining ignorant of the power of demonstration, would hold in doubt those things that have been most truly demonstrated.[84]

The conclusion is that the mercy of God provided to us the truths of salvation and instructed us "to hold by faith even those truths that the human reason is able to investigate. In this way, all men would easily be able to have a share in the knowledge of God, and this without uncertainty or error."[85] Of course, this assumes that one has accurately interpreted the

---

84. St. Thomas Aquinas, *Summa Contra Gentiles*, trans. Anton C. Pegis (Notre Dame: University of Notre Dame Press, 1975), I.4.1–5. "Duplici igitur veritate divinorum intelligibilium existente, una ad quam rationis inquisitio pertingere potest, altera quæ omne igenium humanæ rationis excedit, utraque convenienter divinitus homini credenda proponitur. Sequerentur tamen tria inconvenientia, si hujus veritas solummodo rationi inquirenda relinqueretur. Unum est, quod paucis himinibus Dei cognitio inesset. Secundum inconviens est, quod illi qui ad prædictæ veritatis cognitionem vel inventionem pervenirent, vix post longum tempus pertingerent. Tertium inconveniens est, quod investigationi rationis humanæ plerumque falsitas admiscetur, propter debilitatem intellectus nostri in judicando et phantasmatum permixtionem. Et ideo apud multos in dubitatione remanerent ea, quæ sunt verissime etiam demonstrata, dum vim demonstrationis ignorant, et præipue quum videant a diversis, qui sapientes dicuntur, diversa doceri." The Latin text comes from S. Thomæ Aquinatis, *Summa Contra Gentiles* (Taurini, Italia: Marietti, 1935), I.IV.

85. Ibid., I.4. 6. "Salubriter ergo divina providit clementia, ut ea etiam quæ ratio inves-

text by which God has revealed to us these truths, or that there is even the possibility of an "accurate" or "correct" interpretation of a the biblical text, or any other text.

But if by "understand God's Word" you mean to be able to deal with theological issues and to argue about word meanings, and syntax, and grammar, and "scriptural synergy," an so on, then the answer is "yes!" The interpreter needs to develop a competence in all of these areas to be able to deal with these important and sometimes technical issues. And, the interpreter must be prepared to give an answer and argue his case—to marshal the evidence and to present it to his audience.

We say all of this not to imply that Hanegraaff is not capable of doing this kind of study, but to point out that he has not done it in this book in which he promised to equip the reader to be his own judge. Hanegraaff has not only not presented the necessary information to equip the reader, he has not even presented the necessary information to show the reader that he has done the background work. He simply makes assumptions and then makes assertions without trying to justify or demonstrate his position. And, he presents a view based on his prior eschatological commitment and yet presents this as if this is merely a function of LIGHTS.

And here is a case in point. After quoting from Isaiah, Hanegraaff declares, "Even the most pedantic literalist intuitively recognizes that Isaiah is not literally intending to infer that all hands will literally go limp and that every heart will literally melt. Nor is he literalistically predicting that every Babylonian face will be on fire any more than John is using wooden literalism to prophecy that Revelation's two witnesses will literally emit flames of fire from their mouths (Revelation 11:5)."[86] Now Hanegraaff's claims may be true, but where is his evidence? He doesn't present even the slightest evidence that the reader should not think of these descriptions literally. To claim that they are intuitively recognized is not evidence. Why does he think this is intuitively recognized? Is it beyond the realm of God's miraculous power to make fire actually come out of the mouths of the two witnesses? Is it beyond the realm of God's miraculous power to make every single hand go limp and every single heart melt? Maybe these are hyperboles, but since it is certainly not beyond the realm of God's power to make these things literally happen, then, rather than just declaring his

---

tigare potest, fide tenenda præciperet; ut sic omnes de facili possent divinæ cognitionis participes esse et absque dubitatione et errore."

86. TAC, 32.

view with rhetorical flare as if that is sufficient to convince his reader, Hanegraaff must show us why we should think these are exaggerations.

FANTASY IMAGERY

Fantasy imagery, according to Hanegraaff, is found in such descriptions as enormous red dragons, locusts with human faces, and beasts that resemble leopards with bear's feet and a lion's mouth. Hanegraaff points out that although fantasy images may be composed of parts that are actual things that exist on the earth, it is the combination of various features that produce an "unearthly combination."[87] In this section, his examples are instructive, and he gives his reader an important warning: "Again the danger does not lie in the use of fantasy imagery, but in uncritically impregnating these images with unbiblical notions."[88] Unfortunately, the reader is led to conclude that any notion that deviates from Hanegraaff's own conclusions is necessarily unbiblical.

CONCLUDING THOUGHTS

Hanegraaff concludes this chapter with a helpful, brief recap, and he encourages the reader to "fervently pray that the Spirit, who inspired the Scriptures, illumines our minds to what is *in* the text."[89] This leads the reader into the next chapter, "Illumination Principle."

87. Gordon D. Fee and Douglas Stuart, *How to Read the Bible for All Its Worth: A Guide to Understanding the Bible*, 2d ed. (Grand Rapids: Zondervan, 1993), 233; quoted in TAC, 33.

88. TAC, 35.

89. Ibid., 36.

3

Illumination Principle

Faithful Illumination vs. Fertile Imagination

HANEGRAAFF HAS TITLED HIS third chapter "Illumination Principle." One wonders why this chapter is so titled since nowhere does the chapter actually explain what the illumination principle is or the scriptural basis upon which this principle is built. Besides the vague reference to recommitting to *faithful exegesis*, there is no discussion of the means by which to take advantage of this principle, nor the means by which to adjudicate between true and false claims of illumination. The reader is no more equipped to employ the illumination principle after reading this chapter than before reading it. If the illumination principle is nothing other than doing exegesis, then why even have a chapter dedicated to this single point. Other than the specific issues discussed, which could have been discussed under any of the other chapters, there is no reason even to have this chapter in the book, or ultimately to have this principle in the acronym.

However, there does seem to be one point that is repeatedly made through this chapter with a clarity that is not so evident in the others. That is, the capacity of Hanegraaff's rhetoric to condemn a view using guilt by association. Hanegraaff reports, "Despite being a misreading of data, it is so assumed that those who oppose it are shouted down as reactionaries."[1] But the notion of shouting down one's opponents is not unlike what Hanegraaff himself is doing here. He is not doing it by shouting, but by derogatory terminology, innuendo, and, in this chapter, guilt by association. He first of all assumes his case and then vilifies his opponents, particularly Tim LaHaye, by making it appear that he is bad just because of the accidental associations with Darwinian evolution.

1. TAC, 38.

An illustration of Hanegraaff's tactic appears early in the chapter. Referring to Darwinian evolution, Hanegraaff declares, "Though its underpinnings are racist, luminaries from politicians to playwrights laud its virtues."[2] It is a matter of historical record that the first edition of *Origin of Species* overtly asserted Darwin's belief that the Caucasian race was the superior race. However, even the Darwinian branch of evolutionary biology has claimed to have jettisoned this aspect (maybe they haven't, but they claim to have), and racism is not a necessary adjunct to evolution. I certainly do not accept evolution in any of its forms, but it is also a matter of record that an individual can espouse evolution without being a racist. Why then does Hanegraaff make this comment? He makes reference to racism in order to entice the reader through guilt by association. Since racism is wrong, then evolution must be wrong. This is the kind of rhetoric that amounts to being "shouted down," and the tactic Hanegraaff uses with reference to Darwinian evolution should alert the reader that he is going to use this same tactic on his eschatology opponents.

ON THE ROAD TO ARMAGEDDON

After providing a whirlwind tour of the history of Darwinian evolution, Hanegraaff begins a similar tour of what he believes to be the history of premillennialism. He claims, "In much the same way that Darwin imposed a speculative spin on the scientific data he encountered along the South American coasts of Patagonia, Darby imposed a subjective spin on the scriptural data he encountered in the city of Plymouth."[3] In a similar manner, Hanegraaff has implied that since Darwin was wrong, Darby must be wrong. But that doesn't follow. Even if it is true that Darby put a subjective spin on the scriptural data, that doesn't prove that his conclusions are wrong. It is possible that Darby arrived at a correct conclusion even though he did not use the correct methodology. But according to Hanegraaff, Darby is guilty by association.

In fact, Hanegraaff has imposed upon his reader a rhetorical spin without giving the reader an opportunity to be the judge. This is particularly problematic since he has not even instructed the reader in what constitutes his illumination principle or whether his subjective characterization of Darby derives from this principle or some other. And once

2. Ibid.
3. Ibid., 41.

again Hanegraaff has failed to demonstrate that the claims of the individuals he discusses are necessary parts of a premillennial or dispensational eschatology. It is a matter of historical record that many interpreters from a dispensational perspective have engaged in attempting to date various prophetic events. But, Hanegraaff does not bother to acknowledge that most contemporary dispensationalists and premillennialists have learned from these mistakes. And this is the history of doctrine, that is, theologians and interpreters making mistakes and later generations attempting to learn from these mistakes. Even though there may be many interpreters who still cling to dating practices, that does not disqualify the system. This is nothing else but guilt by association.

THE HEART OF DISPENSATIONALISM

Rapture and Dispensationalism

Apparently Hanegraaff believes that the "heart of dispensationalism" is a pretribulation rapture. He has already made the mistake of claiming that it is dispensationalsim's "cardinal doctrine."[4] Hanegraaff declares, "In 1831—the year Miller announced that he had discovered the time of Christ's return—Darby added a unique twist to the dating game by introducing the concept of a secret coming seven years prior to the second coming of Christ."[5] Contrary to Hanegraaff's implication, it would not take much study or reading to discover that a pretribulation rapture is not the heart of dispensationalism. Dispensationalists propose several different rapture scenarios, as we have already pointed out. And in fact, the rapture of the church is not even distinctively dispensationalist. J. Oliver Buswell, a committed covenant theologian, holds to the notion of the rapture prior to the pouring out of God's wrath. After discussing several passages, Buswell says, "Although these references to salvation 'from wrath' do not definitely state, in themselves, that the rapture of the church will take place before the outpouring of the vials of wrath, yet these references harmonize with that view."[6] In fact, Buswell also holds to the notion of a literal tribulation which, according to Buswell will be "most

4. Ibid., 5.

5. Ibid., 45.

6. J. Oliver Buswell, *Soteriology and Eschatology*, vol. 2, *A Systematic Theology of the Christian Religion* (Zondervan Publishing House, 1962), 389.

severe" and "may well be identified with 'the time of Jacob's trouble' ..."[7] It appears that not only has Hanegraaff attempted to condemn dispensationalism by using a guilt-by-association tactic, he has actually misrepresented what is the heart of dispensationalism.

Division and Mudslinging

Hanegraaff attempts further to disparage Darby's claims by reporting that the Plymouth Brethren "considered it [Darby's notion of a secret coming seven years prior to the second coming of Christ] exegetically indefensible. Thus Darby's system of dividing the Bible divided the Brethren."[8] But, dividing the Brethren or dividing Christians is no evidence that a view is wrong. Every truth-claim, whether true or not, divides between those who believe it and those who don't. And not every division is a bad or destructive division. Many churches that claim to be Christian have been divided when some of the congregation held to the doctrine of inerrancy while others did not. Dividing between these two groups was a beneficial division, separating from those who do not hold to a high view of Scripture. In fact, Hanegraaff's own book is designed to cause division—to divide those who agree with Hanegraaff from those who do not. And, I do not believe that Hanegraaff would think that this is a bad thing. One of the reasons he wrote the book is to make divisions—divisions which he no doubt believes to be beneficial. He wants to divide Christians from what he believes to be errors. So, the fact of division does not necessarily mean that a view is wrong. And sometimes divisions can benefit each of the groups that are divided because a division may end strife and enmity that hinders each group from functioning effectively. So, just because Darby's doctrine caused division says nothing about whether it was right or wrong. Rather, this is simply another rhetorical tactic to try to sling more mud upon the dispensationalists.

Deciding in Advance

Hanegraaff claims, "Thus, to Darby, reading the Bible for all it is worth meant deciding in advance which Scriptures applied uniquely to Israel and which Scriptures applied unequivocally to the church."[9] But we have

7. Ibid., 388–89.
8. TAC, 45.
9. Ibid., 46.

already documented several instances where Hanegraaff does the same thing. And, as we said, doing this is not necessarily a bad thing, especially if you can show that your choices are valid. After all, you can't look at every verse every time you want to say something. The problem is not necessarily that you decide before hand, but that you decide before hand while pretending that you are not. Perhaps Darby was guilty of doing this also, but we have certainly seen Hanegraaff do this.

Nightmarish Ending

Hanegraaff again employs his guilt-by-association tactic: "As Darwin's subjective spin on science led to the nightmare of eugenics, Darby's subjective spin on Scripture leads inexorably toward a nightmarish ending. If LaHaye is right, the time of Jewish Tribulation will indeed be a nightmarish reality beyond imagination."[10] But this comparison is faulty. It was Darwin's evolutionary theories that formed the basis of arguments in favor of eugenics, but eugenics was not a necessary or inevitable result of an evolutionary scheme. What I mean is that, although it may be a logical consequence, it does not necessarily lead to this kind of practice.[11] People often refuse to follow a belief to its logical conclusion. This is clear from the fact that, although eugenics has been abandoned, at least in its overt forms, evolution is still the dominate theoretical scheme. So, even if evolution were in fact true, it can nevertheless be maintained without necessarily leading to eugenics.

However, if LaHaye's scheme is true, then the result is inescapable. And it is not inescapable because it is LaHaye's or anyone else's scheme. If it is true, then it is inevitable because it is true. So, contrary to Hanegraaff's claim, Darby's scheme is not what leads to the nightmarish ending. If it is true, it is the truth that leads to this nightmare, and regardless of how nightmarish it is, the truth is still the truth. In fact, eternally existing in hell, separated from God for all eternity, is a much more nightmarish ending than the terrible yet temporary nightmare of the tribulation. Nevertheless, it is true that some will be eternally separated from God. Hanegraaff's comparison is not only faulty, it ignores the truth. It is yet

10. Ibid., 47.

11. For a further examination of this point see John G. West, *Darwin Day in America* (Wilmington, Delaware: ISI Books, 2007), 369ff.

another piece of rhetoric to entice the reader to Hanegraaff's scheme, something he said he would not do.

Hanegraaff quotes Timothy Weber who claimed, "For the first time, dispensationalists believed that it was necessary to leave the bleachers and get onto the playing field to make sure the game ended according to the divine script."[12] But what could possibly be wrong with promoting the divine script? Is Hanegraaff saying that we should in fact fight against God's plan? Or is he claiming that we should just sit in the bleachers and let God's plan go where it will? In fact, Hanegraaff says, "If the evangelical death march toward the end game of Armageddon is to be subverted, it will be because believers recommit themselves to *faithful illumination*."[13] But if the end game of Armageddon as the dispensationalists define it is the truth, what makes Hanegraaff think faithful illumination will induce any other action except getting on board? Dispensationalists leave the bleachers and get onto the playing field because they believe their eschatological scheme is true, just like Hanegraaff advocates leaving the bleachers and getting onto the playing field to promote his scheme because he thinks it is true. So, recommitting to "faithful illumination" will produce the results Hanegraaff wants only if his scheme is true. Leaving the bleachers and getting onto the playing field is not in itself a bad or undesirable thing.

Hanegraaff characterizes "faithful illumination" as recommitting oneself to "*faithful exegesis*—to mining what the Spirit has breathed into Scriptures as opposed to reading our own predilections into the text."[14] But no one disputes this. The problem is discovering who is doing what. Just because Hanegraaff thinks that dispensationalists are reading into the text rather than mining out of the text does not prove his point, and we have already seen instances in which Hanegraaff is quite adept at reading into the text what is not there.

But he goes on to assert, "Sudden flashes of intuition or inspiration are poor substitutes for the scrupulous study of Scripture."[15] Who would not agree with this? And yet several times Hanegraaff talks about how we "intuitively recognize" certain meanings or conclusions. Should we have

12. Timothy P. Weber, *On the Road to Armageddon: How Evangelicals Became Israel's Best Friend* (Grand Rapids: Baker Book House, 2004), 39; quoted in TAC, 48.

13. TAC, 48 (emphasis in original).

14. Ibid.

15. Ibid.

73

intuitions or not? And so far, Hanegraaff has failed to show any of his own actual "scrupulous study of Scripture." That is not to say that he has not done this. Perhaps he has done much scrupulous study, but he has failed to show it in the pages of this book in which he promised to equip his readers do to precisely that. So far what he has shown his reader is rhetoric, unsubstantiated appeal to passages, unjustified assumptions, *ad hominem abusive* attacks, guilt by association, *consensus gentium* arguments, chronological snobbery, and a host of other tactics. Hanegraaff advocates "a willingness to sacrifice treasured traditions on the altar of biblical fidelity."[16] But Hanegraaff himself has not shown such a willingness. So far all he has shown is disdain for those who advocate a position with which he disagrees. Once again this is not to say that he is not willing to do this. Rather, he has not shown this by any humility or respect for the abilities of others. If Hanegraaff believes he can be "illumined" by the Holy Spirit, does he deny this possibility to those with whom he disagrees? Does he believe it is entirely outside the realm of possibility that he has got it wrong? If he does hold his view with humility, he has failed so far to demonstrate this in the pages of this book. Everyone wants to turn from fruitless eisegesis and march undeterred to the end-game of faithful exegesis. But Hanegraaff writes as if he is the only one who is actually doing this.

TWO DISTINCT PEOPLE

Hanegraaff begins his trek through "faithful illumination" or "faithful exegesis" by addressing the issue of "two distinct people": "We begin by turning our attention to the heart of the dispensational dogma, namely, that God has two distinct peoples—one of whom must be raptured before God can continue his plan with the other."[17] The question Hanegraaff poses is, "Does the illumination of Scripture reveal that God has two categories of people, or does Scripture reveal only one chosen people who form one covenant community, beautifully symbolized by one cultivated olive tree?"[18] Notice how Hanegraaff stacks the deck in the very manner in which he poses the question. When referring to the notion of two categories, he states this in straightforward speech. But when referring to

16. Ibid.
17. Ibid.
18. Ibid.

the notion of one group, he uses the terms "community," and "beautifully" and "one cultivated olive tree." Now who wouldn't opt for the beautiful community symbolized by a cultivated tree?

Now someone may object that we ought to give the reader more credit than to fall for something like that. But, whether the reader falls for it or not is not the point. The point is, rather than give a balanced presentation in which he persuades his reader by the weight of evidence, he attempts to entice the reader by skewed speech and innuendo. This is the very kind of rhetoric that eugenists used to vilify their opponents and present eugenics in the best possible light. Whether he is successful or not is not relevant. The fact is, he ought to be more objective and fair in his presentation. He passionately believes his view is right, and that's not a bad thing. The problem is, he presents his view as if the mere presentation is enough to show that it is correct, and that's not what he promised to do. And even if his view is correct, he ought to present it with a good dose of humility and respect for his Christian brothers.

One Chosen People

Since in the previous section Hanegraaff encouraged the reader to re-commit to *faithful illumination* and *faithful exegesis*, the reader is led to believe that this is what Hanegraaff will be presenting as he discusses the question of two distinct people. Hanegraaff starts off by denying the "two people" position: "First, far from communicating that God has two distinct peoples, the Scriptures from beginning to end reveal only *one chosen people* purchased 'from every tribe and tongue and language and nation' (Revelation 5:9)."[19] As a reader, I was disappointed to discover that Hanegraaff does not actually present any "faithful exegesis" of Rev 5:9. Rather, he simply declares that this passage supports his claim that there is "only *one chosen people*."

The passage in question reads, "And they sang a new song, saying, 'Worthy are You to take the book and to break its seals; for You were slain, and purchased for God with Your blood from every tribe and tongue and people and nation.'"[20] Since the verse begins with the pronoun 'they,' it is

19. Ibid., 49 (emphasis in original).

20. καὶ ᾄδουσιν ᾠδὴν καινὴν λέγοντες· ἄξιος εἶ λαβεῖν τὸ βιβλίον καὶ ἀνοῖξαι τὰς σφραγῖδας αὐτοῦ, ὅτι ἐσφάγης καὶ ἠγόρασας τῷ θεῷ ἐν τῷ αἵματί σου ἐκ πάσης φυλῆς καὶ γλώσσης καὶ λαοῦ καὶ ἔθνους (Rev 5:9).

important to discover its antecedent. The "they" are the "four living creatures" (τὰ τέσσαρα ζῷα, āoz aresset at) referred to in verse 8. However, nowhere in the context is there any reference to the fact that there is only "one chosen people," or that those who have been purchased (ἠγόρασας, sasaroḡe) formed a single "chosen people." So, rather than "faithful exegesis," it appears as though Hanegraaff is doing a bit of eisegesis, again. If it is legitimate to infer that this is a reference to only one chosen people, Hanegraaff needs to show the exegesis that supports this inference. Just because Jesus' blood purchased people from every tribe and tongue and people and nation does not prove that these people form only one group. From all these people whom Jesus' purchased, He could have formed two or more groups. I'm not saying that He did. What I am saying is that the verse Hanegraaff references does not seem to support his claim, and if it does support his claim he needs to present the argument and evidence to show this. Simply quoting it is not sufficient.

One Body

Hanegraaff claims, "As Paul explains, the 'mystery is that through the gospel the Gentiles are heirs together with Israel, members together of *one* body, and sharers together in the promise in Christ Jesus' (Ephesians 3:6)."[21] Perhaps it will be helpful in this instance to provide a bit of the context:

> For this reason I, Paul, the prisoner of Christ Jesus for you Gentiles if indeed you have heard of the dispensation of the grace of God which was given to me for you, how that by revelation He made known to me the mystery (as I have briefly written already, by which, when you read, you may understand my knowledge in the mystery of Christ), which in other ages was not made known to the sons of men, as it has now been revealed by the Spirit to His holy apostles and prophets: that the Gentiles should be fellow heirs, of the same body, and partakers of His promise in Christ through the gospel, of which I became a minister according to the gift of the grace of God given to me by the effective working of His power. (Eph 3:1–7)[22]

21. TAC, 49 (emphasis in original).

22. Τούτου χάριν ἐγὼ Παῦλος ὁ δέσμιος τοῦ Χριστοῦ Ἰησοῦ ὑπὲρ ὑμῶν τῶν ἐθνῶν εἴ γε ἠκούσατε τὴν οἰκονομίαν τῆς χάριστος τοῦ θεοῦ τῆς δοθείσης μοι εἰς ὑμᾶς, ὅτι κατὰ ἀποκάλυψιν ἐγνωρίσθη μοι τὸ μυστήριον, καθὼς προέγραψα ἐν ὀλίγῳ, πρὸς ὃ δύνασθε ἀναγινώσκοντες νοῆσαι τὴν σύνεσίν μου ἐν τῷ μυστηρί

Once again the reader is disappointed that Hanegraaff does not offer any actual exegesis of the passage, just unsubstantiated assertions. Although Hanegraaff had promised to equip the reader to "be the judge," he does not give the reader any information with which to be the judge. And, as before, the text does not say what Hanegraaff claims that it says. Hanegraaff's translation of verse 6 reads, "members together of *one* body." However, the word 'one' does not actually occur in the verse. The verse is laid out below with a word-for-word translation.

Table 1: Ephesians 3:6

εἶναι	τὰ	ἔθνη	συγκληρονόμα
to be	the	Gentiles	fellow receivers
καὶ	σύσσωμα	καὶ	συμμέτοχα
and	co-members	and	co-participants
τῆς	ἐπαγγελίας	ἐν	Χριστῷ
of the	promise	in	Christ
Ἰησοῦ	διὰ	τοῦ	εὐαγγελίου
Jesus	through	the	Gospel

The word that is translated "members together of one body" is the single Greek word σύσσωμα (aṁossus). This word occurs only here in the NT, and it does not occur in the Greek OT. According to BDAG, the word means "belonging to the same body,"[23] and according to the *Greek-English Lexicon of the New Testament Based on Semantic Domains*, it refers to "a person who is a member of a group, with the emphasis upon his coordinate relation to other members of the group—'co-member.'"[24] So, neither the word nor the text states that there is only one body, but that the Gentiles are members of the same body on an equal standing with other members of this body. The fact that these members form one body

ῳ τοῦ Χριστοῦ, ὃ ἑτέραις γενεαῖς οὐκ ἐγνωρίσθη τοῖς υἱοῖς τῶν ἀνθρώπων ὡς νῦν ἀπεκαλύφθη τοῖς ἁγίοις ἀποστόλοις αὐτοῦ καὶ προφήταις ἐν πνεύματι, εἶναι τὰ ἔθνη συγκληρονόμα καὶ σύσσωμα καὶ συμμέτοχα τῆς ἐπαγγελίας ἐν Χριστῷ Ἰησοῦ διὰ τοῦ εὐαγγελίου, οὗ ἐγενήθην διάκονος κατὰ τὴν δωρεὰν τῆς χάριτος τοῦ θεοῦ τῆς δοθείσης μοι κατὰ τὴν ἐνέργειαν τῆς δυνάμεως αὐτοῦ (Eph 3:1–7).

23. BDAG (2000), s.v. "σύσσωμος."

24. *Greek-English Lexicon of the New Testament Based on Semantic Domains* (1989), 11.9.

does not exclude the fact that there is another body about which Paul is making no mention in this context. In other words, neither the word nor the context states that there is *only* one body. It merely states that there is one body.

What is even more egregious about Hanegraaff's use of this verse is the way he renders the verse. He says, "As Paul explains, the 'mystery is that through the gospel Gentiles are heirs together with Israel . . .'"[25] However, the word 'Israel' does not occur in this verse, and in fact the word is used only once in the entire book of Ephesians and that is in chapter 2 verse 12. So Hanegraaff has completely misrepresented the verse by the way he presents it. Now, maybe there is a legitimate reason for inserting this word, but Hanegraaff doesn't alert the reader that he has inserted the word. He simply presents his insertion as if it is a part of what "Paul explains," when in fact it was not. Now if it was some innocuous word that translators usually insert to make better English, I could understand not drawing attention to it. But, that's not the case here. If there is a good reason for inserting the word, Hanegraaff ought to explain it and justify his putting it in a verse in which it does not appear, or he ought at least to tell the reader that he has put this word here but that it is not a part of the original. Hanegraaff's presentation is disingenuous at best.

And, once again Hanegraaff has given his understanding of a passage without any explanation of how he has arrived at this conclusion and without any indication of his exegetical process. Also, a straightforward, plain and proper, natural, commonsense reading of the text does not necessarily support Hanegraaff's claim. Likewise, it does not contradict his claim either. But, the point is, Hanegraaff is supposed to be equipping the reader to be the judge, but instead of equipping the reader, or even showing the reader how he arrived at his conclusions, he is simply declaring what he thinks the text says. This is neither "faithful illumination" nor "faithful exegesis." This is simply unsubstantiated assertion.

Old Testament Terminology

Hanegraaff claims, "the precise terminology used to describe the children of Israel in the Old Testament is ascribed to the church in the New Testament. Peter calls them '*a chosen people*, a royal priesthood, a holy nation, a people belonging to God, that you may declare the praises of

25. TAC, 49.

him who called you out of darkness into his wonderful light' (1 Peter 2:9).
Ultimately, they are the one chosen people of God, not by virtue of their
genealogical relationship to Abraham, but by virtue of their genuine relationship to 'the living Stone—rejected by men but chosen by God' (1 Peter
2:9). The true church is true Israel, and true Israel is truly the church."[26]
But notice that the text of 1 Peter does not say "*the* chosen people" or "*the*
royal priesthood" or "*the* holy nation" or "*the* people belonging to God"
(ὑμεῖς δὲ γένος ἐκλεκτόν [*a* chosen people], βασίλειον ἱεράτευμα [*a*
royal priesthood], ἔθνος ἅγιον [*a* holy people], λαὸς εἰς περιποίησιν
[*a* people for (God's) possession], ὅπως τὰς ἀρετὰς ἐξαγγείλητε τοῦ
ἐκ σκότους ὑμᾶς καλέσαντος εἰς τὸ θαυμαστὸν αὐτοῦ φῶς·" (1 Pet
2:9). Greek does not have an indefinite article like the 'a' or 'an' in English.
That's why in the translations in brackets, the indefinite articles are in italics. But, Greek does have a definite article like 'the' in English (it occurs
in above quote as τὰς), and this article is not used in any one of these
instances. In fact, there is nothing in this context that would necessarily
indicate that there is only one such group. There is a group, but this text
does not exclude the possibility that there is also another group.

True Church and True Israel

Hanegraaff quotes a portion of 1 Pet 2:4, and at the end of the paragraph
asserts, "The true church is true Israel, and true Israel is truly the church."[27]
It is not clear whether Hanegraaff sees 1 Pet 2:4 as somehow supporting
his assertion. The text reads: "And coming to Him as to a living stone
which has been rejected by men, but is choice and precious in the sight of
God."[28] Neither any statement in this verse nor in the context necessarily
indicates the conclusion that Hanegraaff proposes. Hanegraaff does not
state why he thinks this verse relates to his point, and again, he has not
presented any "faithful exegesis" that would indicate how he arrived at
this conclusion.

26. Ibid. (emphasis in original).

27. Ibid.

28. πρὸς ὃν προσερχόμενοι λίθον ζῶντα ὑπὸ ἀνθρώπων μὲν ἀποδεδοκιμασμέ
νον παρὰ δὲ θεῷ ἐκλεκτὸν ἔντιμον (1 Pet 2:4).

One Covenant Community

Hanegraaff claims that the Old and New Testaments "reveal only one chose people," and "they reveal only *one covenant community*."[29] He argues,

> While that one covenant community is physically rooted in the offspring of Abraham—whose number would be like that of "the stars" of heaven (Genesis 15:5) or "the dust of the earth" (Genesis 13:16)—it is spiritually grounded in one singular Seed. Paul makes this explicit in his letter to the Galatians: "The promises were spoken to Abraham and to his *seed*. The Scripture does not say 'and to *seeds*,' meaning many people, but 'and to your seed' meaning one person, who is Christ" (Galatians 3:16). As Paul goes on to explain, "If you belong to Christ, then you are Abraham's seed, and heirs according to the promise." (v 29)[30]

Once again Hanegraaff quotes from and points to Bible verses, but makes no attempt to demonstrate that his understanding of these verses is correct or how they serve to support his claims. The fact that Jesus is the one ground of all saved people does not necessarily indicate that there is only one group, and the fact that all who belong to Christ are Abraham's seed and heirs of the promise likewise does not necessarily demonstrate that there is only one group. Many groups could still be Abraham's seed and remain distinct groups. In fact, the descendants of Ishmael are Abraham's seed, but no one would think they and the Jews form one group. If this supports Hanegraaff's argument, that is not clear just from citing the verses. Hanegraaff needs to argue for his conclusion, especially since other competent interpreters have arrived at different conclusions. The practice of "faithful exegesis" usually involves interacting with these contrary views to show why one's own view ought to be accepted. Hanegraaff is not engaging in exegesis at all. Rather, he is simply engaging is propaganda.

Twice Hanegraaff refers to Gal 3:16. The passage reads:

> Brethren, I speak in terms of human relations: even though it is a man's covenant, yet when it has been ratified, no one sets it aside or adds conditions to it. Now the promises were spoken to Abraham and to his seed. He does not say, "And to seeds," as to many, but to one, "And to your seed," that is, Christ. What I am saying is this: the Law, which came four hundred and thirty years later, does not

29. TAC, 49 (emphasis in original).
30. Ibid.

invalidate a covenant previously ratified by God, so as to nullify the promise. (Gal 3:15–17)[31]

Again there is nothing in these verses that necessarily indicates that there is only one covenant community. In this context, Paul is working to convince the Galatian Christians that the efforts of the flesh and the law are not the way to become more Christ-like. This is about sanctification, not justification. At least, this is what many competent scholars claim. Although all who are born again are born again on the same basis, that is, by grace through faith, and since that faith is illustrated paradigmatically in Abraham, all who believe as Abraham did are his seed. But, this does not require one covenant community since there are several covenants in the Old Testament. Even if we accept the possibility that this passage may be talking about this, we have no "faithful exegesis" from Hanegraaff that could serve to convince anyone. All we have are quotes and claims. It is certainly true that "If you belong to Christ, then you are Abraham's seed, and heirs according to the promise," but this does not say anything about there being "only one covenant community." Where is the exegesis?

what do you think "one" means?

Israel's National Destiny

Hanegraaff declares, "To suggest that Israel must 'fulfill her national destiny as a separate entity after the Rapture and Tribulation and during the Millennium' is an affront to the One Seed in whom all the promises made to Abraham have reached their climax."[32] But where is the exegesis to support this declaration? Simply declaring it doesn't make it so, and simply citing and quoting verses doesn't do it either. Jehovah's witnesses quote and cite verses to support their views. Hanegraaff requires more from them than he is willing to give in support of his own view.

Hanegraaff then quotes from Keith Matheson: "The promises made to literal, physical Israelites were fulfilled by a literal, physical Israelite, Jesus the Messiah. He is the Seed of Abraham."[33] There are a number of

31. Ἀδελφοί, κατὰ ἄνθρωπον λέγω· ὅμως ἀνθρώπου κεκυρωμένην διαθήκην οὐδεὶς ἀθετεῖ ἢ ἐπιδιατάσσεται. τῷ δὲ Ἀβραὰμ ἐρρέθησαν αἱ ἐπαγγελίαι καὶ τῷ σπέρματι αὐτοῦ. οὐ λέγει· καὶ τοῖς σπέρμασιν, ὡς ἐπὶ πολλῶν ἀλλ' ὡς ἐφ' ἑνός· καὶ τῷ σπέρματί σου, ὅς ἐστιν Χριστός. τοῦτο δὲ λέγω· διαθήκην προκεκυρωμένην ὑπὸ τοῦ θεοῦ ὁ μετὰ τετρακόσαι καὶ τριάκοντα ἔτη γεγονὼς νόος οὐκ ἀκυροῖ εἰς τὸ καταργῆσαι τὴν ἐπαγγελίαν (Gal 3:15–17).

32. TAC, 50.

33. Keith A. Matheson, *Dispensationalism: Rightly Dividing the People of God?*

81

problems with this proposal. If the promises made to the literal, physical Israelites were fulfilled in the literal, physical Jesus, then is He presently reigning, literally and physically, over the kingdom of Israel according to the borders prescribed by God to Abraham in Genesis? It would appear that He is not since much of the land in that area is ruled over and controlled by other groups. It will not do to say that Christ is reigning over His kingdom spiritually, and that people who are born again and live in that land are the subjects of His kingdom. That's not what Matheson said. He said the "literal, physical" promises were literally and physically fulfilled in Jesus. But that just does not seem to be the case, and where are any passages that say this? Once again Hanegraaff does not provide any argumentation to prove his point. He has progressed from simply quoting Bible verses to simply quoting the claims of others, but simple quotations are not "faithful exegesis." Why should anyone think that these literal and physical promises have been fulfilled in Jesus the Messiah? Where does the text say this? Where is the evidence that this is true? Where is the faithful exegesis? Where are the tools so we can be the judge?

Hanegraaff goes on to assert, "The faithful remnant of Old Testament Israel and New Testament Christianity are together the one genuine seed of Abraham and thus heirs according to the promise. This remnant is not chosen on the basis of religion or race but rather on the basis of relationship to the resurrected Redeemer. Clothed with Christ, men, women, and children in every age and from 'every tongue and tribe and nation' form one and only one covenant community."[34] Whether we are the one genuine seed or not does not address the question of whether there is only one covenant community. It is interesting that God gives a different statement about His choosing Israel than the one Hanegraaff gives:

> For you are a holy people to the Lord your God; the Lord your God has chosen you to be a people for His own possession out of all the peoples who are on the face of the earth. The Lord did not set His love on you nor choose you because you were more in number than any of the peoples, for you were the fewest of all peoples, but because the Lord loved you and kept the oath which He swore to your forefathers, the Lord brought you out by a mighty hand and redeemed you from the house of slavery, from the hand of Pharaoh king of Egypt. (Deut 7:6–8)

(Phillipsburg, NJ: P & R, 1995), 29; quoted in TAC, 50.

34. TAC, 50.

So YHWH is Racist after all? Not Surprised.

כִּי עַם קָדוֹשׁ אַתָּה לַיהוָה אֱלֹהֶיךָ בְּךָ בָּחַר יְהוָה
אֱלֹהֶיךָ לִהְיוֹת לוֹ לְעַם סְגֻלָּה מִכֹּל הָעַמִּים אֲשֶׁר 6
עַל־פְּנֵי הָאֲדָמָה:

לֹא מֵרֻבְּכֶם מִכָּל־הָעַמִּים חָשַׁק יְהוָה בָּכֶם וַיִּבְחַר
בָּכֶם כִּי־אַתֶּם הַמְעַט מִכָּל־הָעַמִּים: 7

כִּי מֵאַהֲבַת יְהוָה אֶתְכֶם וּמִשָּׁמְרוֹ אֶת־הַשְּׁבֻעָה
אֲשֶׁר נִשְׁבַּע לַאֲבֹתֵיכֶם הוֹצִיא יְהוָה אֶתְכֶם בְּיָד
חֲזָקָה וַיִּפְדְּךָ מִבֵּית עֲבָדִים מִיַּד פַּרְעֹה מֶלֶךְ־ 8
מִצְרָיִם:

(Deut 7:6–8)

God says He chose Israel because they were the fewest of all peoples and because He set His love upon them and made an oath with their fathers. It says nothing about a relationship with the resurrected Redeemer. Now I would not want to deny that perhaps the basis of God's choosing Israel was a relationship with the resurrected Redeemer. But Hanegraaff has not argued for this view, nor has he made any attempt to show, even if this is the case, how it relates to the argument about one covenant community. Once again I ask, "Where is the faithful exegesis?"

TWO DISTINCT PLANS

This section purports to deal with the claim that there are two distinct plans, at least according to the claims of dispensationalists. Hanegraaff, to the contrary, claims, "Just as there is one chosen people who form one covenant community characterized in Scripture by one cultivated olive tree, so too there is only *one distinct plan* for what Ephesians 2:15 characterizes as 'the one true humanity' of God."[35] The text of Eph 2:15 reads, "by abolishing in His flesh the enmity, the Law of commandments in ordinances, so that in Himself He might make the two into one new man, establishing peace" (Eph 2:15).[36] Once again Hanegraaff has misrepresented

35. Ibid., 51.

36. τὸν νόμον τῶν ἐντολῶν ἐν δόγμασιν καταργήσας, ἵνα τοὺς δύο κτίσῃ ἐν αὐτῷ εἰς ἕνα καινὸν ἄνθρωπον ποιῶν εἰρήνην (Eph 2:15).

the text. The text does not say "one true humanity." In fact, the word 'true' (Greek ἀληθινός) does not even occur in the entire book of Ephesians. Nevertheless, on the basis of this and a couple of other texts, Hanegraaff denies that there are two plans. He argues, "First, far from the dispensational *postponement* of God's original plan *for* Israel, Scripture reveals the distinct *progression* of the divine plan to establish *through* Israel a new humanity (Ephesians 2:15) in a new homeland (Romans 4:13; Hebrews 12:18, 22)."[37] What Hanegraaff fails to explain is, if this is a progression of the divine plan, then why is it designated a *new* man. The designation "new" (καινὸν, noniak) seems to imply the abrogation of an "old" man, perhaps along the lines of the replacement of the Old Covenant with the New. And, if there was an "old" humanity that is replaced with the new humanity, does this imply a distinction in plans, or a "postponement" of God's plan for Israel? At least this designation and these questions should be addressed.

In fact, the idea of the postponement of God's plan for Israel is not a distinctly dispensational belief. With reference to the establishing of the kingdom, Richard Pratt, a Preterist author, argues, "At a time when other prophets were speaking of the imminent fulfillment of eschatological expectations, Daniel learned that the eschaton had been postponed because of a lack of repentance. As a result, the early postexilic community faced an anomalous situation. The imminent eschatological expectation of Jeremiah had been realized in part, but it had also been delayed."[38] The eschatological expectation of the complete restoration of the people to their land, and the complete fulfillment of the inheritance of all the land specified in the Abrahamic covenant, were, according to Pratt, "postponed" and "delayed" because of Israel's lack of repentance. God brought them back into the land to prepare them for the next step in His plan to bring Israel back to the relationship they had rejected. When Hanegraaff argues against the notion of postponement, he is not arguing against only a dispensationalist view, but against also the view of some Preterists.

Hanegraaff claims that the land promises to Abraham become "a tangible reality when Joshua leads the children of Israel into Palestine."[39]

37. TAC, 51.

38. Richard L. Pratt, Jr., "Hyper-Preterism and Unfolding Biblical Eschatology," in *When Shall These Things Be?* ed. Keith A. Matheson (Phillipsburg, New Jersey: P&R Publishing, 2004), 145.

39. TAC, 52.

Of course this does not happen. For example, the tribe of Dan could not inherit the land that was allotted to them: "Then the Amorites forced the sons of Dan into the hill country, for they did not allow them to come down to the valley; yet the Amorites persisted in living in Mount Heres, in Aijalon and in Shaalbim; but when the power of the house of Joseph grew strong, they became forced labor" (Judg 1:34–36).

וַיִּלְחֲצ֧וּ הָאֱמֹרִ֛י אֶת־בְּנֵי־דָ֖ן הָהָ֑רָה כִּי־לֹ֥א נְתָנ֖וֹ לָרֶ֥דֶת לָעֵֽמֶק׃	34
וַיּ֤וֹאֶל הָֽאֱמֹרִי֙ לָשֶׁ֣בֶת בְּהַר־חֶ֔רֶס בְּאַיָּל֖וֹן וּבְשַֽׁעַלְבִ֑ים וַתִּכְבַּד֙ יַ֣ד בֵּית־יוֹסֵ֔ף וַיִּֽהְי֖וּ לָמַֽס׃	35
וּגְבוּל֙ הָאֱמֹרִ֔י מִֽמַּעֲלֵ֖ה עַקְרַבִּ֑ים מֵהַסֶּ֖לַע וָמָֽעְלָה׃	36

(Judg 1:34–36)

Judges indicates that other tribes either did not inherit all the land that was allotted to them, or that they could not drive out the inhabitants of the land. This hardly sounds like the promises to Abraham have become a "tangible reality."

Hanegraaff goes on to claim, "Though the land promises reached their zenith under Solomon—whose rule encompassed all the land from the Euphrates River in the north to the River of Egypt in the south (1 Kings 4:20–21; cf. Genesis 15:18)—the land vomited out the children of the promise just as it had vomited out the Canaanites before them."[40] Hanegraaff needs to do more than simply make his claim and cite a couple of verses. According to Thomas Constable, "This does not mean that the Abrahamic Covenant was fulfilled in Solomon's day (Gen 15:18–20), for not all this territory was incorporated into the geographic boundaries of Israel; many of the subjugated kingdoms retained their identity and territory but paid taxes (*tribute*) to Solomon. Israel's own geographic limits were 'from Dan to Beersheba' (1 Kings 4:25)."[41] In other words, it is simply misleading for Hanegraaff to claim that Israel's "rule" encompassed the land from the Euphrates to the River of Egypt and that this

40. Ibid., 52–53.

41. Thomas L. Constable, "1 Kings," in *The Bible Knowledge Commentary: Old Testament*, ed. John F. Walvoord and Roy B. Zuck (Wheaton, Illinois: Victor Books, 1985), 497.

fulfills Abraham's promise. The promise to Abraham was not that Israel would only *rule* the land, but that they would possess the land. To rule and to possess are not the same thing, and it is simply a historical fact that Israel did not possess all the lands they ruled. It seems characteristic of Hanegraaff's tactic conveniently to neglect to present all of the evidence. This is another instance of selective reporting. As Constable points out, 1 Kgs 4:25 states, "So Judah and Israel lived in safety, every man under his vine and his fig tree, from Dan even to Beersheba, all the days of Solomon." In other words, the actual boundaries of the land that Israel inhabited was "from Dan to Beersheba," not from the Euphrates to the River of Egypt.

The comments from Constable may not convince those who have a Preterist (or Exegetical Eschatology) perspective, but what this shows is that there are other ways to understand this verse, and Hanegraaff simply is not doing the "faithful exegesis" that one needs to do to support his position. In fact, once you look at the whole of Scripture (isn't that what Hanegraaff advocates in his "Scriptural Synergy" principle?), it looks like the text actually contradicts Hanegraaff's claim, and by leaving out this critical verse (1 Kgs 4:25), Hanegraaff's assertions become disingenuous claims.

It is interesting that Hanegraaff would point out that, "As God had promised Abraham real estate, he had also promised him a royal seed,"[42] and yet not realize that since Christ is the literal fulfillment of the promised royal seed, it follows that land promises will also be fulfilled literally. Of course, Hanegraaff thinks that they have been fulfilled literally in the settling of the land under Joshua. However, the text indicates that this did not in fact occur, and Hanegraaff has presented no faithful exegesis to persuade the reader otherwise.

The Gap

Hanegraaff objects to the notion of a gap. He exclaims, "Further, as there is no dispensational postponement in the plan of God, so too there is no parenthesis in the purposes of God."[43] It seems also characteristic of Hanegraaff to mischaracterize his opponents' views. Dispensationalists do not claim that there is a simple "postponement" in the plan of God. Dispensationalists argue that there is a postponement in Israel's prom-

42. TAC, 53.
43. Ibid., 54.

ised possession of the land, but that this is all part of God's overall plan from the beginning which has not been postponed. Again, the way Hanegraaff characterizes the view, he prejudices the reader before presenting the case.

He goes on to say, "The pretext for a parenthesis during which there is a postponement in God's plans for Israel and the commencement of a plan for a church age is the product of a peculiar reading of prophecy. The main focus of the dogma is Daniel."[44] Why does Hanegraaff persist in using emotionally volatile terms to characterize the views of his opponents? The term 'dogma' is calculated to call up stereotypical images of a hard-nosed, unthinking "Bible thumpers." Of course this view is neither a pretext nor a dogma, in the derogatory sense of these words, and there is no question that Hanegraaff is using them in a derogatory sense. His frequent invectives and innuendos, inflammatory terminology and misrepresentations leave no room for doubt. Indeed, dispensationalists believe that they can present evidence and support for their view just as Hanegraaff believes there is support and evidence for his view. The primary difference between dispensationalists and Hanegraaff seems to be that dispensationalists actually present evidence and actually do exegesis. Hanegraaff simply makes inflammatory accusations and points to Bible verses. He doesn't actually do any "faithful exegesis."

Hanegraaff says, "The very notion that the Old Testament prophets did not see 'The Valley of the Church,' which 'did not exist before its birth at Pentecost' and 'will come to an abrupt end at the Rapture,' is flatly false. The Old Testament prophets not only saw the 'Valley of the Church,' they announced it! Peter—speaking after the birth of the church at Pentecost—could not have said it any more plainly: '*All the prophets* from Samuel on, as many as have spoken, have *foretold* these days' (Acts 3:24)."[45] This is a classic misunderstanding of this verse. Let me illustrate by referring to the crucifixion, death, burial, and resurrection of Christ. There are a myriad of passages in the Old Testament to which exegetes have pointed that clearly "foretold" these events. Gen 3:15 states, "He shall bruise you on the head, and you shall bruise him on the heel." Ps 22:16 declares, "They pierced my hands and my feet."[46] Isaiah 53 is a classic text to which exegetes point.

44. Ibid.

45. Ibid.

46. Although the Hebrew text, which is verse 17, reads : כָּאֲרִי יָדַי וְרַגְלָי, which could be translated, "as a lion my hands and feet," both the Greek and the Syriac testify that the

Notwithstanding these and others, in 1 Cor 2:6–8, Paul announces, "Yet we do speak wisdom among those who are mature; a wisdom, however, not of this age nor of the rulers of this age, who are passing away; but we speak God's wisdom in a mystery, the hidden *wisdom* which God predestined before the ages to our glory; which none of the rulers of this age has knew [ἔγνωκεν, neḳonge]; for if they had known [ἔγνωσαν, naŝonge] it they would not have crucified the Lord of glory."[47] Here Paul clearly asserts that the crucifixion of Jesus was a hidden mystery, which none of the rulers of this age knew. Now that it has been revealed to us "through the Spirit [διὰ τοῦ πνεύματος, sotamuenp uot aid]," Paul can look back into the Old Testament and see all those places where these events were foretold. Now, if such a momentous event was hidden, why is a "by-product of a fertile imagination" to think that the age of the Bride of Christ would be hidden? Peter is saying the same thing. Once this mystery has been made known, we can now look back into the OT and see the wisdom of God, how these events were there all the time, foretold but hidden.

Someone may argue that this is a reference to the spiritual powers, not to earthly powers. But that doesn't work since the text does not make this distinction. And it makes little sense to say that it was hidden only from the unbelievers, not from the believers. This notion is particularly nonsensical since we can see in the lives of the disciples that it was hidden from them. Even when Jesus specifically asserted that He was going to be put to death for them, Peter was ready to fight to prevent it. Rather than developing clever vilifications by which to demean his opponents, Hanegraaff ought to be engaging in some "fertile exegesis."[48]

Hebrew text has been pointed by the Masoretts in such a manner as to change the way the text reads. The consonantal text would have been left unchanged by the Masoretts, although the pointing would have been altered to change the obvious meaning.

47. Σοφίαν δὲ λαλοῦμεν ἐν τοῖς τελείοις, σοφίαν δὲ οὐ τοῦ αἰῶνος τούτου οὐδὲ τῶν ἀρχόντων τοῦ αἰῶνος τούτου τῶν καταργουμένων· ἀλλὰ λαλοῦμεν θεοῦ σοφίαν ἐν μυστηρίῳ τὴν ἀποκεκρυμμένην, ἣν προώρισεν ὁ θεὸς πρὸ τῶν αἰώνων εἰς δόξαν ἡμῶν, ἣν οὐδεὶς τῶν ἀρχόντων τοῦ αἰῶνος τούτου ἔγνωκεν· εἰ γὰρ ἔγνωσαν, οὐκ ἂν τὸν κύριον τῆς δόξης ἐσταύρωσαν (1 Cor 2:6–8).

48. Someone will no doubt retort, "Well! You ought to do your own 'fertile exegesis.'" The difference is, unlike Hanegraaff, I did not claim that I was going to do "faithful exegesis" (TAC, 3), nor did I claim that I was going to put tools in the hands of my readers so as to make them the judges. Hanegraaff claimed both of these, and he also promised he would not attempt to "entice you to embrace a particular model of eschatology" (TAC, 3). However, by his tactics he is doing precisely what he promised he would not do.

Proper Exegesis

After attacking the whole question of whether an author of a sermon is Ephraem or Pseudo-Ephraim, Hanegraaff declares, "At issue is not pseudo-Ephraim but proper exegesis."[49] That may be, but what is at issue in Hanegraaff's book is any exegesis at all. We would, as Hanegraaff asserts, "be better served to examine the pages of Scripture,"[50] but there is more to examining the pages of Scripture than making claims and citing passages. The reader's hopes are raised by the promise of some actual exegesis when Hanegraaff says, "An appropriate place to begin is Paul's first letter to the Thessalonians."[51] The reader's hopes are soon dashed with the realization that Hanegraaff is going to make only "a cursory exegesis,"[52] which actually turns out to be no exegesis at all.

Hanegraaff appeals to 1 Thessalonians 4 and 1 Corinthians 15, but he doesn't even quote either passage, although he does quote a portion of one verse from 1 Thessalonians. He claims that Bible scholars have "duly noted" that these passages are parallel, but he doesn't actually examine any pages of Scripture, nor does he identify any of these Bible scholars.[53] Hanegraaff argues, "Nowhere does the text say that when Christ comes down from heaven 'with a loud command, with the voice of the archangel and with the trumpet call of God' (1 Thessalonians 4:16) that Christ will hover with us in midair, suddenly change directions, and escort us to mansions in heaven while all hell breaks out on earth."[54] Of course, no one claims that Christ will "hover with us in midair." The use of this kind of misrepresentation is called the Fallacy of Argument from Innuendo. This fallacy consists of persuading someone to accept a conclusion by the use of words to mislead, implying or suggesting a conclusion, but not directly asserting the conclusion. In this case, Hanegraaff uses words to ridicule his opponents' views.

49. TAC, 57.

50. Ibid.

51. Ibid.

52. Ibid.

53. The endnote #56 at the end of the paragraph on page 58 of TAC presents some confusion. When one looks at the endnotes on page 246, there are actually two endnotes with the number 56. The first one corresponds to the endnote number 56 on page 58, and the second one corresponds to the endnote number 57 on page 58. Hanegraaff is not actually citing any scholars in support of his assertion.

54. TAC, 58.

But notice that Hanegraaff offers no "examination of Scripture" by which he might refute contrary arguments. Notice also that Hanegraaff conveniently omits verse 17: "Then we who are alive and remain will be caught up together with them in the clouds to meet the Lord in the air, and so we shall always be with the Lord" (1 Thess 4:17).[55] This verse actually says we will meet the Lord "in the air" (εἰς ἀέρα, area sie). If this verse does not have the plain and proper meaning it seems to have, then Hanegraaff ought to explain why. Hanegraaff declares, "Nor would the Thessalonians have understood Paul this way,"[56] and he quotes N. T. Wright: "Paul conjures up images of an emperor visiting a colony or province. The citizens go out to meet him in open country and then escort him into the city. Paul's image of the people 'meeting the Lord in the air' should be read with the assumption that the people will immediately turn around and lead the Lord back to the newly remade world."[57] A problem with Wright's characterization, however, is that the text says nothing about escorting Christ anywhere. Why should any reader think that "the people will turn around" any more than Christ will "change directions"? And why does Christ need to be escorted anywhere?

None of these questions, nor many others, are even considered by Hanegraaff. He merely takes Wright at his word, as if what N. T. Wright says is necessarily accurate. Other equally competent NT scholars take a different view. And Hanegraaff does not "examine the pages of Scripture," which he said we would be better off doing. Notice that when others are exegeting some ancient writer, Hanegraaff squelches this activity by charging that it is better to examine Scripture (this sounds like the claims of the arrogant Corinthians, "I follow Christ," 1 Cor 1:12). But, it is apparently OK for Hanegraaff to quote the exegesis of someone else rather than examine the Scriptures.

Throughout this section, Hanegraaff has neither demonstrated that dispensationalists hold to "two distinct plans," nor has he done any "faithful exegesis" or "proper exegesis," or even examined any Scripture, to support

---

55. ἔπειτα ἡμεῖς οἱ ζῶντες οἱ περιλειπόμενοι ἅμα σὺν αὐτοῖς ἁρπαγησόμεθα ἐν νεφέλαις εἰς ἀπάντησιν τοῦ κυρίου εἰς ἀέρα· καὶ οὕτως πάντοτε σὺν κυρίῳ ἐσόμεθα. (1 Thess 4:17).

56. TAC, 58.

57. N. T. Wright, "Farewell to the Rapture," *Bible Review*, August 2001, <http://www.ntwrightpage.com/Wright_BR_Farewell_Rapture.pdf > (accessed January 26, 2007); quoted in TAC, 58.

his view or to show that the contrary view is wrong. Whether dispensationalists actually hold to the view of two distinct plans, as Hanegraaff claims, is not the issue. The issue is, Hanegraaff has not done any exegesis either to demonstrate this or to demonstrate that it is not the correct view. This is a pattern that is repeated throughout this book.

TWO DISTINCT PHASES

At the beginning of this section, Hanegraaff refers to the notion that God has two distinct people as a "presupposition."[58] Once again, this kind of language seems to be calculated to cast his opponents' views in a bad light. The notion that God has two distinct people is not a "presupposition." Rather, it is a conclusion to which some theologians and exegetes have arrived after examining many passages of Scripture. Whether this conclusion is correct or not is not at issue here. Rather, what is at issue is the fact that Hanegraaff, whether deliberately or not, prejudices his reader's perspective against Hanegraaff's opponents by using this kind of misrepresentation and decidedly inflammatory language.

Hanegraaff claims, "the faithful illumination of Scripture reveals neither a secret coming of Christ followed by a seven-year Tribulation, nor a second chance for sin and salvation following the second coming of Christ."[59] Unfortunately for his readers, Hanegraaff never explains what constitutes "faithful illumination." If illumination is faithful exegesis, as Hanegraaff indicates earlier in this chapter,[60] the illumination principle seems superfluous since exegesis encompasses the whole of Hanegraaff's LIGHTS, or at least it supposed to. Understand! I am not saying that the illumination of the Holy Spirit is superfluous. I am saying, if Hanegraaff's "illumination principle" is no different than "faithful exegesis," then this principle, in his acronym LIGHTS, seems superfluous. Nevertheless, Hanegraaff has articulated no steps, no processes, no means by which to distinguish "faithful illumination" from whatever is not this. It appears, since Hanegraaff offers no basis of distinction, that faithful illumination amounts to nothing more than accepting his eschatological model.

And again Hanegraaff engages in misrepresentation in order to disparage his opponents' views. No dispensationalist claims that after the

---

58. TAC, 59.
59. Ibid.
60. Ibid., 48.

second coming that there will be "a second chance for sin and salvation."[61] If any particular interpreter makes this claim, it is not a claim of dispensationalism, and Hanegraaff's argument is with that person, not with this eschatological perspective.

Hanegraaff claims, "First, the very notion of a *secret coming* is without biblical precedent."[62] Hanegraaff claims that there is no "collection of verses that can be construed to communicate a secret coming prior to the second coming of Christ. Instead, the notion of a secret coming, as pretribulational rapturists readily admit, is 'a deduction from one's overall system of theology.'"[63] Of course the dispensationalists will argue that there is indeed a collection of verses that yield this understanding. But, the fact that the pretribulation rapture is "a deduction from one's overall system of theology" is no mark against the view. Hanegraaff's view that illumination is equivalent to "faithful exegesis" is likewise a deduction from his own system. There is no verse, and no collection of verses, that indicate this doctrine. In fact, the word 'illumination' ($\phi\omega\tau\iota\sigma\mu\acute{o}\varsigma$, somsītohp) occurs only twice in the entire NT (1 Cor 4:4, 6), and neither one of these says anything about illumination being equivalent to "faithful exegesis." That a doctrine is a deduction from a system does not necessarily make the doctrine unscriptural or wrong. It is up to Hanegraaff to demonstrate this, not merely use name-calling or character assassination to try to make his view seem viable.

Hanegraaff claims that LaHaye's deduction about a "secret coming during which *only* the church will be raptured . . . stands in stark contrast to Jesus's teachings."[64] Hanegraaff deduces this from Jesus' statement in Jn 5:28–29. Hanegraaff's translation reads, "a time is coming when *all* who are in their graves will hear his voice and come out—those who have done good will rise to live, and those who have done evil will rise to be condemned."[65] The text actually says, "Do not marvel at this; for an hour is coming, in which all who are in the tombs will hear His voice, and will come forth; those who did the good to a resurrection of life, those who

---

61. Ibid., 59.

62. Ibid., 60.

63. Ibid.

64. Ibid. (emphasis in original).

65. Ibid. (emphasis in original).

committed the evil to a resurrection of judgment."[66] Hanegraaff asserts, "The plain and literal sense of our Lord's words suggests a moment in the future when both the righteous and the unrighteous will be resurrected and judged together."[67] But if that is the case, then how does Hanegraaff deal with Rev 20:5? "The rest of the dead did not come to life until the thousand years were completed. This is the first resurrection."[68] This verse certainly seems to indicate that not all will be raised at the same time, and the fact that the text refers to "the first resurrection" implies that there will be at least a second resurrection. In fact, Rev 20:6 says, "Blessed and holy is the one who has a part in the first resurrection; over these the second death has no power, but they will be priests of God and of Christ and will reign with Him for a thousand years."[69] If those who have a part in the first resurrection are saved, indicated by the fact that the second death has no power over them, then it follows that there will be no unsaved in this resurrection, which this verse identifies as the first resurrection. Also, verse 5 indicates that after the first resurrection, the rest of the dead are not raised until after the millennial kingdom, 1,000 years later. In fact, it seems that Hanegraaff's claim that, "The notion that believers will be raptured during a secret coming of our Lord 1,007 years prior to the resurrection of unbelievers is thus an imposition on the text,"[70] is the one that stands in stark contrast to the plain and proper statements of Scripture.

Also, the statement that "all who are in the tombs will hear His voice, and will come forth," does not necessarily indicate that this will all happen at the same time. In 1 Cor 15:22 Paul says, "For as in Adam all die, so also in Christ all will be made alive,"[71] but this does not mean that everyone will die and be made alive all at the same time. Rather this is common way of referring to future events without having to go through the trouble

66. μὴ θαυμάζετε τοῦτο, ὅτι ἔρχεται ὥρα ἐν ᾗ πάντες οἱ ἐν τοῖς μνημείοις ἀκούσουσιν τῆς φωνῆς αὐτοῦ καὶ ἐκπορεύσονται οἱ τὰ ἀγαθὰ ποιήσαντες εἰς ἀνάστασιν ζωῆς, οἱ δὲ τὰ φαῦλα πράξαντες εἰς ἀνάστασιν κρίσεως (Jn 5:28–29).

67. TAC, 60.

68. οἱ λοιποὶ τῶν νεκρῶν οὐκ ἔζησαν ἄχρι τελεσθῇ τὰ χίλια ἔτη. αὕτη ἡ ἀνάστασις ἡ πρώτη (Rev 20:5).

69. μακάριος καὶ ἅγιος ὁ ἔχων μέτρος ἐν τῇ ἀναστάσει τῇ πρώτῃ· ἐπὶ τούτων ὁ δεύτερος θάνατος οὐκ ἔκει ἐξουσίαν, ἀλλ᾽ ἔσονται ἱερεῖς τοῦ θεοῦ καὶ τοῦ Χριστοῦ καὶ βασιλεύσουσιν μετ᾽ αὐτοῦ τὰ χίλια ἔτη (Rev 20:6).

70. TAC, 60.

71. ὥσπερ γὰρ ἐν τῷ Ἀδὰμ πάντες ἀποθνῄσκουσιν, οὕτως καὶ ἐν τῷ Χριστῷ πάντες ζῳοποιηθήσονται (1 Cor 15:22).

of enumerating each one. To claim that the word 'hour' (ὥρα, aīoh) indicates that they will occur at the same time does not work either. The word 'hour' here is figurative for a time when it will occur. If someone wants to take this literally, then they have to explain why the resurrection will take an hour. Is Jesus saying that it will take an hour to raise these people? In Jn 4:21 Jesus says, "Woman, believe me, an hour [ὥρα, aīoh] is coming, when neither in this mountain, nor in Jerusalem, will you worship the Father."[72] Here the word 'hour' certainly does not mean that people will worship God for only an hour. Rather, this is a figure of speech referring to a time in the future when this will take place. Now, whether this is convincing or not is not the point. The point is, "faithful exegesis" requires that Hanegraaff must "examine the pages of Scripture" and present evidence to support his position. But, he doesn't to do this.

Seven-Year Tribulation

Hanegraaff challenges the reader, "search as you may, you will not find a *seven-year Tribulation* in the biblical text."[73] There are two problems with this statement. First of all, try as you may and you will not find "Trinity" in the biblical text either. The simple fact that you cannot find this explicitly stated in Scripture in this manner is no necessary mark against its truth. There is such a thing as valid inferences, and dispensationalists believe that the seven-year tribulation is a valid inference from certain passages. Second, Dan 9:27 seems to indicate precisely this, at least this is what dispensationalists claim. Whether this can be maintained is another question. The point is, Hanegraaff makes these kinds of assertions without the least consideration for the mass of exegesis and argumentation that has been done over this issue. Where is Hanegraaff's faithful illumination that supports this claim? Where is the faithful exegesis? Hanegraaff chides LaHaye for providing "precious little by way of evidence," but Hanegraaff provides none at all. He claims that LaHaye "pontificates that John's revelation divides the Great Tribulation into 'into [*sic*] two periods . . .'" and yet Hanegraaff has done nothing by way of examination or exegesis that might exclude him form the same charge of pontificating.

---

72. πίστευέ μοι, γύναι, ὅτι ἔρχεται ὥρα ὅτε οὔτε ἐν τῷ ὄρει τούτῳ οὔτε ἐν Ἱεροσολύμοις προσκυνήσετε τῷ πατρί (Jn 4:21).

73. TAC, 61.

Redemption of Our Bodies

Referring to Paul's statement in Rom 8:18–25, Hanegraaff claims, "Paul points out that the liberation of creation goes hand in hand with the redemption of our bodies."[74] But nowhere does Paul say that this is a temporal relationship. Paul says the creation awaits the revealing of the children of God and that the whole of creation will be set free from its slavery to corruption. But Paul does not say when this will occur, whether these events will occur at precisely the same moment, or whether one is separated by some time from the other. Hanegraaff inferred (deduced?) this from the text. He referred to reading into the text and pressing statements into a particular mold, but this is precisely what he is doing here by making the text imply a time frame when none is implied. He says, "The notion that our bodies are redeemed at the rapture and the earth is liberated from its bondage to decay approximately 1,007 years later is without biblical precedent," and yet there is nothing in the text that would forbid this understanding. Hanegraaff offers no exegesis to the contrary and in fact offers none to support his own claims.

THE END OF THE MATTER IS THIS . . .

The remainder of this chapter involves Hanegraaff's continued railing against the claims of LaHaye. As such they have little to do with dispensationalism generally speaking. Hanegraaff's complaints against LaHaye are not necessarily complaints against dispensationalism since the beliefs of LaHaye are not necessarily beliefs of dispensationalism generally speaking.

Also, the pattern of making claims, citing verses, quoting parts of verses, and quoting some statements from some people is the pattern followed in the remainder of this chapter. Hanegraaff never attempts to do any actual exegesis. He never demonstrates how the verses or people relate to his points. He never interacts with those who argue a different interpretation or a different point of view, he simply ridicules them. He never examines passages of Scripture that seem to contradict his point. Without showing how he handles objections and different interpretations or different verses that seem contrary to his conclusions, how is he going to equip anyone to do faithful exegesis? And, this is all part of the chapter on the "illumination principle," none of which is actually related by

74. Ibid., 64.

Hanegraaff to this principle. In fact, after going through this chapter, the reader knows a bit more about where Hanegraaff stands, but he doesn't know anything more about the illumination principle or about "faithful exegesis" or how to do it—unless, of course, the illumination principle is simply quoting verses, citing verses, quoting those who agree with you, and making unsubstantiated, unproven claims, and ridiculing and vilifying one's opponents. If this is the illumination principle, then perhaps we should just move on to the next principle and see if there is anything more there.

4

Grammatical Principle

"It Depends on the Meaning of the Word Is"

H ANEGRAAFF BEGINS THIS CHAPTER reminiscing about the "grammatical gyrations" of President Clinton. He refers to the fact that
even children are able to grasp complex grammatical constructions and
to understand meaning. He connects this with Bible study by saying,
"When it comes to interpreting Scripture, we should not suppose that the
rules of grammar mysteriously change."[1] It is no doubt true that the rules
of grammar do not "mysteriously change," but Hanegraaff has ignored the
fact that the rules of grammar do not necessarily have a one-to-one corre-
spondence from one language to the other. There are certainly principles
of grammar that are the same for all languages, but more often than not it
is not these general principles that cause the differences of opinion among
commentators. When Hanegraaff encourages the reader to remember the
basic rules of grammar, Hanegraaff needs to understand that some of
the rules of English grammar may not exactly correspond to some of the
rules of grammar of the original languages of the Bible.

Hanegraaff first of all confuses grammar and semantics. When he
says, "'this' means 'this,'"[2] this may not be simply a matter of meaning.
As we have pointed out before, 'this' can mean 'this,' in two instances and
yet still have different referents. Whether 'this' means 'this' is a semantic
issue. Whether 'this' is functioning as a demonstrative or a substantive
is a grammatical or syntactical issue. The confusion of these principles
throughout this chapter should cause the reader to exercise particular
caution. Hanegraaff seems to be unfamiliar with grammar, syntax, and
semantics and the peculiar part each plays in communicating meaning.

1. TAC, 72.
2. Ibid.

Simply because one knows a few basic principles of grammar does not necessarily mean that he is equipped to do grammatical exegesis, particularly since exegesis of the Bible involves the grammar, syntax, and semantics of Greek, Hebrew, and Aramaic, not English. Hanegraaff declares, "In fact, the moment dispensationalists such as LaHaye utter such statements, our baloney detectors must surely flash, 'Warning! Grammatical gyrations ahead!!!'"[3] The reader of this book should perhaps turn on another detector: "Caution! Confusion of grammatical, syntactical, and semantic categories ahead! Writer unfamiliar with the languages!!"

THIS GENERATION

Hanegraaff begins his foray into the field of grammar by discussing the use of the term 'this' in Jesus' Olivet Discourse. Hanegraaff declares, "Allow me to state the obvious. Our Lord is not grammatically challenged in the least!"[4]

Of course the problem is not with Jesus' grammar. It is with Hanegraaff's understanding of it. He says, "Had he wanted to draw the attention of his disciples to a generation nineteen hundred years hence, he would not have confused them with the adjective *this*."[5] Since Hanegraaff does not actually indicate to which verse he is referring when he makes this comment, the reader can only surmise that he is referring to the statement by Jesus quoted by Gerald Sigal in a quote Hanegraaff earlier provided. That is from Matt 24:34: "Truly I say to you, this [αὕτη, etuah] generation will not pass away until all these things take place."[6] In a great demonstration of grammatical prowess, Hanegraaff mislabels the word 'this' as an adjective. Although the word is functioning adjectivally in this instance, which is a syntactical function, the word is actually a demonstrative pronoun, its grammatical category. Now it is quite easy to make such mistakes, but for someone who is harping on the finer points of grammar in order to critique his opponents, he needs to be able correctly to identify the parts of speech involved.

3. Ibid., 77.

4. Ibid.

5. Ibid.

6. ἀμὴν λέγω ὑμῖν ὅτι οὐ μὴ παρέλθῃ ἡ γενεὰ αὕτη ἕως ἂν πάντα ταῦτα γένηται (Matt 24:34).

Hanegraaff quotes Kenneth Gentry about the meaning of this term: "As Dr. Kenneth Gentry has aptly noted, 'this generation,' in the context of the Olivet Discourse, is 'a nonapocalyptic, nonpoetic, unambiguous, didactic assertion.'"[7] With all of this we can certainly agree. However, not a single one of these categories says anything about the sense-reference distinction. Hanegraaff says, "Thus, there is no mysterious esoteric meaning locked up in the grammar."[8] And of course this is true also. But again, it completely misses the point. It is neither a matter of grammar nor semantics that is at issue. The word 'this' can mean 'this' in a hundred contexts and have a different referent in each one. The question here is not a question of meaning, or grammar, but of referent. To what is Jesus referring when He says "this." Hanegraaff believes that He is referring to the generation to whom He is speaking, but this is not confirmed by referring to questions of grammar and meaning. So, all of the quoting and claims about grammar have nothing to do with the issue of to whom Jesus is referring. Hanegraaff says we should put on our "baloney detectors" when reading LaHaye, but when reading Hanegraaff, maybe we should turn on our "Missing the Point" detectors.

Hanegraaff goes on to say, "When Jesus said, 'When *you* see standing in the holy place "the abomination that causes desolation" spoken of through the prophet Daniel' (Matthew 24:15), his disciples did not for a moment think he was referencing a far future generation."[9] Besides the fact that the text does not say anything about what the disciples were thinking, and besides the fact that Hanegraaff has no way of verifying his speculations about what they were thinking, the point is beside the point. The disciples were notorious for misunderstanding Jesus' words. So, even if we could verify that they were not thinking about a far future generation, this does not say anything about whether that is what Jesus was saying.

However, Hanegraaff has gotten closer to the issue when he speculates that the disciples were not thinking that Jesus was "referencing" a far off generation. The question is a question of reference, but Hanegraaff has presented no evidence that Jesus is not making such a reference. Appeals to meaning do not approach this question. It is a *non sequitur* to move

7. TAC, 77.
8. Ibid.
9. Ibid.

from statements about the meaning of the term to conclusions about the reference of the term. It does not follow that because 'this' means 'this' that 'this' cannot be referencing something different in each instance.

Hanegraaff notes that the expression "this generation" appears quite frequently in the Gospels, and he undertakes to consider some of these uses. By way of addressing some of Hanegraaff's claims about this expression, I have put together a brief examination of each of the uses of the term in Matthew's Gospel.

ΓΕΝΕΑ AND ITS REFERENTS

In the debate about how the word 'generation' (γενεάν) is used by Jesus in Matt 24:34, reference is often made, as Hanegraaff does, to the other instances in which Jesus uses this term in Matthew's Gospel. It is claimed that in each case Jesus is clearly referring to the generation existing during the time that Jesus is ministering on earth. Most argue that Jesus is referring to His immediate audience. If this is the case, it is claimed, then this goes a long way in arguing that Jesus is using the same expression with the same meaning in the passage in question. The focus in the debate concerns the *meaning* of the term, but this may not be the question that should be asked.

What Is a Referent?

In examining these other instances, we will attempt to refocus the debate to consider what is called the "referent" of the term. Terms can have both sense and reference. "Sense" roughly indicates the term's meaning, and "referent" indicates that to which the term pertains or relates.[10] For example, the expressions 'morning star' and 'evening star' have different meanings, but the same referent. The expression 'morning star' means a bright, shining object in the sky that can be seen from certain points on the earth in the early morning hours. The expression 'evening star' means a bright, shining object in the sky that can be seen from certain points on the earth in the early evening hours. So, these two expressions have differ-

10. This distinction was initially articulated by Gottlob Frege in the article "Funktion und Begriff" ("Function and Concept") published in 1891. However, this distinction is probably most frequently associated with Frege's later article "Über Sinn und Bedeutung" ("On Sense and Reference") published in *Zeitschrift für Philosophie und philosophische Kritik*, vol. 100 (1892), pages 25–50. However, our popular use here does not exactly correspond to Frege's view.

ent senses or meanings, but they both refer to Venus. Also, a word can be used in different contexts with the same meaning but have different referents. The word 'father' can be used in different contexts to refer to different persons even though in each occurrence the word has the same meaning, "a male biological parent." In our case, we must not ask only what does the term mean, but to whom or to what does the term refer? This question must be addressed in each instance. The differences in the debate are not primarily a question of sense-meaning, but of referent.

The Meaning of 'Generation'

Hanegraaff spends much time referring to the meanings of terms. He claims, "Legendary dispensationalist Dr. C. I. Scofield suggested that generation did not mean 'generation' it meant 'race.'"[11] He goes on to say,

> Scofield went so far as to say that, as "all lexicons" reflect, the Jewish "race ... will be preserved ... a promise wonderfully fulfilled to this day." One might presume that because this premise is postulated in a popular reference Bible, it is true. In reality, however, it is not. As noted by Gary DeMar, a perusal of popular lexicons reveals that the word "generation" in the context of Matthew's gospel references an interval of time, not an ethnic race of people. For example, Thayer's *Greek-English Lexicon of the New Testament* defines the Greek word *genea* as '*the whole multitude of men living at the same time.* Mt. xxiv.34; Mk. Xiii. 30; Luke i.48.' Thayer cites Matthew 24:34 and Mark 13:30 in support of translating *genea* as 'generation.' Thayer does not apply the 'race' translation to Matthew 24:34. A check of other lexicons and theological dictionaries will show that *genea* in Matthew 24:34 is translated 'generation'—'those living at the same time'—not 'race.'"

Once again, however, Hanegraaff has confused categories. Lexicons and dictionaries are not designed to dictate the referent of a word in a given context. Lexicons and dictionaries are designed to report the various uses of a word in a given language at a given point in the history of that language. A lexicon will also cite or reference passages that the lexicographers believe represent those uses. Lexicons and dictionaries are not prescriptive reference works. Rather, they are descriptive reference works. They do not prescribe how words must be used. Rather, they describe how words are being used. Additionally, Thayer's lexicon is not the standard

11. TAC, 79.

Greek lexicon. The Bauer-Arndt-Gingrich Lexicon (BDAG) has been the standard New Testament Greek lexicon for many years. According to BDAG, γενεά indicates "the sum total of those born at the same time, expanded to include all those living at a given time and freq. defined in terms of specific characteristics, *generation, contemporaries*."[12] Notice that BDAG does not specify which time period, only that the word can be used to refer to a group in a given time period. Hanegraaff seems correct in rejecting the meaning "race" in Matt 24:34.

Considering Specific Passages

Matthew 11:16

The first instance of this expression is found in Matt 11:16: "But to what shall I compare this generation [τὴν γενεὰν ταύτην, ñetuat naeneg ñet]? It is like children sitting in the market places, who call out to the other *children*."[13] In this instance, the term 'generation' seems to mean "those living at a given time." To whom does the expression "this generation" refer? In this context Jesus is talking about those who have been willing to find fault with John the Baptist on the one hand and with Jesus on the other. It seems that the referent in this instance is the people who were alive at the time Jesus is making these statements, that is, His immediate audience.

Matthew 12:39

The second instance is found in Matt 12:39 "But He answered and said to them, 'An evil and adulterous generation [γενεά, aeneg] craves for a sign; and no sign will be given to it but the sign of Jonah the prophet;'"[14] In this instance Jesus does not use exactly the same expression as is found in 11:16 where He says, "this generation," but this passage is often referenced in the debate and must be considered. Here again the question is not a question of meaning only but of referent also. And, once again the meaning seems to be "those living at a given time," and the referent seems to be

12. BDAG (2000), s.v. "γενεά."

13. Τίνι δὲ ὁμοιώσω τὴν γενεὰν ταύτην; ὁμοία ἐστὶν παιδίοις καθημένοις ἐν ταῖς ἀγοραῖς ἃ προσφωνοῦντα τοῖς ἑτέροις (Matt 11:16).

14. ὁ δὲ ἀποκριθεὶς εἶπεν αὐτοῖς· γενεὰ πονηρὰ καὶ μοιχαλὶς σημεῖον ἐπι—ζητεῖ, καὶ σημεῖον οὐ δοθήσεται αὐτῇ εἰ μὴ τὸ σημεῖον Ἰωνᾶ τοῦ προφήτου (Matt 12:39).

the people who are alive at the time Jesus is making these claims. In fact, in this context, the referent seems to be the very people who have asked Jesus about a sign.

Matthew 12:41, 42, 45

The third instance is Matt 12:41: "The men of Nineveh will stand up with this generation [τῆς γενεᾶς ταύτης, šetuat saeneg šet] at the judgment, and will condemn it because they repented at the preaching of Jonah; and behold, something greater than Jonah is here."[15] This and the next two instances, Matt 12:42 and 45, are in the same context, so they can be treated together. These texts are:

> Matt 12:42: "*The* Queen of *the* South will rise up with this generation [τῆς γενεᾶς ταύτης, šetuat saeneg šet] at the judgment and will condemn it, because she came from the ends of the earth to hear the wisdom of Solomon; and behold, something greater than Solomon is here."[16]

> Matt 12:45 "Then it goes and takes along with it seven other spirits more wicked than itself, and they go in and live there; and the last state of that man becomes worse than the first. That is the way it will also be with this evil generation [τῇ γενεᾷ ταύτῃ, aeneg ̄et ̄etuat]."[17]

In the above verses, there doesn't seem to be any other way to take these expressions than as meaning "those living at a given time" with referents being the people to whom Jesus is talking at the time.

Matthew 16:4

In Matt 16:4, we find the following: "An evil and adulterous generation [γενεά] seeks after a sign; and a sign will not be given it, except the sign

---

15. ἄνδρες Νινευῖται ἀναστήσονται ἐν τῇ κρίσει μετὰ τῆς γενεᾶς ταύτης καὶ κατακρινοῦσιν αὐτήν, ὅτι μετενόησαν εἰς τὸ κήρυγμα Ἰωνᾶ, καὶ ἰδοὺ πλεῖον Ἰωνᾶ ὧδε (Matt 12:41).

16. βασίλισσα νότου ἐγερθήσεται ἐν τῇ κρίσει μετὰ τῆς γενεᾶς ταύτης καὶ κατακρινεῖ αὐτήν, ὅτι ἦλθεν ἐκ τῶν περάτων τῆς γῆς ἀκοῦσαι τὴν γῆς ἀκοῦσαι τὴν σοφίαν Σολομῶνος, καὶ ἰδοὺ πλεῖον Σολομῶνος ὧδε (Matt 12:42).

17. τότε πορεύεται καὶ παραλαμβάνει μεθ᾽ ἑαυτοῦ ἑπτὰ ἕτερα πνεύματα πονηρότερα ἑαυτοῦ καὶ εἰσελθόντα κατοικεῖ ἐκεῖ· καὶ γίνεται τὰ ἔσχατα τοῦ ἀνθρώπου ἐκείνου χείρονα τῶν πρώτων. οὕτως ἔσται καὶ τῇ γενᾷ ταύτῃ τῇ πονηρᾷ (Matt 12:45).

of Jonah.' And He left them and went away."[18] This statement by Jesus is almost identical to the one in 12:39. The only difference is the last part of the sentence. Here Jesus says, "except the sign of Jonah," (εἰ μὴ τὸ σημεῖον Ἰωνᾶ, añoI noiemes ot⁻em ie), whereas in 12:39 He says, "but the sign of Jonah the prophet" (εἰ μὴ τὸ σημεῖον Ἰωνᾶ τοῦ προφήτου, uotehporp uot añoI noiemes ot⁻em ie). The two English translations are more different from each other than the two Greek phrases are from each other: the Greek idiom, 'εἰ μὴ' (em ie) is translated by the English word 'but' in 12:39 and by the English word 'except' in 16:4. In spite of these rather minor differences, the expressions are identical, and the meaning and the referent for 16:4 seems to be virtually the same as in 12:39, namely, "those living at a given time," and the people who were alive at the time Jesus is talking.

Matthew 17:17

Again, in Matt 17:17 we find a similar expression used by Jesus: "And Jesus answered and said, 'You unbelieving and perverted generation [γενεά], how long shall I be with you? How long shall I put up with you? Bring him here to Me.'"[19] Here Jesus is directly addressing the people whom He characterizes as an unbelieving and perverted "generation" (γενεά). There seems to be no question that the meaning is "those living at a given time," and the referent of the term is the people to whom Jesus is speaking.

Matthew 23:36

The last use to consider before our verse is Matt 23:36: "Truly I say to you, all these *things*[20] will come upon this generation [τὴν γενεὰν ταύτην]."[21] This also seems to be an instance of meaning "those alive at a given time" and referring to those at this time. However, there is a curious statement made by Jesus in verse 35: "so that upon you may fall *the guilt of* all the righteous blood shed on earth, from the blood of righteous Abel

18. γενεὰ πονηρὰ καὶ μοιχαλὶς σημεῖον ἐπιζητεῖ, καὶ σημεῖον οὐ δοθήσεται αὐτῇ εἰ μὴ τὸ σημεῖον Ἰωνᾶ. καὶ καταλιπὼν αὐτοὺς ἀπῆλθεν (Matt 16:4).

19. ἀποκριθεὶς δὲ ὁ Ἰησοῦς εἶπεν· ὦ γενεὰ ἄπιστος καὶ διεστραμμένη, ἕως πότε μεθ' ὑμῶν ἔσομαι; ἕως πότε ἀνέξομαι ὑμῶν; φέρετέ μοι αὐτὸν ὧδε (Matt 17:17).

20. In this and the subsequent instances, the word 'things' is not actually present in the Greek text. It is, however, implied by the neuter plural demonstrative pronoun, 'these' (ταῦτα).

21. ἀμὴν λέγω ὑμῖν, ἥξει ταῦτα πάντα ἐπὶ τὴν γενεὰν ταύτην (Matt 23:36).

to the blood of Zechariah, the son of Berechiah, whom you murdered between the temple and the altar."[22] We have discussed this earlier, but here we want to exam the passage in greater detail. The curious part of this statement is that Jesus accuses the scribes and Pharisees of murdering Zechariah between the temple and the altar. The exact accusation is found in the latter part of the verse: "whom you murdered." This is a translation of the relative clause, "ὅν ἐφονεύσατε" (etasuenohpe noh). The verb 'murdered' is a second person, plural verb translated "you murdered." The event to which Jesus seems to be referring is found in 2 Chron 24:21: "So they conspired against him [Zechariah] and at the command of the king they stoned him to death in the court of the house of the Lord."[23] The murder of Zechariah took place during the reign of Amaziah, king of Judah, between 796–767 BC. Assuming for the moment that this is the Zechariah to whom Jesus is referring, the question is, why does Jesus say these scribes and Pharisees murdered Zechariah? They certainly could not have murdered a Zechariah who lived several hundred years before them. Jesus had already pointed out how they claimed to be different from their fathers who murdered the prophets (23:30), but by killing the ones Jesus would send to them, and ultimately killing Jesus, they demonstrated that they were of the same spirit as those who killed the prophets. In other words, in spite of their disclaimers, they were in fact the same kind of people as their fathers—evil and unbelieving.

Gary DeMar attempts to avoid the unpleasant consequence of this use of the second person pronoun. He argues, "while it's common to link the Zechariah of Matthew 23:35 with the Zechariah of 2 Chronicles 24:20–21, I don't believe it should be."[24] Why doesn't he believe it should be? Because, "The Zechariah of 2 Chronicles is identified as 'the son of Jehoiada,' while Zechariah of Matthew 23:35 is said to be the 'son of Berechiah.'"[25] Unfortunately for DeMar's assertion, it takes only a little familiarity with the Hebrew language to learn that Hebrew has no sepa-

---

22. ὅπως ἔλθῃ ἐφ᾽ ὑμᾶς πᾶν αἷμα δίκαιον ἐκχυννόμενον ἐπὶ τῆς ἀπὸ τοῦ αἵματος "Αβελ τοῦ δικαίου ἕως τοῦ αἵματος Ζαχαρίου υἱοῦ Βαραχίου, ὅν ἐφονεύσατε μεταξὺ τοῦ ναοῦ καὶ τοῦ θυσιαστηρίου (Matt 23:35).

23. וַיִּקְשְׁרוּ עָלָיו וַיִּרְגְּמֻהוּ אֶבֶן בְּמִצְוַת הַמֶּלֶךְ בַּחֲצַר בֵּית יהוה
(2 Chron 24:21).

24. Gary DeMar, "Norman Geisler, 'You,' & 'Zechariah the Son of Berechiah,'" http://www.preteristarchive.com/PartialPreterism/demar-gary_07_01.html.

25. Ibid.

rate word for "son" and "descendant" or "grandson." The Hebrew word "son," serves to indicate a biological son as well as a descendant. In Matt. 23:31 Jesus says, "So you testify against yourselves, that you are sons [υἱοί, ioiuh] of those who murdered the prophets."[26] Of course, the scribes and Pharisees were not the biological sons of those who murdered the prophets, although they may have been the biological descendants. Here the word 'son' is used to indicate someone who has exhibited the same characteristics as an ancestor, regardless of their biological relations. So also, the expression בֶּן־יְהוֹיָדָע ('adayoh°y neb), translated "son of Jehoiada," simply means "descendant of Jehoiada," not biological son. DeMar poses the additional question, "If Jesus meant the Zechariah of 2 Chronicles 24, who was killed 'in the court of the house of the LORD' (2 Chronicles 24:21), then why didn't He say 'the son of Jehoiada' in order to avoid any confusion?"[27] Apparently, the only confusion is in the mind of DeMar. There is no confusion for those who do not have an eschatological system to justify. The reason Jesus said "Berechiah" is because this was Zechariah's actual father, and the reason the writer of Chronicles says "son/descendant of Jehoiada" is to make the connection between the evil actions of the Jews in killing Zechariah and Zechariah's important priestly line.

DeMar doesn't want to believe that Jesus is referring to the Zechariah of 2 Chronicles because this presents an insurmountable problem for his interpretation of the reference in Matthew 24. By way of an alternate proposal, DeMar asserts, "In the New Testament, John the baptizer's father's name is Zacharias, but in Greek it's spelled the same way as the Zechariah of Matthew 23:35. Could this be the Zechariah who Jesus said was murdered?"[28] So, rather than referring to the Zechariah of 2 Chronicles, of whom we have an actual biblical record concerning his murder, DeMar opts for a murder of a different Zechariah for whom there is no record, either in the Bible or anywhere else, that he was ever murdered by anyone. Additionally, the context indicates that Jesus is refuting His opponents' claim that they are not like those who murdered the prophets: "Woe to you, scribes and Pharisees, hypocrites! For you build the tombs of the prophets and adorn the monuments of the righteous, and say, 'If we had been in the days of our fathers, we would not have been partners with

---

26. ὥστε μαρτυρεῖτε ἑαυτοῖς ὅτι υἱοί ἐστε τῶν φονευσάντων τοὺς προφήτας (Matt 23:31).

27. DeMar, "Zechariah son of Berechiah."

28. Ibid.

them in the blood of the prophets.' So you testify against yourselves, that you are sons of those who murdered the prophets" (Matt 23:29–31).[29] Yet Zacharias, the father of John the Baptist, is never referred to as a prophet. In Lk. 1:67ff Zacharias prophesies after being filled with the Holy Spirit, but this does not make him a prophet. In 1 Samuel 10:10 the Spirit comes upon Saul so that "he prophesied" (וַיִּתְנַבֵּא, 'ebantiyyaw), and yet Saul turned out neither to be a prophet nor righteous. Jesus is arguing that the scribes and Pharisees are just like those who murdered the prophets, but if the referent of Jesus' statement is Zecharias, who was a priest and not a prophet, then His argument falls flat. The fact that DeMar would opt for a made up murder rather than one that fits the context and the purpose of Jesus' discourse indicates the lengths to which some will go to try to make the text fit their preconceived systems.

DeMar's remarks are directed at the assertion by Norman Geisler that there is "a change in audience reference at 24:9" in which "'you' must be taken generically as 'you of the Jewish nation.'"[30] DeMar says, "There is no indication that the use of 'you' in Matthew 24:9 and following refers to any other audience than the one to whom Jesus is speaking."[31] So, let us grant that DeMar's speculations about Zacharias are possible. Even this move does not help his cause. First of all, it is very likely that not every scribe or Pharisee was in the audience at this time. The organization of Pharisees was divided into distinct communities, some of which lived and functioned in other parts of the land. Also, among the Pharisees were a number of Priests and Levites, some of whom were probably conducting duties at the time. In other words, the life and responsibilities of the Pharisees probably prevented some from being present. Of course someone will say that this is just speculation, and that is true. But, it is no more fanciful speculation than DeMar's claims about a murder of Zacharias for which there is no historical evidence. At lest my speculation is based on historical facts.[32] Given these facts, it is ridiculous to think that Jesus'

---

29. Οὐαὶ ὑμῖν, γαρμματεῖς καὶ Φαρισαῖοι ὑποκριταί, ὅτι οἰκοδομεῖτε τοὺς τάφους τῶν προφητῶν καὶ κοσμεῖτε τὰ μνημεῖα τῶν δικαίων, καὶ λέγετε· εἰ ἤμεθα ἐν ταῖς ἡμέραις τῶν πατέρων ἡμῶν, οὐκ ἂ ἤμεθα αὐτῶν κοινωνοὶ ἐν τῷ αἵματι τῶν προφητῶν. ὥστε μαρτυρεῖτε ἑαυτοῖς ὅτι υἱοί ἐστε τῶν φονευσάντων τοὺς προφήτας (Matt 23:29–31).

30. DeMar, "Zechariah son of Berechiah."

31. Ibid.

32. Much of this information comes from *The Zondervan Pictorial Encyclopedia of*

remarks were directed at only those scribes and Pharisees who happened to be present. It surely applied to all scribes and Pharisees who believed and acted like the one's Jesus is rebuking. So, even if the 'you' is referring to Jesus' immediate audience, it is not confined to this immediate audience. So, Geisler's point that 'you' must be taken generically, that is, it cannot be confined to those who were immediately present, still stands.

Second, it is absurd to think that every scribe and Pharisee in the nation of Israel, or even every one to whom Jesus was talking, actually murdered Zacharias. And yet it is equally absurd to think that Jesus' comments are meant for only those few who actually committed a murder of Zacharias. In fact, the point of Jesus' statement is that all the scribes and Pharisees who thought and acted like these to whom Jesus is talking were guilty of the crime of killing Zacharias, even if they did not actually participate in the actual murder. So, the 'you' in this verse must be taken generically. That is, it must be broader than just the immediate audience of Jesus at this moment. Even if we grant DeMar's speculations, this does not support his point.

Third, DeMar neglected to consider the role of textual criticism in his claims. There are several manuscripts that actually omit the name "Berechiah," including ℵ*, which is the Codex Sinaiticus, and minuscule 1346. Now, the textual evidence against including "Berechiah" is not very convincing, but that's not the point. Since DeMar's argument rests completely on the name 'Berechiah,' he should explain to his readers why he thinks it is original. He is obligated to deal with the textual issue. If there are manuscripts that do not include the name, which implies that this is a scribal error, then how does he explain this? DeMar doesn't deal with this issue, and of course neither does Hanegraaff.

Once again these arguments may not convince anyone, but again, that's not the primary point. We certainly would like to convince our reader that our understanding of 'you' is correct, but our primary point is that neither the arguments of Hanegraaff nor DeMar are as convincing as they may initially sound, and neither of them considers these contrary arguments. DeMar does more exegesis in his article than Hanegraaff does—in fact, Hanegraaff doesn't do any exegesis—and yet it is Hanegraaff's book that is supposed to be equipping the reader to do faithful exegesis.

the Bible, s.v. "Pharisees."

We have reserved the following argument against DeMar's claim for last because it is the longest and, I think, the most devastating. It is important to recall what Jesus said to the scribes and Pharisees:

> Woe to you, scribes and Pharisees, hypocrites! For you build the tombs of the prophets and adorn the monuments of the righteous, and say, "If we had been living in the days of our fathers, we would not have been partners with them in shedding the blood of the prophets." So you testify against yourselves, that you are sons of those who murdered the prophets. Fill up, then, the measure of the guilt of your fathers. You serpents, you brood of vipers, how will you escape the sentence of hell? Therefore, behold, I am sending you prophets and wise men and scribes; some of them you will kill and crucify, and some of them you will scourge in your synagogues, and persecute from city to city, so that upon you may fall the guilt of all the righteous blood shed on earth, from the blood of righteous Abel to the blood of Zechariah, the son of Berechiah, whom you murdered between the temple and the altar. Truly I say to you, all these things will come upon this generation. (Matt 23:29–36)[33]

Jesus is condemning the scribes and Pharisees because they pretended to be righteous, but they were actually as guilty of murder as their fathers were. Jesus tells them that He is going to send prophets, and wise men (σοφοὺς, suohpos), and even scribes, but they will murder them also. It is important now to look at the context of the 2 Chronicles quote:

> They abandoned the house of the Lord, the God of their fathers, and served the Asherim and the idols; so wrath came upon Judah and Jerusalem for this their guilt. Yet He [God] sent prophets to them to bring them back to the Lord; though they testified against them, they would not listen. Then the Spirit of God came on Zechariah

---

33. Οὐαὶ ὑμῖν, γραμματεῖς καὶ Φαρισαῖοι ὑποκριταί, ὅτι οἰκοδομεῖτε τοὺς τά φους τῶν προφητῶν καὶ κοσμεῖτε τὰ μνημεῖα τῶν δικαίων, καὶ λέγετε· εἰ ἤμεθα ἐν ταῖς ἡμέραις τῶν πατέρων ἡμῶν, οὐκ ἂν ἤμεθα αὐτῶν κοινωνοὶ ἐν τῷ αἵμ- ατι τῶν προφητῶν. ὥστε μαρτυρεῖτε ἑαυτοῖς ὅτι υἱοί ἐστε τῶν φονευσάντων τοὺς προφήτας. καὶ ὑμεῖς πληρώσατε τὸ μέτρον τῶν πατέρων ὑμῶν. ὄφεις, γεννήματα ἐχιδνῶν, πῶς φύγητε ἀπὸ τῆς κρίσεως τῆς γεέννης; Διὰ τοῦτο ἰδοὺ ἐγὼ ἀποστέλλω πρὸς ὑμᾶς προφήτας καὶ σοφοὺς καὶ γραμματεῖς· ἐξ αὐτῶν ἀποκτενεῖτε καὶ σταυρώσετε καὶ ἐξ αὐτῶν μαστιγώσετε ἐν ταῖς συναγωγαῖς ὑμῶν καὶ διώξετε ἀπὸ πόλεως εἰς πόλιν· ὅπως ἔλθῃ ἐφ' ὑμᾶς πᾶν αἷμα δίκαιον ἐκχυννόμενον ἐπὶ τῆς γῆς ἀπὸ τοῦ αἵματος Ἄβελ τοῦ δικαίου ἕως τοῦ αἵματος Ζαχαρίου υἱοῦ Βαραχίου, ὃν ἐφονεύσατε μεταξὺ τοῦ ναοῦ καὶ τοῦ θυσιαστηρίου. ἀμὴν λέγω ὑμῖν, ἥξει ταῦτα πάντα ἐπὶ τὴν γενεὰν ταύτην (Matt 23:29–36).

the descendant of Jehoiada the priest; and he stood above the people and said to them, Thus God has said, "Why do you transgress the commandments of the Lord and do not prosper? Because you have forsaken the Lord, He has also forsaken you." So they conspired against him [Zechariah] and at the command of the king they stoned him [Zechariah] to death in the court of the house of the Lord. Thus Joash the king did not remember the kindness which his ancestor Jehoiada had shown him, but he murdered his son. And as he [Zechariah] died he said, "May the Lord see and avenge!" (2 Chron 24:18–22)

וַיַּעַזְבוּ אֶת־בֵּית יהוה אֱלֹהֵי אֲבוֹתֵיהֶם וַיַּעַבְדוּ

אֶת־הָאֲשֵׁרִים וְאֶת־הָעֲצַבִּים וַיְהִי־קֶצֶף   18

עַל־יְהוּדָה וִירוּשָׁלִַם בְּאַשְׁמָתָם זֹאת׃

וַיִּשְׁלַח בָּהֶם נְבִאִים לַהֲשִׁיבָם אֶל־יהוה וַיָּעִידוּ

בָם וְלֹא הֶאֱזִינוּ׃   19

וְרוּחַ אֱלֹהִים לָבְשָׁה אֶת־זְכַרְיָה בֶּן־יְהוֹיָדָע

הַכֹּהֵן וַיַּעֲמֹד מֵעַל לָעָם וַיֹּאמֶר לָהֶם כֹּה

אָמַר הָאֱלֹהִים לָמָה אַתֶּם עֹבְרִים אֶת־מִצְוֺת   20

יהוה וְלֹא תַצְלִיחוּ כִּי־עֲזַבְתֶּם אֶת־יהוה

וַיַּעֲזֹב אֶתְכֶם׃

וַיִּקְשְׁרוּ עָלָיו וַיִּרְגְּמֻהוּ אֶבֶן בְּמִצְוַת הַמֶּלֶךְ

בַּחֲצַר בֵּית יהוה׃   21

וְלֹא־זָכַר יוֹאָשׁ הַמֶּלֶךְ הַחֶסֶד אֲשֶׁר עָשָׂה

יְהוֹיָדָע אָבִיו עִמּוֹ וַיַּהֲרֹג אֶת־בְּנוֹ וּכְמוֹתוֹ   22

אָמַר יֵרֶא יהוה וְיִדְרֹשׁ׃

(2 Chron 24:18–22)

Notice the interesting parallels between these two passages:

Table 2: Parallelism of 2 Chronicles and Matthew

2 Chronicles 24:18–22	Matthew 23:29–36
They have abandoned the Lord God of their fathers	They had abandoned the Lord God of their fathers
The Spirit was upon Zechariah	The Spirit was upon Christ
God sent prophets to them, but they would not listen	Jesus will send prophets to them, but they will not listen
They are guilty of shedding the blood of righteous Zechariah	The are guilty of shedding the blood of righteous Zechariah
May the Lord see and avenge	Destruction will come upon this generation.

These parallelisms are designed to make the connection between the guilt of the scribes and Pharisees. Rather than honoring the prophets as they claimed they were doing, they were actually murdering them just like their fathers did, and the parallel circumstances and actions illustrate their guilt. This also serves to demonstrate that Jesus is in fact referring to the murder of Zechariah in the 2 Chronicles passage. Consequently, the argument concerning the pronoun 'you' in Matthew seems to be unaffected by DeMar's criticisms, and in fact it is not Geisler's argument but it is DeMar's argument that "does not stand up to exegetical scrutiny."[34]

Now, the relevance of these observations about the pronoun 'you' is that even though Jesus is using the second person form of the verb, 'you murdered,' he is not claiming that they actually murdered Zechariah, but that they were just as guilty as those who did. But the 'you' both does and does not refer to the scribes and Pharisees to whom Jesus is speaking. It *does* refer to them in the sense that they are the one's Jesus is directly condemning, but it *does not* refer to them in the sense that they were not the ones who actually murdered Zechariah. So, even though the meaning of the 2nd person pronoun is the same throughout this passage, the referent is different in this verse. What this shows is that a word can have the same meaning, but a different referent, and that figures of speech allow terms to have a broader referent than they would normally have in strictly literal

34. DeMar, "Zechariah the Son of Berechiah."

expressions. This is important when considering the similar problem in 24:34, which we will now consider.

Matthew 24:34

For this verse we will provide a bit more of the context:

> And then the sign of the Son of Man will appear in the sky, and then all the tribes of the earth will mourn, and they will see the Son of Man coming on the clouds of the sky with power and great glory. And He will send forth His angels with a great trumpet and they will gather together His elect from the four winds, from one end of the sky to the other. Now learn the parable from the fig tree: when its branch has already become tender and puts forth its leaves, you know that summer is near; So, you too, when you see all these *things*, recognize that He is near, at the door. Truly I say to you, this generation will not pass away until all these *things* take place. Heaven and earth will pass away, but My words will not pass away. (Matt 24:30–35)[35]

As was the case with the use of 'you' in 23:35, so also there is the possibility that Jesus is using this term in a similar manner here. When Jesus says, "So, you too . . ." (οὕτως καὶ ὑμεῖς, siemuh iak stuoh), He may not be confining the reference specifically to His disciples, but to His disciples and anyone else who might "see all these *things*" (ὅταν ἴδητε πάντα ταῦτα, atuat atnap etedi natoh). In other words, there is precedent for understanding Jesus' use of the second person pronoun in a broader sense than the specific group to whom He is talking. In fact, it is unreasonable to think that the term 'you' refers only to Jesus' immediate audience. If we, as Hanegraaff does, assume that this is talking about the events in 70 AD, then it most certainly cannot be confined to Jesus' immediate audience only. Are we to conclude that only Jesus' immediate audience would

35. καὶ τότε φανήσεται τὸ σημεῖον τοῦ υἱοῦ τοῦ ἀνθρώπου ἐν οὐρανῷ, καὶ τότε κόψονται πᾶσαι αἱ φυλαὶ τῆς γῆς καὶ ὄψονται τὸν υἱὸν τοῦ ἀνθρώπου ἐρχόμενον ἐπὶ τῶν νεφελῶν τοῦ οὐρανοῦ μετὰ δυνάμεως καὶ δόξης πολλῆς· καὶ ἀποστελεῖ τοὺς ἀγγέλους αὐτοῦ μετὰ σάλπιγγος μεγάλης, καὶ ἐπισυνάξουσιν τοὺς ἐκλεκτοὺς αὐτοῦ ἐκ τῶν τεσσάρων ἀνέμων ἀπ᾽ ἄκρων οὐρανῶν ἕως τῶν ἄκρων αὐτῶν. Ἀπὸ δὲ τῆς συκῆς μάθετε τὴν παραβολήν· ὅταν ἤδη ὁ κλάδος αὐτῆς γένηται ἁπαλὸς καὶ τὰ φύλλα ἐκφύῃ, γινώσκετε ὅτι ἐγγὺς τὸ θέρος· οὕτως καὶ ὑμεῖς, ὅταν ἴδητε πάντα ταῦτα, γινώσκετε ὅτι ἐγγύς ἐστιν ἐπὶ θύραις. ἀμὴν λέγω ὑμῖν ὅτι οὐ μὴ παρέλθῃ ἡ γενεὰ αὕτη ἕως ἂν πάντα ταῦτα γένηται. ὁ οὐρανὸς καὶ ἡ γῆ παρελεύσεται, οἱ δὲ λόγοι μου οὐ μὴ παρέλθωσιν (Matt 24:30–35).

"see all these things" in 70 AD? There were certainly many who became Christians between the time Jesus made these statements and 70 AD, and it seems reasonable that all of those Christians would also be included as referents of the term 'you.' To confine this only to Jesus' immediate audience seems very problematic, even for a Preterist (or an Exegetical Eschatologist).

It is specifically verse 34 that uses the term 'generation': "truly I am saying to you that in no way will pass away this generation (ἡ γενεὰ αὕτη) until all these *things* come to be" (my translation).[36] Here is how the uses compare:

Table 3: Comparison of Uses of "Generation"

Matt 11:16	this generation	τὴν γενεὰν ταύτην
Matt 12:39	generation	γενεὰ
Matt 12:41	this generation	τῆς γενεᾶς ταύτης
Matt 12:42	this generation	τῆς γενεᾶς ταύτης
Matt 12:45	this generation	τῇ γενεᾷ ταύτῃ
Matt 16:4	generation	γενεὰ
Matt 17:17	generation	γενεὰ
Matt 23:36	this generation	τὴν γενεὰν ταύτην
Matt 24:34	this generation	ἡ γενεὰ αὕτη[37]

As we have seen, the referent of the expression "this generation" in 24:34 is not necessarily confined to the disciples only, and that for two reasons: 1) we have seen in Matt 23:35 that a word can have the same meaning but different referents, and 2) the sense of the passage would seem naturally to include those who would become Christians after Jesus' resurrection and before 70 AD. However, since the referent is not clear just from the word itself, we must look for other indicators in the text that might point us to the referent. One of these likely indicators is the

---

36. ἀμὴν λέγω ὑμῖν ὅτι οὐ μὴ παρέλθῃ ἡ γενεὰ αὕτη ἕως ἂν πάντα ταῦτα γένηται (Matt 24:34).

37. The difference in spelling of the demonstrative pronoun 'this' in 24:34 is simply a matter of morphology. Whereas 'this' is nominative in 12:34, and therefore does not begin with the letter tau (τ), the other instances use one of the oblique cases, which all begin with the letter tau (τ). They are, nevertheless, the same lexeme.

prior statement of Jesus: "when you see all these *things* [ὅταν ἴδητε πά ντα ταῦτα, atuat atnap eʹedi natoh], recognize that He is near, *right* at the door."[38] This statement seems to indicate that the referent of the words 'you' and 'generation' is the ones who see all these things. This, of course, raises the question, "To what *things* is Jesus referring." Before we pursue this question, we must point out that we are not claiming that the word 'generation' has a different *meaning* in this context. Just like the word 'you' in chapter 23 did not have a different meaning although it had a different referent, so also the word 'generation' here has the same meaning as all the other instances we have considered, but it may have a different referent. In this instance, the difference in referent does not make a difference in the meaning.

Now, to what is Jesus referring when he says, "all these *things*" (πά ντα ταῦτα, atuat atnap). At the very least "these things" seem to refer to the immediately previous "things" Jesus has described:

- sign of the Son of Man will appear in the sky

- all the tribes of the earth will mourn

- they will see the Son of Man coming on the clouds of the sky with power and great glory

- He will send forth His angels with a great trumpet

- they will gather together His elect from the four winds, from one end of the sky to the other

So, the referent of the term 'generation' is that generation who sees these things. But, not just "these things"—literally, "*all* [πάντα, atnap] these things [ταῦτα, atuat]." Jesus actually seems to be saying that the generation that sees *all* of these things will not pass away. This may imply that the *things* to which Jesus is referring are more than just these few that immediately precede our statement. In fact, verse 30 begins with the connector, 'and then' (καὶ τότε, etot iak). This seems chronologically to connect the sign of the Son of Man with the events previously described. This would seem at least to include the events referred to in verse 29: "But immediately after the tribulation of those days the sun will be darkened, and the moon will not give its light, and the stars will fall from the sky,

38. οὕτως καὶ ὑμεῖς ὅταν ἴδητε πάντα ταῦτα, γινώσκετε ὅτι ἐγγύς ἐστιν ἐπὶ θύραις (Matt 24:34).

and the powers of the heavens will be shaken."[39] So, the list seems to have expanded somewhat:

- the sun will be darkened

- the moon will not give its light

- the stars will fall from the sky

- the powers of the heavens will be shaken

- sign of the Son of Man will appear in the sky

- all the tribes of the earth will mourn

- they will see the Son of Man coming on the clouds of the sky with power and great glory

- He will send forth His angels with a great trumpet

- they will gather together His elect from the four winds, from one end of the sky to the other

The list of "things" to which Jesus seems to be referring may ultimately include more, but it does not seem to include less than these. It would be much too involved to investigate if and when these events may have occurred. The point here is that to understand the expression "this generation" to be referring only to the disciples is not as certain a case as Hanegraaff would have us believe. The term 'generation' seems rather to refer to whoever sees *all* these things, not just *some* of them. If these things occurred on or before 70 AD, then the disciples would certainly be included in this referent. If, however, it can be shown that these things have not yet occurred, then the referent to the expression "this generation" would be a yet future group, and this without changing the meaning of the term, without taking the expression out of context, without distorting the text, and without doing the myriad of other less than flattering charges that are made against Futurists by Hanegraaff and others.

ONE COUNTER-ARGUMENT

One argument against the notion that "this generation" may refer to the future is succinctly described by Doug Beaumont. Although Beaumont

---

39. Εὐθέως δὲ μετὰ τὴν θλῖψιν τῶν ἡμερῶν ἐκείων ὁ ἥλιος σκοτισθήσεται, καὶ ἡ σελήνη οὐ δώσει τὸ φέγγος αὐτῆς, καὶ οἱ ἀστέρες πεσοῦνται ἀπὸ οὐρανοῦ, καὶ αἱ δυνάμεις τῶν οὐρανῶν σαλευθήσονται (Matt 24:29).

does not necessarily adhere to the Preterist view expressed in these objections, he does present a helpful summary of the particular arguments we wish to address:

> Preterists point out that this face-value interpretation is so obvious that it is even used by atheists to argue against Christianity [R. C. Sproul, *The Last Days According to Jesus* (Grand Rapids: Baker Book House, 2000), 13]. For example, Bertrand Russell, a famous 20th century atheist, includes this allegedly failed prophecy of Jesus to discredit His claim to be the Messiah [Bertrand Russell, *Why I am Not a Christian* (New York: Touchstone, 1957), 16]. Russell's argument is echoed by many others as well.
>
> Preterists charge Futurists with attempting to rescue this alleged non-fulfillment of Christ's words by moving the prophecy into the future. Atheists do not accept this and, oddly, Futurists themselves will not allow this move with other groups. Ron Rhodes in his book, Reasoning from the Scriptures with the Mormons [(Eugene, OR: Harvest House Publishers, 1995), 68] attacks Joseph Smith's prophetic claims by noting several of Smith's false prophecies. Rhodes emphasizes an obvious failure concerning Smith's prophecy in *Doctrine and Covenants* 84:3–5 that the building of the Mormon temple in Missouri would occur within "this generation." ["For verily this generation shall not all pass away until an house shall be built unto the Lord." Triplet version (Salt Lake City, UT: The Church of Jesus Christ of Latter Day Saints, 1981)]. Yet in other writings, Rhodes refutes those who use the very same argument against Jesus' claim to be a prophet by resorting to the "race" argument or by stating that this refers to "the generation that witnesses the signs" [Norman L. Geisler and Ron Rhodes, *When Cultists Ask: A Popular Handbook On Cultic Misinterpretations* (Grand Rapids: Baker Books, 1997), 126–27]. Why, it must be asked, is this an acceptable argument when attempting to vindicate Christ, but not when defending Joseph Smith? (Indeed, D&C 84:3–5 references Mt. 24 :34 in its explanatory footnotes).[40]

Our own examination of the referent of the word 'generation' is just as much a "face value" interpretation as the one proffered by Preterists, and the reference to Bertrand Russell does not help their case. Russell

---

40. Doug Beaumont, "CHAPTER NINE (?) CAN JESUS TELL TIME? Alleged Time Indicators in the Olivet Discourse," (unpublished manuscript). We must stress the fact that the arguments presented by Mr. Beaumont are not his arguments, nor is he necessarily advocating these. He is simply summarizing and comparing the arguments of the belligerents.

also argued that God must have a cause. Russell has a history of mis-understanding Christianity and the Bible, and the reference to Russell shows only that misunderstanding the text is not a practice owned by Christians.

Also, there is in fact no inconsistency in Rhodes' arguments. The problem is, once again, the difference between the referents in each case, not the time factor. With reference to the Mormons, Rhodes points out that the referent for Smith's prophecy was the generation of people to whom he was speaking. However, this cannot be assumed in the Matthew passage. The referent in Jesus' prophecy is the generation of people who "see all these things." Additionally, the claim that Futurists attempt "to res-cue this alleged non-fulfillment of Christ's words by moving the prophecy into the future," could in fact have been used against a Preterist in 55 AD. An atheist would say, "Jesus' prophecy did not come true." The Preterist would say, "It's in the future." So, simply pointing out that it is in the future is not a valid criticism. Had there been any Preterists in 55 AD they would have done the same thing Futurists do today.

ONE OBJECTION

The following objection has been proposed against the previous argument:

> A Pretererist saying this in 55 AD would still be within the time frame asserted by Jesus. An atheist could not very well argue that a prophecy said to come to pass within a generation (i.e. by 70 AD) that was unfulfilled in 55 AD was therefore false. That would be like me claiming that Jesus will return in 2020 and someone argu-ing in 2015 that I was wrong because it had not happened yet.

But this objection does not seem to work because the same can be said for the Futurist, that is, either that generation is now, or it has yet to come to be. According to the Futurist interpretation, the Futurist is still within the time frame also. The understanding of its fulfillment is predicated on the referent of the term 'generation.' For the Futurist to say its fulfillment is in the future would be no different than a Preterist in 55 AD saying, "the fulfillment is still in the future." The Preterist would argue, "The prophecy said that this generation would not pass away before these things are fulfilled. At 55 AD we have not reached the *termius ad quim* of the generation. The end of the generation isn't here yet. So, you can't say it is a failed prophecy. There is still time before the end of this generation is reached." But, the Futurist says the same thing. "The prophecy said this generation would not pass away before these things are fulfilled. At 2006 we have not reached the *terminus ad quim*. The end of the generation that sees these things isn't here yet. In fact, that generation may not have even begun. So, you can't say it is a failed prophecy. There is still time before the end of the generation that sees these things is reached."

ANOTHER ASPECT TO ΓΕΝΕΑ

Genea and the Kind of People

There is another aspect to the question of the term 'generation' that must be considered. Look again at the statement of Jesus in Matt 12:39: "But He answered and said to them, 'An evil and adulterous generation [γενεά] craves for a sign; and no sign will be given to it but the sign of Jonah the prophet;'"[41] Now there seems to be no question that the time frame for the referent of the term 'generation' is the time when Jesus is speaking. But, who are the *persons* included in the referent? It seems obvious that Jesus is not referring to everyone in the entire world at the time. This is clear enough from the fact that it was the Jews who sought for a sign, while the Greeks sought wisdom (1 Cor 1:22: "For indeed Jews ask for signs and Greeks search for wisdom").[42] Also, it is more than likely the case that Jesus is not including His own disciples in this group either, or any other Jews who believed into His name. In fact, in the context of chapter 12, the referent seems particularly to be the Jewish leaders who were opposing Him. In other words, the people to whom Jesus is referring in this reference are the evil people who, being alive at the time, were opposing Jesus and His teaching. So, the term 'generation,' although referring to people alive at the time, is a reference to a kind of people, not only a temporally defined group. The Jews at this time were the kind of people who do not trust God or Christ and are the evil generation who seeks for a sign.

Additionally, the adjective 'adulterous' (μοιχαλὶς, silahciom) has specific reference to the covenant people. Israel was an adulterous people because they broke the covenant relation with God and went playing the harlot with other gods (Ezek 16:41 et. al.), like an unfaithful spouse who

---

41. The Greek passage for this verse has already been given in footnote 14.

42. ἐπειδὴ καὶ Ἰουδαῖοι σημεῖα αἰτοῦσιν καὶ Ἕλληνες σοφίαν ζητοῦσιν (1 Cor 1:22).

breaks the covenant of marriage and commits adultery. This term would not apply to the non-Jews because no other nation had a covenant relation with God, nor was any other people referred to as God's wife (e.g., Ezek 16:32). So, the referent to the term 'generation' in 12:39 would seem to be an evil, unbelieving Jew—not just any Jew, and not any non-Jews at all. So, Jesus is not referring to everybody, and He is not identifying certain individuals. Rather He is referring to a certain *kind* of person. The kind of person who is an evil, unbelieving Jew.

Now, if this is the case in 12:39, it would seem to follow that because the next three instances (Matt 12:41, 12:42, and 12:45) are in the same context, that this would be true of these uses as well. But, when we look at the other instances, save for the moment 24:34, it seems to be the case that these instances can be understood similarly. Consider for example Matt. 11:16: "But to what shall I compare this generation? It is like children sitting in the market places, who call out to the other *children*."[43] In verses 18 and 19 Jesus explains, "For John came neither eating nor drinking, and they say, 'He has a demon!' The Son of Man came eating and drinking, and they say, 'Behold, a gluttonous man and a drunkard, a friend of tax collectors and sinners!' Yet wisdom is vindicated by her deeds."[44] To whom is the pronoun 'they' in verse 18 referring? It must be referring back to the persons designated as "this generation," indicating what it is they say that is like what children in the market places say. But, it is clear from the Gospel accounts that not everyone did this. There were many people who believed into Jesus' name who were not guilty of this kind of evil. Certainly Jesus' own disciples would not have been included in this group. So, once again it seems to be a reference, not to specifically identified individuals, but to the kind of person that acts and thinks this way. I'm not talking about a race, but about the kind of person, regardless of race, who is an unbeliever and did the kinds of things indicated in the text.

This also seems to apply to Matt 16:4 since this statement is almost identical to the one in 12:39. What about the remaining instances? Matt 17:17: "And Jesus answered and said, 'You unbelieving and perverted generation, how long shall I be with you? How long shall I put up with you?

---

43. The Greek for this verse is given in footnote 13.

44. ἦλθεν γὰρ Ἰωάννης μήτε ἐσθίων μήτε πίνων, καὶ λέγουσιν· δαιμόνιον ἔχει. ἦλθεν ὁ υἱὸς τοῦ ἀνθρώπου ἐσθίων καὶ πίνων, καὶ λέγουσιν· ἰδοὺ ἄνθρωπος φάγος καὶ οἰνοπότης, τελωνῶν φίλος καὶ ἁμαρτωλῶν. καὶ ἐδικαιώθη ἡ σοφία ἀπὸ τῶν ἔργων αὐτῆς (Matt 11:18–19).

Bring him here to Me.'"[45] This instance is particularly interesting because the persons to whom Jesus is speaking are not the Jewish leadership, but the man whose son was suffering, and possibly even His own disciples. Whereas in the other instances there seems to be no reason to think that a characterization like "evil and adulterous generation" would refer to Jesus' own disciples, in this instance this implication seems to be that even Jesus' own disciples are included in the referent. Why would this be the case? Because in this instance Jesus' disciples are acting just like those unbelieving and evil people who do not trust in God. This would be similar to Paul in 1 Corinthians 2 calling the Corinthian believers "natural"—not that they were in fact natural or unsaved men, but that they were acting like natural men, men of the flesh (σαρκίνοις, sionikras). Matt 17:17 seems to strengthen the idea that the referent to the term 'generation' is not primarily a quantitative reference, but a qualitative reference. Even the disciples, when they act like the evil unbelievers, are part of "this generation."

Finally, Matt 23:36 seems to use the term in the same manner: "Truly I say to you, all these *things* will come upon this generation."[46] This is particularly clear in this instance where we have already argued that the word 'you' refers to the people who are guilty of murder, whether in the time of Zechariah, or in the time of Jesus' earthly ministry. In other words, looking at each of the instances of the use of the term 'generation,' excepting for the moment 24:34, the term seems to refer qualitatively, not quantitatively—it is a certain kind of people. This conclusion seems to be fortified in this last instance by the context. Consider verse 35: "so that upon you may fall all the righteous blood shed on earth, from the blood of righteous Abel to the blood of Zechariah, the son of Berechiah, whom you murdered between the temple and the altar."[47] The expression 'upon you may come the blood' (ἔλθῃ ἐφ' ὑμᾶς πᾶν αἷμα, amiah nap samuh hpe‐ehtle) is an idiomatic expression indicating their guilt. The NET Bible captures this idea with its rendering of 23:36: "I tell you the truth, this generation will be held responsible for all these things!" This is a stern warning to all who would follow the practices of the scribes and Pharisees. So ultimately, the

---

45. The Greek for this verse is given in footnote 19.

46. The Greek for this verse is given in footnote 21.

47. ὅπως ἔλθῃ ἐφ' ὑμᾶς πᾶν αἷμα δίκαιον ἐκχυννόμενον ἐπὶ τῆς γῆς ἀπὸ τοῦ αἵματος Ἄβελ τοῦ δικαίου ἕως τοῦ αἵματος Ζαχαρίου υἱοῦ Βαραχίου, ὃν ἐφονεύ σατε μεταξὺ τοῦ ναοῦ καὶ τοῦ θυσιαστηρίου (Matt 23:35).

term 'generation,' at least in this instance, refers primarily to a kind of people, not exclusively to a people of a given time.

Qualitative and Quantitative Referents in Matthew 24:34

How does this relate to 24:34? If, as the Preterists assert, we should take this instance in the same way as the others, it would seem that the primary emphasis in this text is not the time reference, but the quality of the people who are referred to as "this generation" regardless of the time in which they live. What kind of people are the people that will not pass away? There is nothing in the text to indicate that Jesus is necessarily referring to these people as evil people. In all of the other instances, the references to the fact that the people were evil were specifically stated in the context. But, no such statement occurs here. So, it is not necessarily the case that the generation is an evil generation. They may in fact be evil, but the text does not say one way or another. The only qualitative reference that seems likely is that the generation that will not pass away is qualified as a people who "see all these things." In other words, the qualifying identification of the referent to "this generation" is not that they are evil, but that they are the ones who see all these things.

Just like the other instances of the use of the word 'generation,' the primary characterization of the generation is not temporal but qualitative—not when the generation exists, but the kind of people they are. The fact that in each of the previous instances 'generation' refers to people who were alive at the time Jesus is making these statements is only a secondary aspect of the referent. These people are referred to, not simply because they are alive at this time, but because they are the kind of people they are. Similarly, in 24:34 the kind of people who will not pass away are a kind of people who are witnesses of "all these things." The time factor seems to be in the background. There is certainly a sense of "when" in the characterization. "This generation" is the generation that exists *when* all these things are seen, but the "when" is not determined by whether they are the generation present when Jesus is saying these things. Rather, the "when" is determined by when all these things are seen. Now, the generation that sees all these things may be the generation of Jesus' immediate audience, or they may be a generation that still has not existed yet. Nevertheless, since we have already argued that the generation is the generation that sees these things, whenever these things occur(red), this qualitative aspect

to the reference seems to support the earlier conclusion that "this generation" is not *necessarily* the disciples. This conclusion does not violate the
context and the prior uses of the term in Matthew, nor does it change the
meaning. Rather it is consistent with the other uses and fits the context
of chapter 24.

Conclusion

Hanegraaff's claims and assertions about the term 'generation' in Matt
24:34 are misguided at best. Hanegraaff concentrates on the meaning of
the term when in fact it is the referent of the term that is the question that
needs to be addressed. That the referent is the primary concern does not
predispose the answer to be either a Futurist or a Preterist (or Exegetical
Eschatologist) interpretation. We did not address the question of whether
these "things" have occurred or are yet to occur. Rather, we argued that
the generation who sees "all these things" is the referent that identifies
the generation about whom Jesus is speaking, and that the term is primarily qualitative in reference rather than quantitative in reference. In
other words, Jesus is more concerned with the kind of person than when
the person lives. Not only has Hanegraaff confused categories. He has
oversimplified a complex issue and completely missed the whole point
of Jesus' warning. Once again, even if this does not convince anyone, the
point is that Hanegraaff has failed to deal with the issues. He has not done
any "faithful exegesis," nor has he given his reader the tools to "be the
judge."

THE PRONOUN 'YOU'

Hanegraaff now turns to the question of the use of the pronoun 'you.' He
starts off by telling a story about the use of the pronoun 'you.' This is another logical fallacy. It is called a bad analogy. The experience of Hanegraaff
talking to his children has no specific relationship to Jesus talking to His
disciples, and it completely misses the point. Suppose Hanegraaff is talking to his children and he says, "I tell you the truth, this day will certainly
not pass away until I have taken *you* all to Disney World." Now suppose
there is an ice cream stand down the street named "Disney World Ice-
cream," and Hanegraaff's children go there all the time. In fact, they go
there so often that when Daddy says, "Let's go to Disney World," the kids
know that he is referring to the ice cream stand, not the amusement park.

However, if you were visiting the Hanegraaff family and did not know about this idiom that the family shared, you might think that Hanegraaff was referring to the actual amusement park, not to some ice cream stand. And when you discovered that you were actually going to an ice cream stand, and not the amusement park, you might get upset that Hanegraaff has cruelly misled his children. However, when the whole circumstance is explained, you understand.

Now, it may be the case that Hanegraaff is like the visitor who just doesn't understand what Jesus is saying because he is not privy to information necessary to make an appropriate judgment. Now my adaptation of Hanegraaff's scenario may not convince anyone, but, again, that's not the point. The point is, Hanegraaff's cute story has nothing to do with the issue at hand. The question is, to what is Jesus referring when He makes His statements, and sometimes there is more to it than simply looking up the meaning of a pronoun, or telling a cute story. We have already dealt with the substance of these arguments, and the material here is simply an extended version of the earlier arguments.

THE ADVERB 'SOON'

Hanegraaff's arguments about the word 'soon' are an extended version of the arguments that appear earlier. It appears that the "this generation" argument, the "pronoun you" argument, and the "adverb soon" arguments are the only arguments he has. Once again he spends a lot of time and words missing the point. In fact, this entire chapter is a demonstration of how Hanegraaff does not understand either grammar, syntax, or semantics. Every one of his arguments has been proposed before, and every one has been answered. Emphatic assertions, citations, references to passages, and the like do not demonstrate his point. He has failed to do any grammatical exegesis, or any exegesis of any kind. I was hoping that after the disappointment of the previous chapter that there might be more substantial argumentation in this chapter. However, there is nothing new in this chapter that merits any serious consideration. Perhaps the substantial argumentation is yet to come. Let us move on to the chapter on the historical principle and hope for more.

5

Historical Principle

Historical Realities vs. Historical Revisionism

Hanegraaff begins this chapter on the historical principle by recounting events surrounding the discovery and publication of the Gospel of Judas. He notes how scholars have lent an air of credibility to the myriad of speculations about this find and how this credibility has led many to question the veracity of the Word of God. Hanegraaff leads into a discussion of the historical principle by proposing, "To answer such questions requires a familiarity with the historical principle of e^2, which is to say that in order to properly evaluate ancient manuscripts, we must take into account their historical legacy."[1] Employing the acronym LEGACY, Hanegraaff purposes to discuss the "factors historians consider in determining the historical viability and meaning of ancient manuscripts."[2] Hanegraaff spends several pages explicating the parts of this acronym, which he will then apply to the study of the eschatological questions that are the theme of his book. We will give a very brief synopsis of each point of the acronym.

- The 'L' stands for 'Location,' which has to do with where a document or artifact was found.

- The 'E' stands for 'Essence,' which has to do with basic thrust or theme of the contents of the manuscript, captured in the question, "What is its essence?"

- 'G,' of course, stands of 'Genre,' a topic that has been discussed by Hanegraaff already.

1. TAC, 98.
2. Ibid.

25

- The letter 'A' is for 'Author.' This addresses the question of who wrote the manuscript.

- The 'C' is for 'Context,' which relates to the "historical milieu within which a manuscript was written ..."

- 'Y' stands for 'Years.' This refers to the dating of the manuscript.

Under the pretense of critiquing critical scholars such as Bart Ehrman, Hanegraaff furtively propagates his eschatological perspective. For example, Hanegraaff recounts how Ehrman charges the authors of the Gospels with anti-Semitism and how Jesus was mistaken and misguided about the eschaton. According to Hanegraaff, Ehrman claimed that Jesus prophesied the end of the world as an event that was to occur almost immediately. Hanegraaff counters Ehrman's speculations when he says, "If fact, Jesus did not predict the end of the world! Rather, Jesus was predicting an apocalypse now—within a generation the Jews would experience destruction of their city and its temple."[3] As we have demonstrated, however, this is not what Jesus was prophesying. Both Ehrman and Hanegraaff have misunderstood the text.

LOCATION

Under the topic "Location," Hanegraaff will deal with the question of the dating of the book of Revelation. He claims that LaHaye's dispensationalism "hinges on proving that the book of Revelation was written long after the destruction of the temple in AD 70."[4] Although it would certainly bolster the dispensational position if this could be proven, the dating of the book is not as critical an issue for dispensationalism as it is for Preterism (or Exegetical Eschatologism). Even if Revelation was written before 70 AD, it is still possible, albeit more difficult, to argue that its prophecies are about the future beyond 70 AD. However, if it can be demonstrated that the book was written after 70 AD, Preterists (or Exegetical Eschatologists) would have a near impossible task of trying to convince anyone that its prophecies are actually only history about the destruction of Jerusalem.

3. Ibid., 106.
4. Ibid., 109.

What John Has In Mind

Hanegraaff begins his discussion of this topic by pointing out that the letters to the seven churches of Asia Minor indicate that the message of the book is "relevant to the whole church throughout the whole of history."[5] He then declares, "Nowhere in Revelation is there any indication that John has two thousand years of church history in mind."[6] Of course this is the very question that is under scrutiny, and Hanegraaff has, again, asserted his position without providing any support.

Must Soon Take Place

Appealing to the same misunderstanding, Hanegraaff declares, "Rather, as John makes clear in the prologue, his letter concerns things that 'must *soon* take place' (Revelation 1:1). Indeed, says John, 'the time is *near* (Revelation 1:3).'"[7] Rev 1:1 reads, "The Revelation of Jesus Christ, which God gave Him to show to His bond-servants, the things which must soon [ἐν τάχει, ne iehcat] take place; and He sent and communicated by His angel to His bond-servant John, who testified to the word of God and to the testimony of Jesus Christ, to all that he saw. Blessed is he who reads and those who hear the words of the prophecy, and heed the things which are written in it; for the time is near [ἐγγύς, sugge]."[8] The phrase "must soon take place" is a translation of the phrase ἃ δεῖ γενέσθαι ἐν τάχει (iahtseneg ied ah iehcat ne). This phrase is set out in Table 4 with a word-for-word translation below.

Table 4: Revelation 1:1

ἃ	δεῖ	γενέσθαι	ἐν	τάχει
which	it is necessary	to become	in	speed

5. Ibid., 110.

6. Ibid.

7. Ibid.

8. Ἀποκάλυψις Ἰησοῦ Χριστοῦ ἣν ἔδωκεν αὐτῷ ὁ θεὸς δεῖξαι τοῖς δούλοις αὐτοῦ ἃ δεῖ γενέσθαι ἐν τάχει, καὶ ἐσήμανεν ἀποστείλας διὰ τοῦ ἀγγέλου αὐτοῦ τῷ δούλῳ αὐτοῦ Ἰωάννῃ, ὃς ἐμαρτύρησεν τὸν λόγον τοῦ θεοῦ καὶ τὴν μαρτυρίαν Ἰησοῦ Χριστοῦ ὅσα εἶδεν. Μακάριος ὁ ἀναγινώσκων καὶ οἱ ἀκούοντες τοὺς λόγους τῆς προφητείας καὶ τηροῦντες τὰ ἐν αὐτῇ γεγραμμένα, ὁ γὰρ χαιρὸς ἐγγύς (Rev 1:1–3).

The word in question is τάχει (iehcat). According to BDAG the word can be used to mean "a very brief period of time, with focus on speed of an activity or event, *speed, quickness, swiftness, haste*."[9] In fact, there is a variant reading in Rev 2:5 that uses this word. It could be translated, "I am coming to you speedily ..." (ἔρχομαι σοι ταχύ, uhcat ios iamohcre).[10] Whether the variant is accepted or not, it does illustrate this use of the term. The variant reading indicates not that Jesus is necessarily coming to them in the very near future. Rather, what Jesus seems to be saying is, when He comes, it will happen *quickly*. We have made this point before. The word does not necessarily mean that something is going to happen in the near future. Rather, it can be used to refer to something that will happen quickly, but not necessarily soon.

BDAG gives another possible meaning for this word: "pert. to a relatively brief time subsequent to another point of time, ἐν τάχει as adverbial unit *soon, in a short time*."[11] BDAG references Rev. 1:1 under this meaning. However, BDAG also places this verse under the first meaning: "*quickly* Rv 2:5 v.l." This cannot be a reference to 2:1 since the word does not occur in that verse. In fact, if we accept the variant in 2:5, then the word occurs in only three places in the book of Revelation, 1:1, 2:5, and 22:6. So, it is not "clear" even in BDAG that John is saying these things were going to happen soon. Rather, John could be saying, whenever they do happen, they will happen quickly. Now these are the possible meanings of this word, and for Hanegraaff simply to ignore the lexical information is not "faithful exegesis." It is in fact selective reporting.

The Time Is Near

The word 'near' occurs in the clause, "for the time in near" (ὁ γὰρ χαιρὸς ἐγγύς, sugge soriahc rag oh). The phrase is set out below in Table #5 with a word-for-word translation. The word translated "for," γὰρ (rag), is a postpositive. In Greek, some words, called postpositives, will occur in the sentence or clause as the second or third word of the clause or sentence, yet the constraints of English require that we put this conjunction first in the clause, "for the time ..."

---

9. BDAG (2000), s.v. "τάχος."

10. This variant is attested in the Byzantine Majority, the Vulgate, and the Syriac.

11. BDAG (200), s.v. "τάχος."

Table 5: Revelation 1:3

ὁ	γὰρ	χαιρὸς	ἐγγύς
the	for	time	near

The word "near" (ἐγγύς, sugge, pronounced "engoos"), according to BDAG, has several possible meanings:

1.   pert. to being in close proximity spatially, *near, close to.*

2.   pert. to being close in point of time, *near.*

3.   pert. to being close as experience or event, *close.*[12]

BDAG references Rev 1:3 under meaning 2 above, that is, close in point of time, near. So, at first this seems to support Hanegraaff's assertion. However, Hanegraaff has made an illicit assumption. He has assumed without argument that what is near is the fulfillment of the prophecies. However, John does not specify what is near other than that the time is near. Time for what? One might surmise that, in the context of verse 3, the phrase refers to the prophecies of the book and the things written in it: "Blessed is he who reads and those who hear the words of the prophecy, and heed the things which are written in it; for the time is *near*" (Rev 1:3). However, this is not a necessary conclusion. In fact, since the phrase itself is not clear, to assume that this is what is meant, and then to use the verse to prove your point is called circular reasoning. Hanegraaff has assumed what must be proven, and he has not demonstrated that his assumption is correct, nor has he shown his reader any "faithful exegesis" that would serve to equip his reader to be the judge. Also, the word 'near' is a relative term. John could be saying, "compared to the centuries we have been waiting for the kingdom, the time is near." So, this would not have to indicate a nearness in any absolute sense. Now these alternate ways of looking at this text may not convince anyone, but, again, that's not the point. The point is, Hanegraaff has simply assumed his interpretation without any argument or faithful exegesis, he has not attempted to deal with contrary views, and he has not provided the reader with any tools so that he can be the judge.

Hanegraaff declares, "As it is wrongheaded to suggest that Revelation symbolizes seven consecutive historical eras, from the apostolic church in

12. BDAG (2000), s.v. "ἐγγύς."

Ephesus to the apostate church in Laodicea . . ." Why is it "wrongheaded" to suggest this? Hanegraaff has not proven that it is wrongheaded. He simply ridiculed the position as if his rejection of it is sufficient to prove that it is wrongheaded. Where is the exegesis? By rejecting Scofield's musings, Hanegraaff has not thereby demonstrated that this view is wrongheaded in principle or in fact. Other interpreters have adopted this view and eliminated those aspects that have been criticized by Hanegraaff. So, Hanegraaff's argument against Scofield is not an argument either against the interpretation in principle, or dispensationalism in general. He is merely arguing against one interpreter who does not necessarily represent the mainstream of dispensational interpretation of the book of Revelation.

ESSENCE

Hanegraaff begins the section on essence by declaring, "The essence of Revelation is the unveiling of a bride."[13] This is an interesting observation since the book itself indicates that its essence is the revelation of Jesus Christ. This entire section is basically a presentation of Hanegraaff's views on various topics in the book of Revelation. Very little if any "faithful exegesis" is done. The methodology is the assertion, without exegetical foundation, of a position and then building upon that unproven position.

The Harlot

For example, Hanegraaff criticizes other commentators for attempting to identify the harlot of Revelation with the Roman Catholic church: "Like LaHaye, hundreds of prophecy experts misidentify the great prostitute as the contemporary Roman Catholic Church."[14] Contrary to this view, Hanegraaff proposes, "The application of the historical principle of e^2, however, demonstrates that this is a clear case of mistaken identity. In biblical history only one nation is inextricably linked to the moniker 'harlot.' *And that nation is Israel!*"[15] There is no question that Israel is labeled 'harlot' more than any other nation in the Old Testament text. However, the passages in Revelation that refer to the harlot do not require that this nation be "inextricably linked to the moniker 'harlot,'" as Hanegraaff says,

13. TAC, 115.
14. Ibid., 119.
15. Ibid.

and there are other nations that are referred to by this label. Isaiah refers to Tyre as a harlot, and Nahum refers to Nineveh with the same label.

> Now in that day Tyre will be forgotten for seventy years like the days of one king. At the end of seventy years it will happen to Tyre as in the song of the harlot: Take your harp, walk about the city, O forgotten harlot; Pluck the strings skillfully, sing many songs, that you may be remembered. It will come about at the end of seventy years that the Lord will visit Tyre. Then she will go back to her harlots [הָנֶתָ֑ה, ḥatñaz^ew] wages and will play the harlot with all the kingdoms on the face of the earth. Her gain and her harlots wages will be set apart to the Lord; it will not be stored up or hoarded, but her gain will become sufficient food and choice attire for those who dwell in the presence of the Lord. (Isa 23:15–18)[16]

> Woe to the bloody city, completely full of lies and pillage; her prey never departs. The noise of the whip, the noise of the rattling of the wheel, galloping horses and bounding chariots! Horsemen charging, swords flashing, spears gleaming, many slain, a mass of corpses, and countless dead bodies they stumble over the dead bodies! All because of the many harlotries of the harlot [זוֹנָ֔ה, ḥañoz], the charming one, the mistress of sorceries, who sells nations by her harlotries and families by her sorceries. (Nah 3:1–4)

Now, once again this is not designed to convince anyone that the term 'harlot' in Revelation is not referring to Israel. This may be the case. However, what this does show is that Hanegraaff needs to present more evidence than simply his own assertions that the harlot in Revelation is Israel. Even though 'harlot' is applied to Israel throughout the Old Testament, this does not prove that the passages in Revelation are referring to Israel. Hanegraaff gives a brief synopsis of the message of Hosea, but none of this proves or even supports his claim. My response to his proclamations is, So! What if every passage in the Old Testament used the term 'harlot' to refer to Israel. That does not guarantee that it is being used that way in Revelation. This needs to be demonstrated from the text of Revelation by "faithful exegesis," not by simple assertion. Supposed similarities between claims in Revelation and various Old Testament books does not prove the claim either. These may be shown to be supporting

---

16. It is debatable whether the title "Tyre" is being used as a figurative title for Israel. Even if this is the case, Tyre functions as an appropriate symbol for the harlot, Israel. If the term 'harlot' did not apply to Tyre, then Tyre would not function as a symbol.

claims once it has been established by "faithful exegesis" of the book of Revelation, but Hanegraaff has not done that.

Hanegraaff claims that the identity of the harlot in Revelation is "self-evident." But, if it is self-evident, then why does anyone need Hanegraaff's arguments? What is self-evident is evident in itself. As Aquinas said, "Those propositions are said to be self-evident that are known immediately upon the knowledge of their terms."[17] But, a knowledge of the terms 'harlot' and 'Israel' does not produce the immediate knowledge that these terms are referring to the same entity, especially since there are other instances in the OT in which the term 'harlot' is used of other nations.

Hanegraaff claims, "If Revelation was written in the mid-nineties during the reign of Domitian, apostate Israel would already have been destroyed. If, on the other hand, Revelation was written in the mid-sixties, the quintessential case of mistaken identity could not possibly have taken place."[18] As we have already demonstrated, "apostate Israel" was not "destroyed" in 70 AD. In 135 AD Israel was able to mount a full-fledged war against Rome—the Bar Kochba rebellion. So, not only is Hanegraaff mistaken about the history—in his chapter on the literal principle we have demonstrate that he is mistaken about the history—it follows from this that his understanding of the description about destruction cannot apply to Israel. Both Daniel and Revelation describe a total destruction that lays the land waste. This simply did not occur in 70 AD. In fact, although Jerusalem was devastated, it was not rendered uninhabitable. Peter Schäfer notes that after the 70 AD war, the Roman legion *legio X Fretensis* was actually headquartered in Jerusalem.[19] Contrary to Hanegraaff's claims, history shows that in fact the 70 AD war was not the end either of Judaism or Jerusalem. Many Jews actually moved back into Jerusalem almost immediately after the war. However, after the Bar Kochba war Jerusalem became a Roman colony, and, as David Duncan notes, "The Jews were forbidden on pain of death to set foot in the new Roman city. Aelia [Jerusalem] thus became a completely pagan city, no doubt with the corresponding public buildings and temples."[20] In other

17. Aquinas, *Summa Contra Gentiles*, 1.10.2. "*Illa enim per se esse nota dicuntur, quæ statim, notis terminis, cognoscuntur.*"

18. TAC, 123–24.

19. Peter Schäfer, *The History of the Jews in the Greco-Roman World* (London: Routledge, 2003), 131.

20. David Laird Dungan, *A History of the Synoptic Problem: The Canon, the Text, the*

words, even after the more devastating war of Bar Kochba Jerusalem was not annihilated, but was repopulated as a Roman city. In his chapter on the historical principle, one would expect Hanegraaff accurately to report the historical facts, but he fails to do so.

The 144,000

Hanegraaff claims, "In truth, the number 144,000 excludes neither non-Jewish men nor women. Far from fixated on race and gender, the number 144,000 is focused on relationship. It represents true Israel—not by nationality but by spirituality, not by circumcision of the flesh but by circumcision of the heart."[21] He goes on to claim, "Indeed, the 144,000 are 'a great multitude that no one can could [sic] count, from every nation, tribe, people and language, standing before the throne and in front of the Lamb.'"[22] Hanegraaff failed to quote the entire verse, however. The verse is Rev 7:9, which starts with the phrase, "After these things . . ." (Μετὰ ταῦτα, atuat ateM). In other words, the vision that begins in 7:9 is a different vision than the one about the 144,000, so John is not saying that the great multitude constitutes the 144,000. Besides being poor interpretation, this is also the fallacy of selective reporting.

But what about the fact that the text refers to each tribe of the nation of Israel and specifically states that there will be 12,000 from each tribe? Hanegraaff declares, "To suggest as LaHaye does that '12,000' from each of the twelve tribes means exactly 12,000—not 11,999 or 12,001—must surely stretch the credulity of even the most ardent literalist beyond the breaking point."[23] Why is this the case? Hanegraaff explains: "To begin with, ten of the twelve tribes lost their national identity almost three thousand years ago in the Assyrian exile. The other two, Judah and Benjamin, were largely decimated two thousand years ago by Roman hordes."[24] Of course there are no Scripture passages anywhere that assert or even imply this. Hanegraaff's claim is particularly problematic since there are a number of Scripture passages that indicate that God will bring Israel back into the land: "For behold, days are coming, declares the Lord, when I will

---

Composition, and the Interpretation of the Gospels (New York: Doubleday, 1999), 47.

21. TAC, 125.
22. Ibid.
23. Ibid., 126.
24. Ibid.

restore the fortunes of My people Israel and Judah. The Lord says, I will also bring them back to the land that I gave to their forefathers and they shall possess it" (Jer 30:3).

כִּי הִנֵּה יָמִים בָּאִים נְאֻם־יהוה וְשַׁבְתִּי אֶת־
שְׁבוּת עַמִּי יִשְׂרָאֵל וִיהוּדָה אָמַר יהוה
וַהֲשִׁבֹתִים אֶל־הָאָרֶץ אֲשֶׁר־נָתַתִּי 3
לַאֲבוֹתָם וִירֵשׁוּהָ:

(Jer 30:3)

And again, "the voice of joy and the voice of gladness, the voice of the bridegroom and the voice of the bride, the voice of those who say, Give thanks to the Lord of hosts, for the Lord is good, for His lovingkindness is everlasting; and of those who bring a thank offering into the house of the Lord. For I will restore the fortunes of the land as they were at first, says the Lord" (Jer 33:11).

קוֹל שָׂשׂוֹן וְקוֹל שִׂמְחָה קוֹל חָתָן וְקוֹל
כַּלָּה קוֹל אֹמְרִים הוֹדוּ אֶת־יהוה צְבָאוֹת
כִּי־טוֹב יהוה כִּי־לְעוֹלָם חַסְדּוֹ מְבִאִים 11
תּוֹדָה בֵּית יהוה כִּי־אָשִׁיב אֶת־שְׁבוּת־
הָאָרֶץ כְּבָרִאשֹׁנָה אָמַר יהוה:

(Jer 33:11)

Other passages that seem to indicate the restoration of Israel and Judah include Isa 43:5–7; Jer 12:15; 24:6; Ezek 20:42; 26:25–6; Hosea 12:9; Amos 9:14–5; Zeph 3:20; Zech 10:10. Now, all of these passages would probably be disputed by Hanegraaff, but that is the very point. Why doesn't he deal with any of these passages? In Hanegraaff's own words, "Anyone who has read the Bible even once"[25] would see these passages as at least suggesting that Israel will be restored to the land. If that is not the correct interpretation, then Hanegraaff needs to show why. Doing this is part of what "faithful exegesis" is all about. But Hanegraaff has yet actually to do any exegesis of any kind.

25. Ibid., 119.

Hanegraaff claims, "Furthermore, God's priority is not race but relationship. Christians are portrayed in Scripture as true Israel as a result of their relationship to Jesus, who is described as the Lion of the tribe of Judah."[26] But this says absolutely nothing about whether the 144,000 are Jews or not. God's priority in certainly relationship, but for the 144,000 to be Jews does not in any way usurp or contradict that priority. God can call out whomever He chooses to do whatever job He chooses without contravening or contradicting His priority.

Hanegraaff goes on to assert, "Finally, the pattern of Scripture is to refer to the community of faith, whether Jew or gentile, with Jewish designations."[27] But whether this is a "pattern" or not has yet to be demonstrated by Hanegraaff. Where is the "faithful exegesis" that is supposed to show this? Hanegraaff simply makes these assertions as if the making of them is sufficient. Additionally, what has this got to do with whether the 144,000 are Jews? Even if this is the "pattern of Scripture," it does not follow that every time the nation of Israel appears as a topic in Scripture it must be taken to refer to the community of faith. This also must be argued for, not simply asserted. What difference does it make that the walls of the New Jerusalem are 144 cubits thick? What does this have to do with whether the 144,000 are Jews? Hanegraaff doesn't even bother to make the connection, and he certainly presents no "faithful exegesis" by which his connections might be demonstrated.

He goes on to claim, "It is far more likely that 144,000 is a number that represents the twelve apostles of the Lamb multiplied by the twelve tribes of Israel, times one thousand. The figurative use of the number twelve and its multiples is well established in biblical history."[28] If the number is symbolic, then why enumerate the amount of those that will come from each tribe of Israel, and why even list the tribes at all? What difference does it make that the number twelve and its multiples are used in a figurative sense? Simply pointing out this fact does not demonstrate that these numbers are used this way here. This must be demonstrated from the text of Revelation, not simply asserted. The number twelve and its multiples can be used in a "thousand more examples"[29] for all sorts of

26. Ibid., 126.
27. Ibid.
28. Ibid.
29. Ibid., 127.

things even in other places in Revelation, but that does not prove how it is being used in a given instance. It certainly shows that it is possible that these numbers are figurative, but it doesn't show that they actually are being used this way in this passage. Once again we must ask, where is the "faithful exegesis" that Hanegraaff said he was going to do?

GENRE

In this section, Hanegraaff says he will discuss the importance of genre for "establishing the historical meaning imbedded in the text of Revelation."[30] He claims, "To begin with, Revelation is a letter."[31] Now how does he know that this is a letter? Well, he says, "It starts with a salutation that identifies both the author of the letter and the audience to whom it is addressed ('John, to the seven churches in the province of Asia' [1:4]) and concludes with an ancient epistolary blessing ('The grace of the Lord Jesus be with God's people. Amen' [22:21])."[32] Now, according to Hanegraaff's scenario, the interpreter must discover the genre of a text in order to "establish the historical meaning." But, in order for Hanegraaff to discover that this is a letter, he first read the letter and understood that it began with a salutation, identified the author and audience, and that it concluded with an epistolary blessing. But, if he read this letter and understood these aspects of the letter before determining that it was of the genre letter, does this mean that his understanding of these parts were not "the historical meaning"? After all, he had to read the text and understand these various parts of it in order to discover into which genre it must be classified. But, if, as Hanegraaff claims, we must know the genre in order to get the historical meaning, and since he read the text and understood its parts before he knew which genre it is, it follows that his reading of the parts was not the historical meaning. Either that, or Hanegraaff's characterization of the nature and importance of genre is extremely overstated. The very fact that Hanegraaff was able to read the text and understand its various parts in order to discover into which genre the text could be classified demonstrates that an interpreter does not have to know the genre to get

30. Ibid., 128.
31. Ibid.
32. Ibid.

the historical meaning. Although genre enhances our understanding of meaning, it does not determine meaning.[33]

Assuming for the moment that Revelation is a letter, it follows that chapters 2–3 address "contemporary problems among the seven churches in the province of Asia."[34] Of course we could say the same about 1 Corinthians. It certainly addresses contemporary problems in the church at Corinth. However, that does not negate the fact that the teaching in it applies to any church throughout any age that follows the pattern of practice as found in the Corinthian church. And, the fact that Revelation is, as Hanegraaff admits, "an apocalypse," it becomes entirely possible to understand the letters of chapters 2–3 to have symbolic reference to churches throughout history. To have contemporary relevance and future significance is the very nature of prophecy. So, arguing for the contemporary relevance of the book does not in any way prove that it cannot have future significance or application. This is especially the case since Hanegraaff, again, fails to do any "faithful exegesis" by which to show his reader why he should accept Hanegraaff's assertions.

The Two Witnesses

Hanegraaff alerts the reader to the fact that, "the identity of the two witnesses of Revelation 11 cannot be comprehended apart from a familiarity with the language system employed by the text."[35] Hanegraaff claims, "only someone with the background music of the Old Testament coursing through their minds comprehends that the two witnesses are a metaphorical reference to Moses and Elijah and reflect Old Testament jurisprudence that mandated at least two witnesses to convict of a crime (Deuteronomy 19:15)."[36] Of course the Old Testament jurisprudence called for two actual witnesses, not two metaphorical witnesses. And, even if this is a metaphorical reference to Moses and Elijah, this does not mean that there are not two actual human beings functioning as the two actual witnesses. Jesus referred to John the Baptist as Elijah: "And if you are willing to accept,

---

33. In chapter 2 we discussed this issue, and in note 41 we directed the reader's attention to an article that addresses this issue in greater detail.

34. TAC, 129.

35. Ibid., 130.

36. Ibid., 131.

John himself is Elijah who was to come (Matt 11:14).[37] This must have been a figurative expression, but that did not mean that there was not an actual John the Baptist or an actual Elijah. John the Baptist could stand symbolically for Elijah and at the same time be an actual person. So also, even if the two witnesses "represent the entire line of Hebrew prophets"[38] does not negate the possibility that they are two actual persons. These are not mutually exclusive categories.

Hanegraaff attempts to connect the two witnesses in Revelation 11 with passages in Zechariah. Zechariah refers to a vision of a gold lampstand with seven bowls and seven channels. Of course the passage in Revelation 11 refers to two lampstands, not one. So, in order to make the connection, Hanegraaff has to claim that the text of Revelation has been "reconfigured." But, if the text of Revelation has been reconfigured, how does he know that the one relates to the other? Hanegraaff does not attempt to demonstrate why the one passage should be connected to the other. He simply asserts, "our minds are inexorably drawn to Zechariah's vision ..."[39] But, drawing one's mind inexorably or otherwise does not prove that there is a connection. Other people's minds might be "inexorably" drawn somewhere else. As seems to be his practice, Hanegraaff makes assertions and claims but offers no exegetical ground or justification.

Next, Hanegraaff warns, "we must never . . . attempt to press the language system of Revelation into a literalistic labyrinth. Indeed, the literal-at-all-cost methodology of people like LaHaye is interpretive suicide when it comes to apocalyptic genre."[40] But, nowhere has Hanegraaff proven that LaHaye or anyone else practices a "literal-at-all-cost" methodology. The simple fact that these people do not agree with Hanegraaff's interpretations does not prove that they employ such a methodology. And, to jettison a literal interpretation at various points becomes a convenient way for Hanegraaff to avoid conflicts with the text. He says, "so too the two witnesses will not literally turn their mouths into blow torches on the streets of Jerusalem."[41] Of course, nowhere does the text say they will turn their mouths into blow torches, nor does any interpreter claim

---

37. καὶ εἰ θέλετε δέξασθαι, αὐτός ἐστιν Ἡλίας ὁ μέλλων ἔρχεσθαι (Matt 11:14).

38. TAC, 131.

39. Ibid., 132.

40. Ibid., 132–33.

41. Ibid., 133.

this. The text says, "And if anyone wants to harm them, fire proceeds from their mouth and devours their enemies" (Rev 11:5).[42] There is nothing said about "blow torches." Why does Hanegraaff say this? Because it is inflammatory (excuse the pun) rhetoric to try to make his opponent's view appear worse than it actually is. Besides this, why does Hanegraaff think that God could not cause literal fire to come out of the mouths of two actual human beings? He rejects this possibility because he has already made up his mind that this can't happen. Maybe it won't happen literally, but Hanegraaff has not presented any "faithful exegesis" to show this.

Hanegraaff says, "Nor should we suppose that Moses and Elijah will be literally transported to the twenty-first century in a time machine."[43] Once again he resorts to inflammatory rhetoric and *ad hominem* argument. Such a tactic would be like pointing out that, although Hanegraaff alerts his reader to have "a familiarity with the language system employed by the text," the text was actually written in Greek, and Hanegraaff has already shown his lack of facility in the original languages—Hanegraaff wants his readers to be alert to the language system of the text, but Hanegraaff himself has none. Now that might be construed as a rhetorical *ad hominem* argument. Just because Hanegraaff does not show any facility in the language systems of Greek, Hebrew, or Aramaic does not mean that his interpretations are necessarily wrong. So also, to exaggerate and mis-characterize the claims of one's opponents for rhetorical effect does not prove that what they actually said is wrong. Nevertheless, the fact that Hanegraaff has demonstrated no facility in the original languages is more pertinent to the question of interpretation than Hanegraaff's attempts to use his own inflammatory rhetoric. Earlier Hanegraaff exclaimed that he was disturbed at LaHaye's rhetoric: "What is particularly disturbing is the rhetoric LaHaye reserves for those who do not subscribe to his understanding of what is and is not literal."[44] But, Hanegraaff has consistently demonstrated his own flare at using rhetoric to put his opponent in as bad a light as possible.

---

42. καὶ εἴ τις αὐτοὺς θέλει ἀδικῆσαι πῦρ ἐκπορεύεται ἐκ τοῦ στόματος αὐτῶν καὶ κατεσθίει τοὺς ἐχθροὺς αὐτῶν· (Rev 11:5).

43. TAC, 133.

44. Ibid., 18.

"Soon" and "Near" Again

Again Hanegraaff appeals to the use of the words 'soon' and 'near,' and we have already shown that his understanding of these terms is not a necessary conclusion. No doubt the angel in Rev 22:10 declares that the time is near. But, as Simon Kistemaker points out, "Greek makes a clear distinction between *chronos*, which refers to time as it is divided into hours, days, weeks, months, and years, and *kairos*, which can signify either a favorable time (as during the harvest) or an eschatological time (as in Revelation). ... The wording in 1:3 and 22:10 is identical ... Both passages allude not to calendar or clock time, but to the special time in which the eschatological prophecies are in the process of being fulfilled. In other words, they point to the end of time and thus alert the hearers and readers of Revelation to prepare themselves for the consummation."[45] In other words, the occurrence of the words 'soon' and 'near' do not necessarily support the conclusion to which Hanegraaff has arrived. These words can be taken to refer to "the end of time," as Kistemaker, who is not a dispensationalist, points out. Now the question is not whether Kistemaker's argument is valid. Rather, the question is, why doesn't Hanegraaff deal with these issues? If Hanegraaff is going to maintain that these words indicate events that were expected to take place soon with respect to John, then he needs to prove this case, not merely refer to these words.

Future or Future?

Since it is clear that many of the things prophesied in Revelation did not occur in 70 AD, Hanegraaff has to find some way around this problem. To alleviate this difficulty he declares, "Of course, the fact that the book of Revelation is predominantly focused on fore-future events should not lead anyone to suppose that the imagery of Revelation is exhausted in the holocaust of AD 70."[46] By this move Hanegraaff has introduced the additional problem of determining which prophecies go where and articulating the principles by which each can be identified. If, as Hanegraaff proposes, "the book of Revelation points forward to the final future when Jesus will appear a second time, the problem of sin will be fully and finally resolved, the dead will be resurrected, and the universe will be recre-

45. Simon J. Kistemaker, "Hyper-Preterism and Revelation," in *When Shall These Things Be?* ed. Keith A. Mathison (Phillipsburg, New Jersey: P&R Publishing, 2004), 237.

46. TAC, 134.

ated without the stain of disease, destruction, death and decay (Romans 8:21)," then does this not introduce a 2,000 year parenthesis or gap in the prophecy? And, since it does, why not put other parts of the book at the end as well? On what basis and according to what hermeneutic principle does Hanegraaff decide what is fulfilled "soon" and what is fulfilled "later"? Unfortunately for his readers, Hanegraaff does not either list the principles by which he makes these decisions, nor does he explain them, and he certainly does not equip the reader to be the judge about these problems.

He considers a couple of examples, but he does not indicate the principle or principles by which he relegates these "to final-future realities to describe judgment in their generation."[47] Hanegraaff claims, "While Peter's prophecy [2 Pet 3:10–13] was fulfilled in the destruction of Jerusalem, the events of AD 70 and the cosmic language Peter used to describe them point forward to an even greater day of judgment when the problem of sin and Satan will be fully and finally resolved!"[48] But why should anyone think that Peter's prophecy admits of two fulfillments, or that Peter's prophecy refers to 70 AD at all. Hanegraaff neither delineates nor describes the principles by which he makes these determinations.

The text of 2 Peter states, "But the day of the Lord will come like a thief, in which the heavens will pass away with a roar and the elements will be destroyed with intense heat, and the earth and its works will be burned up. Since all these things are to be destroyed in this way, what sort of people ought you to be in holy conduct and godliness, looking for and hastening the coming of the day of God, because of which the heavens will be destroyed by burning, and the elements will melt with intense heat! But according to His promise we are looking for new heavens and a new earth, in which righteousness dwells" (2 Pet 3:10–13).[49] There is no mention in the text of the destruction of Jerusalem in 70 AD, and, in fact, the heavens did not pass away with a roar, nor were the elements destroyed

47. Ibid., 135.

48. Ibid.

49. ῞Ηξει δὲ ἡμέρα κυρίου ὡς κλέπτης, ᾗ οἱ οὐρανοὶ ῥοιζηδὸν παρελεύσονται στοιχεῖα δὲ καυσόμενα λυθήσεται καὶ γῆ καὶ τὰ ἐν αὐτῇ ἔργα εὑρεθήσεται. τούτων οὕτως πάντων λυομένων ποταπoὺς δεῖ ὑπάρχειν ὑμᾶς ἐν ἁγίαις ἀναστροφαῖς καὶ εὐσεβείαις, προσδοκῶντας καὶ σπεύδοντας τὴν παρουσίαν τῆς τοῦ θεοῦ ἡμέρας δι᾽ ἣν οὐρανοὶ πυρούμενοι λυθήσονται καὶ στοιχεῖα καυσόμενα τήκεται. καινοὺς δὲ οὐρανοὺς καὶ γῆν καινὴν τὸ ἐπάγγελμα αὐτοῦ προσδοκῶμεν, ἐν οἷς δικαιοσύνη κατοικεῖ (2 Pet 3:10–13).

with intense heat. To conclude, as Hanegraaff does, that the destruction of Jerusalem "fulfills the cosmic language"[50] requires a whole lot more explanation than Hanegraaff has provided. And, if the "cosmic language" is fulfilled by the events of 70 AD, then why should we think that "it does not exhaust its meaning"?[51] And, what does it mean to "exhaust meaning"? Peter's prophecy does not simply "suggest" a day of ultimate judgment; there is no reason to think that it is referring to anything else but the future judgment. And Hanegraaff has presented no "faithful exegesis" to overturn the normal, plain and proper, commonsense understanding of the words.

There is simply no basis upon which to think that 2 Pet 3:10–13 refers to the destruction of Jerusalem in 70 AD. The text does not make reference to this event. The descriptions of the text go beyond anything that actually occurred at the time. In fact, as we have shown, the destruction of Jerusalem was not even a major destruction, much less a complete desolation, and much of the land of Israel was undisturbed. The historical facts of the 70 AD war do not do justice to the drastic descriptions in 2 Peter. The normal, plain and proper, commonsense understanding does not indicate a connection between the drastic descriptions of Peter and the far less than total devastation of the events of 70 AD. Therefore, if Hanegraaff wants to maintain this connection, he needs to do much more than simply assert it.

AUTHOR

This section purports to discuss the authorship of Revelation. Hanegraaff approvingly quotes G. K. Beale: "If an unknown author were attempting to identify himself with a well-known Christian figure like the apostle John, he would probably call himself not just 'John' but 'John the apostle.'"[52] This sounds convincing at first, but how likely is it that Beale is aware of this ploy and yet readers of John's time would not be aware of it? Does Beale have so much more insight and understanding than someone who lived in the time of John? Isn't it just as likely that a person passing himself off as the apostle John would think that his readers might expect the true apostle to identify himself simply as "John," and knowing this he would

50. TAC, 135.

51. Ibid.

52. Ibid., 137.

do the same? How likely is it that only modern writers are aware of this ploy? I agree that Revelation "was not written pseudonymously,"[53] but arguments like Beale's seem rather superficial and arrogant. Hanegraaff's arguments, mostly from others, that John the apostle was the author of the book, seem to be strong enough to make John's authorship almost certain. However, contrary to Hanegraaff's claim, identifying John as the author does not shut the door to the possibility that the book was written in about 96 AD. There is sufficient historical evidence to support the notion that John the Apostle lived long enough to produce the book by that date. At the very least Hanegraaff ought to deal with these issues.

CONTEXT

At first one might think that Hanegraaff is using the word 'context' to refer to the place in a given book where a passage occurs. Instead he is referring to "the context in which Revelation was written ..."[54] Hanegraaff believes that he can further demonstrate that Revelation was written "during the reign of the sixth Roman Emperor—Nero Claudius Caesar Augustus Germanicus—better known today for his number than his name."[55] Hanegraaff believes that he "can be absolutely certain that 666 is the number of Nero's name and that Nero is the beast who ravaged the bride in a historical milieu that includes three-and-a-half years of persecution ..."[56]

Six Hundred Sixty-Six—χξϛ

Hanegraaff begins his discussion about Nero with the claim, "First, John identified the Beast as number six of seven kings ..."[57] However, there is nowhere in the text, either prior to or following, that says anything about the beast being number six of seven kings. The text does make reference to a beast that has ten horns and seven heads. The ten horns seem to be a reference to kings since the text states, "and on his horns were ten diadems, and on his heads blasphemous names" (Rev 13:1). However there is no reference to support Hanegraaff's claim about the beast being the sixth of seven kings. It is unfortunate for his readers that Hanegraaff does

53. Ibid.
54. Ibid., 144.
55. Ibid.
56. Ibid.
57. Ibid.

not bother to give any Bible references to indicate from where he obtained this information. It may be because there is in fact no reference that makes this claim to which Hanegraaff can appeal. If this is supposed to be an inference (deduction?) from what the text does say, then Hanegraaff needs to say this, and he needs to argue for this as a valid inference.

He goes on, "He informs his readers that the seven-headed Beast represents both a kingdom and kings of that kingdom."[58] It certainly seems to be the case that the ten horns and the seven heads could be taken to represent kings and kingdoms. However, it is not accurate for Hanegraaff to claim that "He [John] informs his readers . . ." In fact, John does not "inform his readers" that the seven-headed Beast represents kings and kingdoms. Someone might object that this is rather a minor distinction. However, in "faithful exegesis" the interpreter needs to be completely accurate, and sometimes what seem to be minor distinctions can make all the difference. Besides that, Hanegraaff has not done any faithful exegesis by which to support his assertions. Not only are his claims inaccurate, he is misleading his readers by making them think that John has actually stated that these are kings and kingdoms. As valid an inference as it might be, it is nevertheless an inference and should be presented as an inference and not as a statement by John.

Hanegraaff then asserts, "He further makes clear that with 'wisdom' and 'insight,' his first-century readers 'can calculate the number of the beast, for it is man's number.'"[59] We have dealt with this claim before. But, since Hanegraaff states it again, we will refute it again. As we pointed out before, Hanegraaff has actually misrepresented and misquoted the verse. The text actually reads, "Here is wisdom. Let him who has understanding calculate the number of the beast, for the number is that of a man; and his number is six hundred and sixty-six" (Rev 13:18).[60] First of all, Jesus does not say that with wisdom they can calculate the number of the beast. He simply says, "Here is wisdom." Apparently, the statement, "let him who has understanding calculate . . ." is a wise saying. It has nothing to do with claiming that with wisdom anyone can calculate the number of the beast.

58. Ibid.
59. Ibid.
60. ῟Ωδε ἡ σοφία ἐστίν. ὁ ἔχων νοῦν ψηφισάτω τὸν ἀριθμὸν τοῦ θηρίου, ἀριθμὸς γὰρ ἀνθρώπου ἐστίν, καὶ ὁ ἀριθμὸς αὐτοῦ ἑξακόσιοι ἑξήκοντα ἕξ (Rev 13:18).

Second, Jesus does not say that these first-century Christians should or would be able to do this. He simply says, "Let him who has understanding calculate . . ." Whether Jesus expected these first-century Christians to have this understanding is at best unclear. In other words, Jesus is saying, if you have understanding, then you can calculate. You may not have this understanding, and there may not be anyone in the first-century who has this understanding, and those who have this understanding may not actually appear for several years. But this whole point is left open. Jesus does not confine the understanding to any particular age, nor does He claim that first-century readers will be able to do this. He simply says, "If you have understanding, then you must do this."[61]

Third, Hanegraaff claims, "Obviously no amount of wisdom would have enabled a first-century audience to figure out the number of a twenty-first-century Beast."[62] My response to that statement is, Why not? How does Hanegraaff know that they could not have done this? He doesn't present any arguments to support his claim. He merely states that it is "obvious." But the fact is, it is not only *not* obvious, it is eisegesis for Hanegraaff to claim this. Why couldn't a first-century audience figure out the number of a twenty-first-century beast? Nowhere in Scripture is such a possibility outlawed. And, given the fact that God can do whatever is logically possible, couldn't God have helped this first-century audience to figure this out? Couldn't God have given the first-century audience the understanding to calculate the number? Because Hanegraaff does not want the text to mean this, he ignores the power of God to make this happen. Hanegraaff's claim is without support and without foundation.

Hanegraaff talks about how the letters of the alphabet represent numbers. After a couple of examples of this kind of reckoning, Hanegraaff quotes F. W. Farrar who states, "The very look of it [χξϛ] was awful. The first letter was the initial letter of the name of Christ. The last letter was the first double-letter (*st*) of the Cross (*stauros*). Between the two the Serpent stood confessed with its writhing sing and hissing sound. The whole found a triple repetition of 6, the essential number of toil and imperfection."[63] There are a couple of problems with this claim. First, although the letter

___

61. The word translated "let him calculate" (ψηφισάτω, otasihpesp) is actually a third person, imperative verb and better rendered, "he must calculate."

62. TAC, 8.

63. F. W. Farrar, *The Early Days of Christianity* (New York: Cassell & Co., 1889), 470–71; quoted in TAC, 146.

χ is the first letter of the word Χριστὸς, and sigma (ς) is the first letter of the word σταυρὸς, the letter ξ is not the first letter of the word "serpent." In fact, the only word in the New Testament for serpent is ὄφις, hardly giving rise to the association of ξ with "serpent." In fact, if one speculates on what the first-century Christians may have thought about these letters (and this is sheer speculation, there is no historical evidence that any early Christians made these associations or looked on this number in this way), one wonders why the early Christians would not have associated ξ with ξύλον, "tree," since Paul said, "Christ redeemed us from the curse of the Law, having become a curse for us—for it is written, 'Cursed is everyone who hangs on a tree [ξύλον].'" It is fanciful speculation ("fertile imagination"?) that the early Christians looked on this number as "awful." What may have looked awful to Farrar may not have looked awful to a first-century Christian. Also, the number is not three individual sixes, 6-6-6. The number is "Six hundred, Sixty-six" (ἑξακόσιοι ἑξήκοντα ἕξ, ioisokaxeh xeh atnoꝁexeh). So, the additional speculations about a "triple repetition of 6" is also fanciful and ungrounded.

Another problem with Farrar's speculations is that the first century Christians did not use the Greek letters as Farrar presents them, which are, in fact, modern script. What we might identify as lower-case letters, actually called minuscules, did not come into use until the fourth century AD. In the first century, these three letters would probably have looked something like this: the χ would have looked like this **X**; the ξ would have looked something like this **Ξ**; and the ς would have looked like this **C**. These are known as uncial script, which was the way Greek was written until the introduction of the use of vellum and minuscule script. Also, since any writing would have been done by hand and not by machine, the letters could have looked differently depending on who was writing them, just like our handwriting might look different from someone else's. So, Farrar's speculations are not only fanciful, they are historically inaccurate. Not being familiar either with the Greek language or the history of the Greek language, one would not expect Hanegraaff to know this. However, as an exegete, he should have done more research.

But, this does not deter Hanegraaff from expanding his speculations. He goes on to assert, "the number of Nero's name in Greek isopsephism totaled 1,005. However, transliterated from the Greek—Νέρων Καῖσαρ—into Hebrew—קסר נרון—he sum total of 'Nero Caesar' equals exactly 666. Proceeding from right to left, נ= 50; ר= 200; ו= 6; ן= 50; ק= 100; ס= 60; ר= 200 totaling 666."[64] The really absurd aspect of this proposal is that Nero's name was not "Nero Caesar." He was born Lucius Domitius Ahenobarbus. He was called Nero Claudius Caesar Augustus Germanicus, but he was also known as Nero Claudius Caesar Drusus Germanicus. Why calculate Nero's name only on the two names "Nero Caesar" when he was not known merely by those two names.

Besides that, why transliterate the name from Καῖσαι to קסר? It would seem more reasonable to transliterate it to כסר, using the Hebrew כ, *k*, to correspond to the Greek K, *k*, instead of the Hebrew ק, *q*? In fact, John J. Davis, in his book *Biblical Numerology*, actually does use the כ rather than the ק to transliterate Nero's name:

> In antiquity Nero was considered a likely candidate for Antichrist because his name, when written with Hebrew characters, had a numerical value of 666. The numerical analysis of his name is as follows:

נ	=	50
ר	=	200
ו	=	6
ן	=	50
כ	=	100
ס	=	60
ר	=	200
		666[65]

The interesting thing about this calculation by Davis is that he assigns a value of 100 to the letter כ in the above quote, but in an earlier list in the same book he says the value of כ is 20, not 100. This may be a misprint, but it is interesting that he uses the כ instead of the ק in his transliteration. Since neither Hanegraaff nor Davis indicate from where they obtained this transliteration, there is no way to discover which Hebrew letter was actually used.

However, Davis does go on to point out how Irenaeus discouraged such speculations: "Irenaeus, in *Against Heresies*, makes mention of the fact that the term *latinos* was a possible identification because it had a numerical value of 666, although he does not seem to adopt the idea. . . .

---

64. TAC, 146.

65. John J. Davis, *Biblical Numerology* (Grand Rapids: Baker Book House, 1968), 144.

His comment on this number is interesting and instructive."[66] Davis then gives the following quotation from Irenaeus:

> It is therefore more certain, and less hazardous, to await the fulfill-
> ment of the prophecy, than to be making surmises, and casting
> about for any names that may present themselves, in so much as
> many can be found possessing the number.[67]

In other words, the Christians in the early church were more level-headed about such speculations than Hanegraaff. Irenaeus indicated that there were "many" who "can be found possessing the number." So, just because Nero's name might have added up to 666, the fact that there were many who possessed this number indicates that the association with Nero was not necessarily as prominent in the first century as Hanegraaff indicates. As it turns out, the transliteration scheme is not as certain as Hanegraaff would have his readers think.

But if the Hebrew letter ב, *k*, is more likely to have been the transla-tion, why does Hanegraaff use the ק, *q*, instead? Because the *k* does not fit his calculation goals. The numerical value of the Hebrew *k* is 20, so the total would be only 586, not 666. This is the very kind of fanciful manipu-lation (fertile imagination?) for which Futurists have been criticized and maligned. There is no evidence nor is there any reason to think that any of the writers of the New Testament would have even engaged in such fanciful imagination.

But, the fanciful imagination does not end here. Hanegraaff goes on to try to explain why a transliteration of the Latin "Nero Caesar" into Hebrew does not produce 666.

> As John's letter was increasingly circulated among Latin-speaking
> audiences, biblical scribes aided them in identifying the Beast by
> transliterating the Latin spelling—"Nero Caesar"—into Hebrew—
> נרו קסר. The sum of the letters in the Hebrew transliteration
> from the Latin form of his name totals 616, just as the Hebrew
> transliteration of the Greek (Νέρων Καῖσαρ), which includes an
> additional letter, renders 666. Subtract the additional letter in the
> Hebrew transliteration from 666, and you are left with 616—two

66. Ibid., 144–45.

67. Irenaeus, *Against Heresies* (Alexander & Donaldson), Book V, chap. 30, p. 559; quoted in Davis, *Biblical Numerology*, 145.

seemingly unrelated numbers that both amazingly lead you to the same doorstep, that of a beast named Nero Caesar.[68]

One of the most absurd aspects of this fanciful speculation is that long before the New Testament times, the Hebrew language had fallen out of popular use, and very few if any Christians would have been able to read Hebrew. Hebrew fell out of use during the Babylonian captivity, and when the tribes of Judah and Benjamin began to return to the land after the edict of Cyrus in 538 BC, the Hebrew people no longer used the Hebrew language, rather the *lingua franca* of the people was Aramaic. The Hebrew language was used by the priests and scribes and maybe some male children of very wealthy parents who could afford to send their sons to learn from the scribes. The Hebrew language was falling out of use and in danger of being lost, which is why the Masorets developed the vowel pointing system that is commonly used today by non-native Hebrew speakers.

Also, the absurd association of 616 and 666 is an amazing slight of hand. First of all, before Jerome (ca. 342–419 AD) produced what is now called the Latin Vulgate in about 390–405 AD, there were only portions of the Bible that appeared in Latin translations. These odd portions are collectively referred to as the Old Latin. The Old Latin portions were not translated from the Hebrew Bible, but were rather translated from the Septuagint, the Greek version of the Old Testament:

> When and where it was that the earliest attempts were made to translate the Bible into Latin has been much disputed. In the opinion of most scholars today the Gospels were first rendered into Latin during the last quarter of the second century in North Africa, where Carthage had become enamoured of Roman culture. Not long afterward translations were also made in Italy, Gaul, and elsewhere. The wooden and literalistic style that characterizes many of these renderings suggests that early copies were made in the form of interlinear renderings of the Greek.[69]

According to the above quote from Bruce Metzger, the Gospels were not translated into Latin until the last quarter of the second century. That would put the translation into Latin some 100 years after the reign of

68. TAC, 146–47.

69. Bruce M. Metzger, *The Text of the New Testament*, 3d ed. (New York: Oxford University Press, 1992), 72.

Nero, and a Latin translation from the Hebrew text was not attempted until Jerome many years later. We can see the influence of the Greek on the Vulgate in the name "Moses."

Table 6: Transliteration Example

	Hebrew	Latin	Greek
Text	מֹשֶׁה	Moyses	Μουσῆν
English Transliteration	hĕsoM	*Mouses*	ñesuoM

As can be seen from the transliterations into English, the Latin of a simple name like *Moyses* is actually rendered from the Greek, not the Hebrew. So, to claim that the name ořeN would have even been known in a Hebrew transliteration form is speculation to the extreme. There simply is no historical evidence that the Old Latin was translated from any other text than the Greek Septuagint, and there is simply no historical evidence that Latin Christians would have been able to read the Hebrew text even if one was available to them. So, it is clear that Hanegraaff's claims about Nero's name are unfounded and border on the kind of fanciful imagination for which he chides LaHaye.

Hanegraaff declares, "Revelation records the first all-out assault of the Beast against the Bride, lasting approximately three and a half years. Prior to AD 64, the church was persecuted by the woman who rides the beast (apostate Israel), but shortly after the Great Fire of Rome, the beast unleashed its full fury against a fledgling Christian church. That Nero started the Great Fire of Rome is historically debatable. That Nero used it as the catalyst for the first state assault against the emerging Christian church is not."[70] The problems with these characterizations is that they just do not fit the historical facts. Nero's persecution probably did not extend beyond the city of Rome, as Church historian Justo González points out:

> It is difficult to know the extent of the Neronian persecution. Christian writers from the later part of the first century, and early in the second, recall the horrors of those days. It is also very likely that both Peter and Paul were among the Neronian martyrs. On the other hand, there is no mention of any persecution outside the city of Rome, and therefore it is quite likely that this persecu-

---

70. TAC, 147.

tion, although exceedingly cruel, was limited to the capital of the Empire.[71]

Church historian Williston Walker states, "The local attack on the church at Rome, while portentous of things to come, had little real effect on the Christian movement, whether at Rome or elsewhere."[72] Kenneth Latourette, arguably one of the most important church historians, says, "Usually ten major persecutions are enumerated, beginning with Nero in the first century and culminating in the one which was inaugurated by Diocletian early in the fourth century. In general they fall into two main chronological groups, the first from Nero to the year 250, *in which they were largely local and probably entailed no great loss of life . . .*"[73] Hanegraaff should have used his own Historical Principle to study the history of the Christian church. Perhaps he would have discovered that such characterizations as he ends up making simply do not fit the facts.

Revelation makes reference to the fact that the beast which John saw "coming up out of the earth, and he had two horns like a lamb and spoke like a dragon . . . causes the earth and those who dwell in it to worship the first beast" (Rev 13:11, 12).[74] John makes reference to these events encompassing the whole earth at least three more times:

- from heaven on the earth in the sight of men. (v. 13)
- he deceives those who dwell on the earth (v. 14)
- telling those who dwell on the earth (v. 14)

He says that the beast was given power to kill all those who would not worship the image of the beast, that "He causes all, both small and great, rich and poor, free and slave, to receive a mark on their right hand or on their foreheads," and "no one may buy or sell except one who has the mark or the name of the beast, or the number of his name" (Rev 13:15–17). It is simply ludicrous to consider these descriptions as fulfilled in the events

71. Justo L. González, *The Early Church to the Dawn of the Reformation*, vol. 1, *The Story of Christianity* (San Francisco: Harper & Row, Publishers, 1984), 35.

72. Williston Walker, et. al. *A History of the Christian Church*, 4th ed. (New York: Charles Scriber's Sons, 1985), 32.

73. Kenneth Scott Latourette, *A History of Christianity* (New York: Harper & Brothers, Publishers, 1953), 85 (emphasis added).

74. ἀναβαῖνον ἐκ τῆς γῆς, καὶ εἶχεν κέρατα δύο ὅμοια ἀρνίῳ καὶ ἐλάλει ὡς δράκων . . . καὶ ποιεῖ τὴν γῆν καὶ τοὺς ἐν αὐτῇ κατοικοῦντας ἵνα προσκυνήσουσιν τὸ θηρίον τὸ πρῶτον (Rev 13:11, 12).

that were localized to the city of Rome—events that had relatively little appreciable impact on the Church as whole and entailed no great loss of life. The notion that the actions of the beast correspond to the actions of Nero must, to use Hanegraaff's own words, "surely stretch the credulity of even the most ardent" Preterist (or Exegetical Eschatologist).[75] Hanegraaff charges LaHaye with doing "violence against the collective memories of those who suffered valiantly in the first Roman persecution of the bride of Christ," but Hanegraaff has done even more grievous harm by doing violence to the history of the Church and to the Word of God by distorting both to try to make them fit his eschatological speculations.

Hanegraaff even distorts history when he claims, "Moreover, it is no mere coincidence that within a year of Nero's suicide, June 9, AD 68, the Roman Empire suffered a near-fatal wound. In a moment, in the twinkling of an eye, a dynasty that had resided in the Julio-Claudia line of Roman Caesars for a century disappeared from the face of the earth. In fact, AD 69 would go down in history as the year of the four emperors—Galba, Otho, Vitellius, and Vespasian."[76] In fact, most Romans were elated at the death of Nero. Tacitus says, "The death of Nero had been welcomed initially by a surge of relief. But it had also evoked a variety of emotions in the senate, the populace, and the garrison of the capital, as well as in all the many legions and legionary commanders."[77] In 70 AD, Vespasian began construction of the Coliseum. In fact, Tacitus, who declares, "My official career owed its beginning to Vespasian, its progress to Titus and its further advancement to Domitain," goes on to report, "Modern times are indeed happy as few others have been, for we can think as we please, and speak as we think."[78] This hardly sounds like the "near-fatal wound" that Hanegraaff claims. One gets the impression that Hanegraaff is grasping at straws to try to make his speculations sound plausible.

It is simply not true that Nero's death brought "near extinction to imperial Rome."[79] Rome had suffered the disaster of civil wars before, some even more devastating than the conflicts of the four emperors. The Social War in 90 BC was "one of the most desperate wars ever fought by

75. TAC, 126.

76. Ibid., 149.

77. Tacitus, *The Histories*, trans. Kenneth Wellesley (Middlesex, England: Penguin Books, 1986), I.4.

78. Ibid., I.1.

79. TAC, 149.

the Romans, because they were fighting against a part of their own military machine."[80] To claim that this took place in the time of the Republic and not the Empire misses the point. The point of Matyszak's statement is that this was the most desperate war ever fought during the whole of the existence of the Roman political entity, whether during the Republic or the Empire. Yet Rome survived this event.

Some years later, Lucius Cornelius Sulla Felix (138–78 BC) instigated another civil war by marching the Roman army into Rome itself: "Never before had a Roman army marched to conquer Rome ..."[81] In the history of Rome, the great military and political empire had suffered devastating events. The descriptions of the devastation of Rome by Tacitus quoted by Hanegraaff could be descriptions of the conflicts that the Republic had experienced more than once. In fact, Tacitus himself says, "There indeed had been times in the past when armies had fought inside the city, twice when Lucius Sulla [Felix] gained control, and once under Cinna. No less cruelty had been displayed then, but now there was a brutish indifference, and not even a momentary interruption in the pursuit of pleasure."[82] To attempt to characterize the time after Nero as a "near fatal wound" is simply beyond credibility. Tacitus characterizes this time as "a year which brought about their death [Sevius Galba and Titus Vinius] and the near destruction of Rome."[83] This was a near destruction of the city of Rome, not of the Roman Empire.

Hanegraaff declares, "For three and a half years the Beast systematically ravished the persecuted bride and sought the ruin of the prostituted bride."[84] But history records that Nero simply did not "systematically ravish the persecuted bride." His persecutions, though terrible, did not extend beyond the city of Rome and did not even come close to "ravishing" the bride. Additionally, all of Hanegraaff's speculations assume that in relevant passages in Revelation the Church is present. This has not been either demonstrated or even argued by Hanegraaff. He asserts it and he assumes it, but he nowhere demonstrates it with any "faithful exegesis." Simply giving references to verses and declaring what he thinks

80. Philip Matyszak, *Chronicle of the Roman Republic* (London: Thames & Hudson, 2003), 155.
81. Ibid., 167.
82. Tacitus, *Histories*, 3.83.
83. Ibid., I.8.
84. TAC, 150.

*If christians "left behind" or "tribulation saints" are on earth in revelation, they are part of the true church, jew/gentile, ect, Scripture never makes distinctions via race or otherwise, see Gal. 3:28-29

they mean does not amount to exegesis, let alone "faithful exegesis." And it certainly doesn't equip the reader to be the judge.

The Siege of Jerusalem in 70 AD

Hanegraaff concludes the section on "Context" by discussing the destruction of Jerusalem in 70 AD. The characterizations of the carnage reported by Hanegraaff no doubt captures to some degree the devastation, destruction, and death of those events. He says, "And on August 30 the unthinkable happened. 'The very day on which the former temple had been destroyed by the king of Babylon,' the second temple was set ablaze. As John had prophesied, 'In one day her plagues will overtake her; death, mourning and famine. She will be consumed by fire, for mighty is the Lord God who judges her (Revelation 18:8).'"[85] Unfortunately for Hanegraaff's claims, however, the Rev 18:8 passage quoted by Hanegraaff is directed at Babylon not Jerusalem. Why does Hanegraaff think that this refers to Jerusalem? Because he thinks Babylon in Revelation is a reference to Jerusalem. He has not bothered to demonstrate this or argue for it. He assumes it, and it seems to be his *modus operandi* to act as if what he assumes must be correct and doesn't need any "faithful exegesis."

It is interesting, however, that with the burning of the temple, one wonders how the abomination of desolation that was, according to Jesus' prediction, to "stand in the holy place" (ἐστος ἐν τόπῳ ἁγίῳ, ne sotseh ⁻oigaȟ opot, Matt 24:15), could have occurred. Hanegraaff avoids the issue. And as we have already shown, as great as the devastation of Jerusalem, the land of Israel was not devastated, nor was the nation of Israel destroyed. This hardly does justice to the descriptions of wide-spread destruction of the Promised Land as are found in Revelation.

YEARS

Hanegraaff argues, "First, if the apostle John were indeed writing in AD 95, it seems incredible that he would make no mention whatsoever of the most apocalyptic event in Jewish history—the demolition of Jerusalem and the destruction of the temple at the hands of Titus."[86] This argument makes no sense at all. First, the "demolition of Jerusalem" in 70 AD was not the most apocalyptic event in Jewish history. In fact, it was not nearly

85. Ibid., 151.
86. Ibid., 153.

as devastating as the destruction of Jerusalem by Nebuchadnezzar in which the people of the southern kingdom were taken into captivity to Babylon. Not only were no people taken into captivity or driven out of the land in 70 AD, but Jerusalem was repopulated by Roman soldiers and Jews almost immediately after the hostilities were over, and in 135 AD the people were able to launch another all-out war against the Romans. Second, if the Revelation is about future events, why would John refer to something in the past? An author includes and excludes material from his composition according to how he sees the material in terms of his theme. That the events of 70 AD were seen by John as not pertinent to his theme is evident by the fact that he does not include that material. It is not "incredible" for an author to decide what he will include and exclude from his own book. And why does Hanegraaff think he is qualified to decide what is incredible for a biblical author to mention or not to mention? Simply because Hanegraaff does not understand why John would not include this material does not mean that it could not have been written after 90 AD. It is incredible to Hanegraaff because he wants his argument to work.

Hanegraaff says, "Imagine writing a history of New York today and making no mention of the destruction of the twin towers of the World Trade Center at the hands of terrorists on September 11, 2001."[87] This is of course a faulty analogy since the book of Revelation is not a history book. Also, it is quite reasonable to write a history of New York and not include anything about the destruction of the twin towers. If the history was about only the positive contributions of a certain organizations head-quartered in New York, or if it was about a history of New York in the twentieth century, or if it were any number of other specialized studies of the history of New York. His continued effort to press faulty analogies—a thesis on terrorism, a history of Jewish struggles—are all beside the point since the book of Revelation is not a history book. As we have pointed out, it is an author's prerogative to decide what he will include and exclude from his own composition, and if Hanegraaff is incapable of grasping this fact, it is no argument for his conclusion. What "stretches credulity," to use Hanegraaff's own words, is not that John would choose not write about the destruction of Jerusalem in a book written twenty-five years after the fact, and that is, after all, written about the future. What "stretches cre-

87. Ibid.

dulity" is that Hanegraaff, or anyone else, would think his argument is a good argument.

Hanegraaff's misrepresentation of the arguments of Norman Geisler borders on abuse. Geisler is arguing about the early dating of the books of the New Testament. This is a general argument about the NT books, not a specific argument about the specific dating of any particular book. To use Geisler's arguments so that it is implied that he is arguing for an early date of Revelation, especially since Hanegraaff knows that this is not what Geisler holds nor is it what he was arguing in this material, is blatantly to misrepresent and misuse this material. This kind of manipulation smacks of desperation.

His final appeal to the fact that John is commanded to "measure the temple of God and the altar" and to "count the worshipers" as if this indicates that Revelation must have been written early simply does not work. This scene could have been a reference to the future temple, which, according to dispensationalists, will be rebuilt before the return of Christ. In fact, in a dispensationalist and premillennial scheme, that this is a reference to the rebuilt temple is supported by the reference to forty-two months, or three-and-a-half years. The dispensational-premillennial scheme holds that Antichrist will set up the abomination of desolation in the middle of the tribulation period, or at the three-and-a-half year mark. Consequently, according to this view, Jerusalem will be trampled down for forty-two months until Christ returns.

But the real problem is not for the Futurist, but for Hanegraaff. Hanegraaff made a big deal out of the fact that, according to his view, if Revelation was written in 95 AD. it should certainly have made reference to the destruction of the Temple. But, an even more significant argument is, if Revelation was written before 70 AD, and if this is supposed to be a command to measure the Temple before its destruction, why is its destruction not mentioned? Unlike Hanegraaff's argument that confuses a prophecy with a history, this question fits the Preterist's (or Exegetical Eschatologist's) assumption that the book is a prophecy about the destruction of Jerusalem and the Temple. Here John is commanded to measure the Temple and its altar, and yet there is absolutely no mention of the destruction of the city or the Temple. This is an ineluctable problem of Hanegraaff, and yet Hanegraaff does not even bother to acknowledge the problem, much less try to deal with it.

In summary, none of Hanegraaff's arguments are successful. First, it is not "unreasonable" for Revelation not to include a reference to the destruction of Jerusalem. What is unreasonable is to confuse a book of prophecy for a book of history. Secondly, it is not incredible to omit a reference to Christ's prediction since it was already past and, again, Revelation is not a history book. Finally, Geisler's arguments about the NT documents is a general, not a specific reference, and Hanegraaff has misrepresented and misused these arguments to his own ends.

WHAT'S AT STAKE

In this section, Hanegraaff again engages in a guilt-by-association argument. Having portrayed Ehrman and other critical scholars as purveyors of "antihistorical sophistry" and proponents of a late date of Revelation, Hanegraaff attempts to implicate LaHaye on the basis of the accident that he also holds to a late date. This is the same as lumping Hank Hanegraaff in with the Jehovah's Witnesses because neither one believes that the 144,000 in Revelation refer to a future called-out group of Jews. Such a characterization would be untrue and unfair, but this is exactly Hanegraaff's strategy. Just as his guilt-by-association tactics fail to implicate LaHaye, so his LEGACY acronym fails to demonstrate his claims. To claim that because Revelation "is principally a book that describes what is about to take place in the twenty-first-century" that it must thereby "have been largely irrelevant to first-century Christians" is likewise to claim that the prophecies of the coming of the Messiah in Gen. 3:15 are largely irrelevant to Moses and Israel on the plains of Moab, or that the prophecy of the virgin birth in Isaiah were largely irrelevant to Ahaz and Israel. That Revelation is a prophecy of future events no more makes it irrelevant to its initial audience than any Old Testament prophecies about future events were irrelevant to those who were the recipients of those writings. In fact, Hanegraaff's claim is a favorite argument among critical scholars to impugn the integrity of many OT books. That Hanegraaff keeps company with critical scholars on this issue does not thereby make him a proponent of higher criticism. Similarly, just because LaHaye advocates a late date does not make him a theological companion of Bart Ehrman.

There is no argument against Hanegraaff's claim that the book of Revelation was written to seven literal churches of Asia Minor. But the book of Genesis was written to the people of Israel as they were on the plains of Moab about to enter the promised land. However, that did not mean that the promises and prophecies about Messiah could not have been referring to Jesus who would be born some 1,500 years later. So also, it is possible that the book of Revelation was written to the seven churches of Asian Minor about events that would take place some 2,000 years later. At least this is the position of Futurists, and Hanegraaff's argument is as ineffective against their view of Revelation as is the like argument from critical scholars against Genesis.

Once again Hanegraaff demonstrates his unwillingness to grasp the use of the pronoun 'you.' That Rev 3:10 can be addressed to the church of Philadelphia and also be a prophetic reference to the future seems completely to escape his grasp. Isa 7:14 declares, "Therefore the Lord Himself will give you a sign: Behold, a virgin will be with child and bear a son, and she will call His name Immanuel"—a prophecy directed at Ahaz, king of Judah from 735 to 715 BC—a prophecy that used the pronoun 'you.' According to Hanegraaff's reasoning, this could not have been a prophecy of the virgin birth of Jesus since Jesus was not born in the time of Ahaz. Isaiah says that the Lord would show "you," Ahaz, a sign. But if the sign was about Jesus' virgin birth, then why did God use the pronoun "you"? Hanegraaff's reasoning is just as faulty.

Once again Hanegraaff drudges up the same tired "soon" and "near" arguments. What is "a reprehensible abuse of language," to use Hanegraaff's own expression, is for Hanegraaff to ignore the fact that Revelation was not written in English and that the Greek words do not have a one-to-one relationship to the English words that are used to translate them. What is "a reprehensible abuse of language" is to ignore the actual range of meaning that these Greek words have. What is "a reprehensible abuse of language" is to purport to know what these words mean without actually having any facility in the original languages of the Bible. Hanegraaff's historical principle is a good idea. Not only has Hanegraaff failed even to make his position viable in its application, but by his frequent invectives against LaHaye and his constant *ad hominem abusive* arguments, he has managed to make his position distasteful.

6

Typology Principle

The Golden Key

This chapter begins with the declaration, "Anti-Semitism is a horrific evil—especially when justified in the name of religion."[1] Likewise, casting aspersions on fellow Christians by using a guilt-by-association tactic and justifying it in the name of theological debate is almost as horrific an evil. Simply because Futurists believe that the land promises of God to Abraham will be fulfilled in the future does not make them "Christian Zionists" who "provide a rationale for ethnic cleansing."[2] Even to hint such a thing of all Futurists is unfair stereotyping and *ad hominem abusive* in the extreme, and yet the implications of Hanegraaff's introductory paragraphs are impossible to miss. Hanegraaff is poisoning the well, setting the reader up to reject the claims of Futurists before they are even heard. By his characterizations, Hanegraaff has made sure that his reader doesn't like "Christian Zionists," justifiably or not. The only thing left to do is to describe the beliefs of Futurists in such a way that they sound like those we don't like.

Claims by such individuals as John Hagee such as, "the [Jewish] people wanted him [Jesus] to be their Messiah, but he absolutely refused. . . . The Jews were not rejecting Jesus as Messiah, it was Jesus who was refusing to be the Messiah of the Jews,"[3] play no part in the system of dispensationalism or Futurism. In fact, these kinds of claims are much closer to the Preterists (or Exegetical Eschatologists) who claim that God rejected Israel from being His people. The supposed "Zionist" claims are peculiar to this individual, not dispensationalism, and if Hanegraaff's

1. TAC, 163.
2. Ibid., 169.
3. Ibid., 180.

argument is directed at these Christian Zionists, then his claims are not relevant to dispensationalism or Futurism, since Christian Zionism is not a necessary part of these perspectives. Once again Hanegraaff's argument becomes a conflict between his claims and the individual claims of his opponents, and his conclusions have nothing to say about the truth of dispensationalism or Futurism.

TYPOLOGY

Hanegraaff gives the following explanation of what he means by 'Typology': "A *type* (from the Greek word *typos*) is a person, event, or institution in the redemptive history of the Old Testament that prefigures a corresponding but greater reality in the New Testament."[4] This is a good definition. Hanegraaff goes on to try to associate the hermeneutical principle of typology with the use of the Greek word τύπος (sopyt): "A type is thus a copy, a pattern, or a model (e.g., the scars on Christ's hands) that signifies an even greater reality (e.g., the actual nails that pierced Christ's hands)."[5]

However, Corley, Leme, and Lovejoy point out, "As a hermeneutical method it [typology] must be distinguished from *typos* ('model,' or 'pattern') as it is widely used in the Greek world."[6] These scholars of hermeneutics argue that typology is not a "pattern" or "model," but that it is "a historical and theological perspective . . ."[7] That is, Corley et al. hold that typology is a historical and theological approach that functions as a hermeneutical presupposition to the act of interpretation. The point of this is that Hanegraaff presents his view as if this is the only way to think of it. The fact that there are other points of view about the very nature of typology is important with reference to the arguments that Hanegraaff makes. In fact, since Hanegraaff's view is peculiar to him, and since he promised to give the reader the tools to be the judge, Hanegraaff is obligated to explain why his understanding of the nature of typology is

---

4. Ibid., 169.

5. Ibid., 169–70.

6. Bruce Corley, Steve Leme, and Grant Lovejoy, *Biblical Hermeneutics: A Comprehensive Introduction to Interpreting Scripture* (Nashville: Broadman & Holman Publishers, 1996), 53.

7. Ibid.

contrary to the prevailing view among Christian scholars, and he should present evidence that his view should be accepted.

Contrary to Hanegraaff's characterization, typology is not a cut-and-dried hermeneutical methodology. What one interpreter sees as a type, another denies. There are other positions on the nature of typology, and there are other positions on what is a type and what is its antitype. As a polemical text—that Hanegraaff's book is a polemic is undeniable—Hanegraaff ought to defend his position. The debate is not about whether the New Testament authors employ types. That seems undeniable from the examples in Hebrews to which Hanegraaff points. The debate is over whether there are any additional types that go beyond what is specifically discussed by the New Testament authors.

HANEGRAAFF'S CLASSIC CASE IN POINT

Hanegraaff again reveals his lack of facility in the original languages. Arguing against LaHaye's supposed literalism, Hanegraaff declares, "The reality is that the debate does not revolve around whether one reads the Bible literally or metaphorically but whether old covenant shadows find their final consummation in the person and work of Jesus Christ."[8] In support of his point, Hanegraaff discusses a statement of Jesus:

> A classic case in point involves the words of Jesus, "Destroy this temple, and I will raise it again in three days" (John 2:19). The Jews believed Jesus to be speaking of Herod's temple. Thus, with sarcasm dripping from their voices, they respond, "It has taken forty-six years to build this temple, and you are going to raise it in three days?" (v. 20). However, says John, the temple Jesus had spoken of *"was his body"* (v 21). After Jesus had been "raised from the dead, his disciples recalled what he had said." "Then," says John, *"they believed the Scripture and the words that Jesus had spoken."* (v. 22)[9]

The problem with Hanegraaff's argument is that it does not reflect the difficulty of the underlying Greek text. The NASBU text reads, "The Jews then said, 'It took forty-six years to build this temple, and will You raise it up in three days?'" The text is set out in the table below with a word-for-word translation:

8. TAC, 174.
9. Ibid.

Table 7: John 2:20

εἶπαν	οὖν	οἱ	Ἰουδαῖοι	τεσσερά κοντα
said	therefore	the	Jews	forty
καὶ	ἓξ	ἔτεσιν	οἰκοδομήθη	ὁ
and	six	years	has been built	the
ναὸς	οὗτος	καὶ	σὺ	ἐν
sanctuary	this	and	you	in
τρισὶν	ἡμέραις	ἐγερεῖς	αὐτόν;	
three	days	will raise up	it?	

The translation difficulty is identified and discussed by Daniel Wallace.

> Several grammars list this as a constative aorist, to the effect that it should be translated, "This temple was built in forty-six years."
> The usual assumption is that ναὸς refers to the temple precincts. Josephus indicates that the temple precincts were not completed until Albinus' procuratorship (c. 62–64 CE), in which case the precincts were still in the process of being built when the statement in John 2:20 was made. The idea then would be, "This temple has been in the process of being built for the last forty-six years." There are several problems with this, however, including the meaning of ναὸς in John, the use of the dative's temporal referent, and the use of the aorist. The force of the aorist here may have some impact on the date of the crucifixion.
> First, the NT normally makes a distinction between the ἱερόν and the ναὸς: The ἱερόν refers to the temple precincts (including the courts) while the ναὸς refers to the holy place or sanctuary proper. If that distinction obtains in John 2:20, then the aorist verb οἰκοδομήθη [has been built] would refer only to the sanctuary. Notably, the sanctuary was completed in c. 18–17 BCE. Forty-six years later would be 29–30 CE.
> Second, the dative (τεσσεράκοντα καὶ ἓξ ἔτεσιν) most naturally refers to a point in time, rather than an extent of time. This would fit well with a completion date of the sanctuary ("was built [at a point in time] forty-six years ago").
> Third, there is some difficulty with taking the aorist to speak of an action that was still in process ("this temple has been [in the

process of being] built for the past forty-six years"). The imperfect would be more natural, but not at all required.

These strands of evidence suggest that the aorist is more naturally taken as consummative. If so, and if this pericope occurred in the first year of Jesus' ministry (as its location in John 2 suggests), then Jesus was probably crucified three years later, in 33 CE.[10]

In Wallace's discussion, he refers to a "constative aorist." According to Wallace, a constative aorist "describes the action in summary fashion, without focusing on the beginning or end of the action specifically."[11] As a constative aorist, the verb οἰκοδομήθη (ehīemodokio) would be translated much as it is in most modern translations: "It *took* forty-six years *to build* this temple, and will You raise it up in three days?" However, as Wallace points out, the temple precincts were not completed until about 62 AD. Also, the word that John uses is ναός, which refers to the sanctuary, not ἱερόν, which includes the precincts, and the sanctuary had been completed some 46 years earlier. So, the Jews could not have been saying "it took forty-six years to build" a temple that was not actually built yet, nor could they be saying this about the sanctuary that had been completed 46 years ago.

Wallace indicates that the aorist verb οἰκοδομήθη (ehīemodokio) could be understood as a consummative aorist. A consummative aorist "is often used to stress the cessation of an act or state."[12] As a consummative aorist, the text would be translated, "This temple was built forty-six years ago, and You will raise it up in three days?" This fits well with John's use of the word ναός. Of course this raises the question of how the response of the Jews relates to the statement of Jesus:

Jesus: "Destroy this temple, and in three days I will raise it up."

Jews: "This temple was built forty-six years ago, and You will raise it up in three days?"

The response of the Jews hardly seems to relate to what Jesus said. If the Jews are saying that the temple was built forty-six years ago, how is that a response to the fact that Jesus said He would raise it up in three

10. Daniel B. Wallace, *Greek Grammar Beyond the Basics* (Grand Rapids: Zondervan Publishing House, 1996), 560–61.

11. Ibid., 557.

12. Ibid., 559.

days? However, if, as Wallace proposes, the phrase should be, "the temple was completed 46 years ago," this may in fact have some relevance to what Jesus is saying. For many years there had been many fanatical groups calling for the dissolution of the leading religious groups and a destruction and cleansing of the temple. With all of their clamor, the temple still remained after 46 years. The Jews may have been responding to Jesus as simply another fanatic calling for the dismantling of the current religious system.

However, the NET Bible makes reference to a passage in Ezra 5:16 in which the same word is used in the LXX version to refer to the fact that the building was not complete: "Then that Sheshbazzar came *and* laid the foundations of the house of God in Jerusalem; and from then until now it has been under construction [ᾠκοδομήθη, ehīemodoKo] and it is not *yet* completed."[13] In fact, Sir Lancelot Brenton translates the LXX as follows: "Then that Sabanasar came, and laid the foundations of the house of God in Jerusalem: and from that time even until now it has been building, and has not been finished."[14] The expression, "and has not been finished," along with the way the Aramaic text reads, וּמִן־אֱדַיִן וְעַד־כְּעַן מִתְבְּנֵא וְלָא שְׁלִם: (miľ︤s ʾalᵉw ʾenᵉbtim naᶜk daᶜᵉw niyadᵉʾ nimu), lit. "and from then and until now, was being built, and not completed," it seems clear that this aorist passive verb is being used to assert that the building was under construction up to the point at which the text was written. This seems to be a precedent for taking the statement in John 2 as a direct response to Jesus' claim to be able to raise the temple in three days. The point is not to resolve this issue here, but rather to demonstrate that Hanegraaff seems completely oblivious to the underlying difficulties of the Greek text. For him to assert, "Thus, with sarcasm dripping from their voices ..." completely misses the intriguing possibilities at the level of the Greek text. Once again this demonstrates that Hanegraaff so dramatically oversimplifies complex issues that are often present in the underlying original text that his claims lose all significance and credibility.

---

13. τότε Σασαβασαρ ἐκεῖνος ἦλθεν καὶ ἔδωκεν θεμελίους τοῦ οἴκου τοῦ θεοῦ τοῦ ἐν Ιερουσαλημ καὶ ἀπὸ τότε ἕως τοῦ νῦν ᾠκοδομήθη καὶ οὐκ ἐτελέσθη (Ezra 5:16).

14. Sir Lancelot Charles Lee Brenton, *The Septuagint Version of the Old Testament According to the Vatican Text Translated into English* (London: Samuel Bagster and Sons, 1844), Ezra 5:16.2.512.

THE HOLY LAND

Hanegraaff briefly recounts the land promises to Abraham, Isaac, and Jacob. He goes on to argue, "Christian Zionists are convinced that these promises God made to Abraham, Isaac, and Jacob with respect to the land are unconditional and yet unfulfilled. . . Even cream-of-the-crop dispensationalist scholars contend that the Bible presupposes Israel must yet control an area of land roughly thirty times its present size."[15] Of course, Hanegraaff does not believe this to be the case: "This, however, is far from true."[16] By contrast, Hanegraaff asserts, "Abraham was not merely promised a country thirty times its present size. He was promised the cosmos!"[17] Hanegraaff declares, "while Christian Zionists hyperventilate over tiny areas of land such as the Golan or Gaza, God promises them the globe."[18] It somehow escapes Hanegraaff's notice that if God promised Abraham and his seed "the globe," that this certainly includes "Golan or Gaza" and the other lands that were literal land promises to Abraham and his seed. So, if Abraham's seed are literally going to inherit the globe, then the land promises to Abraham and his seed must be literal as well.

Hanegraaff goes on to claim, "In the fore future, God fulfilled his promise when the children of Israel entered the Promised Land."[19] Of course this did in fact not occur, especially if Abraham was promised the globe. The land that Israel inhabited, by Hanegraaff's own admission, was only 1/30th of the land that was promised. Hanegraaff claims that "God fulfilled his promise to true Israel through Christ, who forever sits on the throne of David."[20] But if God's promise as expressed in Rom 4:13—"Abraham and his offspring received the promise that he would be heir of the world . . ."—should be taken literally, then why should the promises to Abraham, Isaac, and Jacob not be taken literally? And, if God will not actually give the actual land to the physical seed of Abraham as He promised, then how can we be sure that God will give the literal world to the spiritual seed of Abraham? Although Hanegraaff makes several claims in support of his position, he never deals with these complex questions.

15. TAC, 177, 178.
16. Ibid., 178.
17. Ibid.
18. Ibid.
19. Ibid.
20. Ibid.

Fulfilled in Joshua

Hanegraaff argues, "First, the land promises were fulfilled in the fore future when Joshua led the physical descendants of Abraham into Palestine."[21] However, this cannot be the case since, by Hanegraaff's own admission, the borders of the land that was promised to Abraham are actually thirty-times the size of the land that Israel actually inhabited. This claim is also peculiar since the writer to the Hebrews indicates that the land promises were not fulfilled: "All these died in faith, without receiving the promises ..." (Heb 11:12). Hanegraaff quotes several passages in an attempt to make them say that the land promises were fulfilled. But, even if we take these verses the way Hanegraaff presents them—which itself is an extremely questionable point—this leaves unresolved the difference between the promise of God to Abraham and the apparently contradictory claims of the verses to which Hanegraaff points. Either Hanegraaff fails to see this problem—which should be the task of "faithful exegesis," that is, to see and resolve exegetical problems in the text—or he simply refuses to deal with it—which should not be the case if he was actually doing "faithful exegesis."

As Hanegraaff points out, Joshua says, "'You know with all your heart and soul that *not one* of all the good promises the LORD your God gave you has failed. Every promise has been fulfilled; *not one has failed*' (Joshua 23:14)."[22] But, in true form, Hanegraaff gives only enough of the story to support his claim. He fails to deal with the opening statement of Judges: "Now it came about after the death of Joshua that the sons of Israel inquired of the Lord, saying, 'Who shall go up first for us against the Canaanites, to fight against them?' (Judg 1:1). Now, if, as Hanegraaff implies, the land that Israel possessed under the leadership of Joshua actually fulfilled the land promises given to Abraham, why are there still Canaanites in the land who must be driven out? And if, as Hanegraaff implies, the land that Israel possessed under the leadership of Joshua actually fulfilled the land promises given to Abraham, why are the boundaries not even close to the boundaries stipulated by God to Abraham? Hanegraaff's treatment implies that there is a contradiction between the testimony of Scripture concerning God's promises to Abraham, Isaac, and Jacob and the testimony of Scripture concerning the fulfillment of God's promises to Israel.

21. Ibid.
22. Ibid.

Again Hanegraaff fails to see the exegetical problem—which should be seen if one is doing "faithful exegesis," that is, to see and resolve exegetical problems in the text—or he simply refuses to deal with it—which should not be the case if he was actually doing "faithful exegesis."

Once again the point is not to resolve this issue but to point out that Hanegraaff simply has not dealt with the text or with the issues. He simply quotes verses and comments on them as if this settles it. In Hanegraaff's own words, "This, however, is far from true."[23] Hanegraaff has no more settled this issue than he has the myriad of other issues he has raised in this polemic. Simply quoting verses and making comments in accordance with his own presuppositions and his prior eschatological framework are not sufficient to resolve these complex issues. In fact, Hanegraaff seems to be totally oblivious to the presence of these issues.

Fulfilled Through Jesus

Next, Hanegraaff wants to argue that the land promises given to Abraham were fulfilled "in the far future through Jesus who provides true Israel with permanent rest from their wanderings in sin."[24] Quoting John Gerstner—notice that when Hanegraaff introduces a quote from a scholar who supports his view, he introduces him as "Dr. John Gerstner," but when he introduces a scholar who holds a position contrary to his view, he introduces him simply as "Norman Geisler"—Hanegraaff argues that under the "Christian Zionist" position, the Jews end up with land, while under his position, the Jews end up with Christ. Of course, this is a mischaracterization of the case. Under Hanegraaff's view, the Jews end up which Christ while God reneges on His land promises. Under the dispensationalist view, they end up with both Christ and the land they were promised.

Hanegraaff claims, "There is no biblical precedent for supposing that God favors Jews over Palestinians or vice versa."[25] Here again Hanegraaff commits another logical fallacy. This time it is the Misuse of Vague Expressions. This fallacy consists of directing someone to an unwarranted conclusion by assigning a precise meaning to a word, phrase, or statement that is in fact imprecise. In this case, the term "favors" is imprecise. In one

23. Ibid.
24. Ibid., 180.
25. Ibid., 181.

sense, God "favors" Christians over non-Christians since Christians go to heaven and non-Christians do not. Of course the term "favors" in this instance actually gives the wrong impression. It is not that God shows favoritism in an illegitimate way or on the basis of characteristics that makes the favoritism a case of immoral preference. God saves those who trust in Him. Those who do not trust in Him, He does not save. Similarly, God said He chose Israel above all the nations of the earth: "The Lord did not set His love on you nor choose you because you were more in number than any of the peoples, for you were the fewest of all peoples, but because the Lord loved you and kept the oath which He swore to your forefathers, the Lord brought you out by a mighty hand and redeemed you from the house of slavery, from the hand of Pharaoh king of Egypt" (Deut 7:7–8). So, in one sense it is not true that there is "no biblical precedent for supposing that God favors Jews over Palestinians."[26] God chose Israel. He did not choose the Palestinians. In another sense, it is not true that God "favors" one group over another, if by the word "favors" one means illegitimate or immoral preference. God does not choose on the basis of illegitimate or immoral preference. However, God does choose some and not others: "just as He chose us in Him before the foundation of the world, that we would be holy and blameless before Him in love" (Eph 1:4). Hanegraaff disguises his claim with this ambiguous expression so as to lead his readers to a conclusion that he wants, but one that is not justified.

Hanegraaff's denial that the land promises to Abraham will be literally fulfilled raises a serious problem for his view. This problem can be illustrated by an instance in the life of Moses. In Exodus 32, while Moses is on the mountain receiving from God the law written on stone tablets, Israel is at the foot of the mountain committing spiritual adultery. Because of this great sin, God tells Moses, "I have seen this people, and behold they are a stiff-necked people. So, now, leave Me, that My anger might burn against them and I might destroy them. But I will make you a great nation" (Ex 32:9–10). After Moses' intercession for the people, the text states, "So Yahweh had compassion regarding the harm that He had said He would do to His people" (Ex 32:14).[27]

John Currid gives a helpful explanation of Moses' intercession for the nation:

---

26. Ibid.

27. (Ex 32:14). וַיִּנָּחֶם יהוה עַל־הָרָעָה אֲשֶׁר דִּבֶּר לַעֲשׂוֹת לְעַמּוֹ׃

167

Moses presents three arguments to God as to why his wrath ought to turn away from the Hebrews. First, he says, the Israelites are 'your people'—that is, they were the ones whom God had chosen and had delivered from the land of Egypt. Secondly, he points out that the Egyptians would surely mock both God and Israel, saying that Yahweh had merely been toying with Israel and that his plan all along had not been to deliver them, but to destroy them. One of the principal purposes of the exodus and, in particular, the series of plagues, was so that the Egyptians might know who Yahweh was, his power, and his redeeming hand (see 7:5; 8:10; 9:14). If God were now to destroy Israel, Egypt would be convinced of nothing! And, thirdly, Moses makes the point that these Israelites embodied the fulfillment of the promises God had made to Abraham, Isaac and Jacob. God should not go back on his word. It is interesting to note that nowhere does Moses attempt to justify the sins of the Hebrews. That is because they are unjustifiable. Moses rather pleads for the mercy of God on the basis of God's character and promises.[28]

The important argument of Moses for our consideration is the second one that Currid identifies in which Moses argues, "Why should the Egyptians speak, saying, 'With evil *intent* He brought them out to kill them in the mountains and to destroy them from the face of the earth'?" (Ex 32:12). Moses is arguing that if God destroys Israel, the Egyptians will claim that either God had planned evil for Israel all along or that God was impotent and unable to fulfill His promises. But this same argument can be lodged against Hanegraaff's claim that God has abandoned the physical land promises that He made to Israel. Had God planned all along to reject physical Israel? Does this imply, at least as far as the nations would think, that God had an evil intent with reference to Israel, or that God was impotent and unable to fulfill His promises? This kind of response to God's rejection of Israel is implied in God's statement in Isa 52:5: "*Again* the Lord declares, 'Those who rule over them howl, and My name is continually blasphemed all day long.'"

With reference to this verse, Oswalt points out, "God's name is held in contempt because it appears to the watching world that Israel's belief in God was false. He had been forced by the superior power of the gods

28. John D. Currid, *Exodus: Chapters 19–40* (Darlington, England: Evangelical Press, 2001), 275–76.

to surrender his people."[29] In Romans, Paul applies this text to the sins of Israel: "You who boast in the Law, through your breaking the Law, do you dishonor God? For 'the name of God is blasphemed among the Gentiles because of you,' just as it is written" (Rom 2:23–24). As John Murray observes, "The thought in the apostle's application of the text is that the vices of the Jews give occasion to the Gentiles to blaspheme the name of God. The reasoning of the Gentiles is to the effect that a people are like their God and if the people can perpetrate such crimes their God must be of the same character and is to be execrated accordingly. The Jews who claimed to be the leaders of the nations for the worship of the true God had become the instruments of provoking the nations to blasphemy."[30]

In the same manner, would not God be subject to blasphemy by the watching nations if He rejected Israel and reneged on the land promises as Hanegraaff claims? Is God not able or simply not willing to establish them in the land and give to them the inheritance as He promised? Is the sin of Israel so great that God cannot or will not forgive them? And if God is either not able or not willing to fulfill His promises to Israel as He said, will He do the same to us who believe? If God alters the parameters of His promises to Israel, can He not also alter the parameters of His promises to us? If God abandoned Israel because of their sins, could He not also abandon us because of our sins?

The fact is, God has not rejected His people. As Paul emphatically declares, "I say then, God has not rejected His people, has He? May it never be! For I too am an Israelite, a descendant of Abraham, of the tribe of Benjamin. God has not rejected His people whom He foreknew" (Rom 11:1, 2). God will restore Israel to a right relationship with Him. Neither their sins nor ours are too great that God cannot overcome and save. God is faithful concerning His promises, and He will complete the work that He began in the nation of Israel, and He will also complete the work that He has begun in us. As God declares, "Is My hand so short that it cannot ransom? Or have I no power to deliver?" (Isa 50:2). All Israel will be saved (Rom 11:26), and because God will fulfill His promises to the nation of Israel, as He has said, we also can trust God to fulfill the promises He has made to us. Hanegraaff's view brings into question the very faithfulness

---

29. John N. Oswalt, *The Book of Isaiah: Chapters 40–66* (Grand Rapids: William B. Eerdmans Publishing Company, 1998), 363.

30. John Murray, *The Epistle to the Romans* (Grand Rapids: Wm. B. Eerdmans Publishing Company, 1968), 85.

of God to keep His promises without changing the parameters of their fulfillment.

CONCLUSION TO THE TYPOLOGY PRINCIPLE

The biggest difference between a live debate and a written critique is that in the live debate, once you have demonstrated that your opponent's view is false, your opponent must stop continuing to make the same assertions over and over. However, when you are critiquing a book, once you have shown that the author's claims are false, you can't stop the writer from writing. All you can do is stop reading the book. Since we have already demonstrated that Hanegraaff's claims are false, and since the remainder of this chapter is a constant rehashing of the same faulty arguments, we will simply move on to the next chapter in hopes that we will find something more substantive there.

7

Scriptural Synergy

The Code Breaker

THE FINAL PRINCIPLE IN Hanegraaff's LIGHTS, the Scriptural Synergy principle, is, as Hanegraaff depicts it, "that the whole of Scripture is greater than the sum of its parts. We cannot comprehend the Bible as a whole without comprehending individual passages, and we cannot comprehend individual passages apart from comprehending the Bible as a whole. Individual passages of Scripture are synergistic rather than deflective with respect to the whole of Scripture. Indeed, scriptural synergy demands that individual Bible passages may never be interpreted in such a way as to conflict with the whole of Scripture."[1] Apparently, what this means on a practical level is that, "no part of Scripture can be interpreted in such a way as to render it in conflict with what is clearly taught elsewhere in Scripture."[2] This sounds like a good principle, until one asks a couple of questions:

1. When you talk about something being "clearly taught elsewhere in Scripture," what makes you think that in those other places something is "clearly taught"?

2. When you say, "clearly taught," whose interpretation of that other part of Scripture are you using?

In other words, the problem here is, those other parts of Scripture that you are supposed to use to balance your interpretation of the one part must also be interpreted. And, if an interpreter has misinterpreted

---

1. TAC, 228–29.
2. R. C. Sproul, *Knowing Scripture* (Downers Grove, IL: InterVarsity Press, 1977), 47.

the one part, how do you know that he has not also misinterpreted the other parts?

Another problem arises for those to whom the Gospel must be preached. Since, according to Hanegraaff, "we cannot comprehend the Bible as a whole without comprehending individual passages, and we cannot comprehend individual passages apart from comprehending the Bible as a whole," this raises a grim specter for the unsaved:

3. Does this mean that for a person to comprehend what the Scripture says in one part about his need to be saved, he must comprehend all of Scripture? If so, who can be saved?

This principle also implies that no one actually "comprehends" either the Bible as a whole or any of its parts. The very fact that there are debates and controversies over what particular passages say demonstrates that no one actually "comprehends" any particular part of Scripture, and, according to Hanegraaff's principle, no one actually "comprehends" the Bible as a whole. Since no one actually comprehends the Bible as a whole, then this means that no one can comprehend any particular part, and these debates are condemned never to be resolved.

Another serious problem with Hanegraaff's principle is that either it implies that Hanegraaff believes he comprehends all of the Bible, or the claim itself is self-referentially incoherent. If it is the case that no one can comprehend the whole Bible without comprehending all of its parts, then either Hanegraaff arrogantly believes that he comprehends all of its parts, or he does not comprehend the Bible as a whole. This is a simple Disjunctive Syllogism:

$P \lor Q$ Either Hanegraaff has comprehended all the parts or he has not comprehended the whole.

$\sim P$ He has not comprehended all the parts.

$\therefore Q$ Therefore, he has not comprehended the whole.

Since it would seem to be the height of arrogance for anyone to think that he has "comprehended" the whole Bible, then it follows that Hanegraaff, unless he is actually claiming that he *has* comprehended the whole, has not comprehended the parts of the Bible. This argument is a simple Modus Ponens:

A ⊃ C If Hanegraaff has not comprehended the whole, then he has not comprehended the parts.

A Hanegraaff has not comprehended the whole (conclusion of the previous argument).

∴ C Therefore, he has not comprehended the parts.

But if Hanegraaff does not comprehend the Bible as a whole or its parts, then why does he think that he can tell Tim LaHaye, or anyone else, what any passage means? So, unless Hanegraaff actually believes that he has comprehended the whole of the Bible, then, according to his own scriptural synergy principle, he has not comprehended the parts of the Bible, and it follows that he has no business telling anyone what any passage of the Bible means. Either that, or Hanegraaff's scriptural synergy principle is simply bogus.

Not only does his scriptural synergy principle imply that unless Hanegraaff, or anyone else, has actually comprehended the whole Bible, he has not comprehended the parts, and he is either exceedingly arrogant or just wrong, but his principle is also self-referentially incoherent. If Hanegraaff has not comprehended the whole Bible or the parts, then he does not know what comprehending the whole Bible looks like. Since he does not know what comprehending the whole Bible looks like, then he has no standard by which to judge whether someone else has comprehended the whole Bible or not. In other words, he has no standard of measure, and it is self-referentially incoherent for Hanegraaff to claim that he has a standard that he does not have and cannot know.

If an interpreter must comprehend the whole before he can comprehend the parts, then he can never comprehend the whole since the comprehension of the whole must be accomplished through the comprehension of the parts, which cannot be done until you comprehend the whole. In other words, you can't do A until you do B, but you can only get to B through A, which means you can never even get started. There is a law on the books in a Southern state that is similar to Hanegraaff's principle. It states, "When two cars come head on, and stop facing each other, neither car can move until the other one goes around it." Both this law and Hanegraaff's scriptural synergy principle, the way he has stated it, are simply absurd.

Apparently, what Hanegraaff is trying to get at is the principle that has been articulated by the Reformers, namely, the analogy of faith. The analogy of faith asserts, as R. C. Sproul puts it, "no part of Scripture can be interpreted in such a way as to render it in conflict with what is clearly taught elsewhere in Scripture."[3] In fact, the section in Sproul's book from which Hanegraaff took the same quote is titled "The Analogy of Faith." But, the analogy of faith never proposed that an individual must comprehend all of Scripture before being able to comprehend a given part. Unless Hanegraaff is equivocating on the word 'comprehend,' his principle is simply a false principle. It never was the analogy of faith.

Besides the obvious incoherence of Hanegraaff's principle, there is no guarantee that the application of this principle will yield a correct understanding of Scripture. The problem is, since each part of Scripture must be interpreted by an interpreter, then the whole of Scripture is interpreted by the interpreter. So, just because an interpreter relates one part to another, or one part to the whole, does not guarantee the accuracy of his conclusions since he may just as easily have misunderstood (miscomprehended?) the whole as well as the part. So, when Hanegraaff claims, "the principle of scriptural synergy . . . should have prohibited LaHaye from supposing that Christ's 'coming on clouds' metaphor was directed toward a twenty-first-century audience,"[4] Hanegraaff is illegitimately assuming that his understanding of the whole is the correct standard by which to judge how LaHaye has comprehended this part. But, if Hanegraaff is wrong about his understanding of the whole, then his scriptural synergy principle falls flat on its face. And, nowhere in this entire book has Hanegraaff demonstrated that he has either comprehended the whole of the Bible or that he has comprehended it correctly. It follows that his criticism of LaHaye based on his scriptural synergy principle, again, falls flat on its face.

In fact, it would be just as easy, and just as legitimate, for LaHaye to claim that, using Hanegraaff's scriptural synergy principle, that it should have prohibited Hanegraaff from supposing that Christ's 'coming on clouds' metaphor, if it even is a metaphor, was directed toward a first-century audience without looking forward to a far future fulfillment. If it could be shown that LaHaye's understanding of the whole of the Bible,

3. Ibid., 46.
4. TAC, 229–30.

according to Hanegraaff's principle, is correct, then Hanegraaff must concede that LaHaye is right about this part and he, Hanegraaff, is wrong. But, we have already shown that Hanegraaff's principle, the way he has defined it, is self-referentially incoherent. So, neither LaHaye nor anyone else needs to appeal to a comprehension of the whole of the Bible to show that Hanegraaff is simply wrong on the parts. All anyone else needs to do is to show that Hanegraaff's interpretation is wrong. But, Hanegraaff, by the establishing of his own principles, must first comprehend the whole Bible in order to show that LaHaye's understanding of a given passage is wrong. But, Hanegraaff has neither done this, nor has he demonstrated anywhere that he has done this. By his own principle, Hanegraaff's criticism of LaHaye, or anyone else, is invalid.

SUPREME RULE

In this section, Hanegraaff argues that his scriptural synergy principle is the "the primary rule of hermeneutics."[5] This expression, "the primary rule of hermeneutics," is a quote from Sproul. However, nowhere in Sproul's account of the analogy of faith does he explain this principle in terms of comprehending the whole and comprehending the parts. Hanegraaff flatters his principle by implying that it is the same as the analogy of faith: "Indeed, scriptural synergy, or what the Reformers referred to as the 'analogy of faith,' . . ."[6] But, as we have shown, Hanegraaff's scriptural synergy principle and the analogy of faith are not the same. Although both principles have to do with not interpreting any part of Scripture so that it contradicts what is clearly taught elsewhere, Hanegraaff's principle goes far beyond what the Reformers meant by the analogy of faith. Consequently, when it comes to evaluating Hanegraaff's critique of his nemeses, the reader must keep in mind that Hanegraaff's scriptural synergy principle is an impossible principle either to sustain or to apply, and Hanegraaff is not employing the Reformed principle of analogy of faith.

As a point meant to support his principle of synergism, Hanegraaff again brings up the Jn. 2:19 passage. He says, "The consequences of reading the Bible literalistically rather than synergistically are disastrous. When Jesus said, 'Destroy this temple, and I will raise it again in three days,' (John 2:19), the Jews interpreted his words in a woodenly literal

5. Ibid., 230.
6. Ibid.

fashion."[7] But we have already shown that Hanegraaff's characterization of this passage is wrong. The difference between the Jews' understanding and John's comment that Jesus was speaking of His body is not a case of literal verses spiritual meaning. Rather, it is a difference of the referents of the term 'temple.' The Jews understood Jesus to be literally referring to the actual Temple, whereas Jesus was literally referring to His actual body. This is not a question of a literalistic or a spiritualizing interpretation of prophecy. This is a matter of the distinction between sense and reference. Jesus' body was an actual, physical temple in which the fullness of the Godhead dwelt. This is not spiritualizing. It is simply a matter that the Jews misunderstood to which temple Jesus was literally referring. Besides that, literal interpretation and synergistic interpretation have not been shown by Hanegraaff necessarily to be in conflict. It is entirely reasonable that, at least theoretically, an interpreter could employ both a literal and a synergistic methodology

Additionally, Hanegraaff actually misquotes Jesus' words. Hanegraaff's quote reads, "Destroy this temple, and I will raise it again in three days."[8] By contrast, Jesus actually says, "Destroy this temple, and in three days I will raise it."

Table 8: John 2:19

λύσατε	τὸν	ναὸν	τοῦτον	καὶ
Destroy	the	temple	this	and
ἐν	τρισὶν	ἡμέραις	ἐγερῶ	αὐτόν.
in	three	days	I will raise	it.

Notice that there is no word "again" in the text. Jesus did not say He would "raise it again" as Hanegraaff renders it. At first, this may seem a trivial difference, but when you think about it, it can be dangerously misleading. There was no time in the past in which Jesus' body was destroyed so that He has to raise it up "again." So, there was no reason for Jesus to say "again." However, if Jesus had used the word 'again,' then the Jews' understanding of what Jesus was saying would have been perfectly reasonable. The Temple of Jerusalem had been destroyed in the past and was

7. Ibid., 231.

8. Ibid.

being rebuilt. If Jesus had said "I will raise it up again," it would have been entirely reasonable for the Jews to think that He was talking about the Temple. But, Jesus did not use the word "again." Now the point here is not to convince anyone of this reasoning but to show how Hanegraaff's treatment of the text lacks rigor and accuracy. It also demonstrates, once again, a lack of facility with the original languages. If Hanegraaff's treatment of the text lacks rigor and accuracy, what does that say about his interpretations of the text. Maybe it says nothing, but the reader deserves more than simply Hanegraaff's word that this is what the text says or means. The reader deserves a demonstration and "faithful exegesis" that what Hanegraaff is claiming is actually the case. As yet he has failed to present any demonstration or "faithful exegesis" that anything he has claimed in this entire book should be taken as accurate, correct, or even likely.

Neglecting the Scriptural Synergy Principle

Hanegraaff argues, "Chapter 3—Illumination Principle of e^2 contains an equally graphic example of what occurs when the principle of scriptural synergy is neglected in the course of biblical interpretation. For example, when Jesus in his Olivet Discourse prophesied a tribulation 'unequaled from the beginning of the world until now—and never to be equaled again' (Matthew 24:21), he was clearly using prophetic hyperbole. If this literary reality is not comprehended, Scripture devolves into hopeless contradiction."[9] But why should anyone think this is "clearly" prophetic hyperbole? Hanegraaff does not justify this classification nor does he show how this "devolves" into "hopeless contradiction." In fact, the only reason to take this as prophetic hyperbole is if you have already accepted Hanegraaff's eschatology. And Hanegraaff doesn't bother to give the reader any "faithful exegesis" to convince the reader that his understanding is correct or even likely. If an interpreter has a different eschatological perspective, it would be just as "clearly" literal to him, and Hanegraaff has not offered any "faithful exegesis," not even anywhere in his book, that his eschatological perspective should be preferred over anyone else's. In fact, Hanegraaff promised in the beginning of his book that his purpose "is not to entice you to embrace a particular model of eschatology."[10] But, by

9. Ibid., 231–32.
10. Ibid., 3.

making statements such as "he was clearly using prophetic hyperbole" is calculated to do just that.

In support of his assertion, Hanegraaff quotes verses from Daniel and Ezekiel. But simply quoting verses is not "faithful exegesis." It may be the case that Hanegraaff has misunderstood these verses also. In fact, the quote from Daniel is not necessarily prophetic hyperbole either. When Daniel said, "for under the whole heaven there has not been done like what was done to Jerusalem," he was not talking merely about the destruction of the city.

וַיָּקֶם אֶת־דְּבָרָיו אֲשֶׁר־דִּבֶּר עָלֵינוּ וְעַל
שֹׁפְטֵינוּ אֲשֶׁר שְׁפָטוּנוּ לְהָבִיא עָלֵינוּ רָעָה
גְדֹלָה אֲשֶׁר לֹא־נֶעֶשְׂתָה תַּחַת כָּל־הַשָּׁמַיִם
כַּאֲשֶׁר נֶעֶשְׂתָה בִּירוּשָׁלָם:

12

(Dan 9:12)

Daniel was also talking about the fact that the covenant God of Israel had abandoned His people to this fate. It was the whole situation to which Daniel was referring, not just to the destruction of the city. Consequently, Daniel's statement is not a "prophetic hyperbole," but was literally true. Never in the history of the people of God has the covenant God ever abandoned His people to such a fate.

Once again this may not convince anyone, but it shows that Hanegraaff's interpretation is not the only one and that Hanegraaff needs to do more than just cite verses. He needs seriously to interact with the exegesis of other interpreters, not just vilify and attach them with *ad hominem abusive* fallacies. In fact, this also shows both the weakness and the strength of his "scriptural synergy" principle. The weakness is that when Hanegraaff appeals to other verses in the application of his scriptural synergy principle, his interpretation of the other verses are just as subject to his interpretation as the verse he is trying to support. So, the scriptural synergy principle is only as good as the interpretations of the verses to which Hanegraaff appeals. Its strength is that it can be used to show that a given interpretation needs more exegetical support. In other words, the strength of Hanegraaff's scriptural synergy principle is that, when he appeals to other verses, the very application of his principle highlights the weakness of his own presentation. Hanegraaff needs to present some "faithful exegesis." His scriptural synergy principle demonstrates that "clearly."

Hanegraaff's appeal to Isaiah does not work either. He argues, "Failure to properly apply the principle of scriptural synergy in the same discourse causes dispensationalists to miss the fact that Christ uses the words sun, moon, and stars in precisely the same way as did the Old Testament prophets. As documented under the grammatical principle in chapter 4, when Jesus declared 'the sun will be darkened, and the moon will not give its light; the stars will fall from the sky, and the heavenly bodies will he shaken' (Matthew 24:29; cf. Mark 13:24–25; Luke 21:25), he was quoting the prophet Isaiah."[11] Hanegraaff then quotes Isa 13:9–10. The focal point of his quote is the last two lines: "*The stars* of heaven and their constellations will not show their light. The rising *sun will be darkened and the moon will not give its light*."[12] Once again Hanegraaff has misquoted the text. The NASBU translation reads, "For the stars of heaven and their constellations will not flash forth their light; The sun will be dark when it rises and the moon will not shed its light" (Isa 13:10). The Hebrew text is set out in Table 9 below.

Table 9: Isaiah 13:10

←				
לֹא	וּכְסִילֵיהֶם	הַשָּׁמַיִם	כּוֹכְבֵי	כִּי־
not	and their constellations	the heavens	stars of	For
בְּצֵאתוֹ	הַשֶּׁמֶשׁ	חָשַׁךְ	אוֹרָם	יָהֵלּוּ
in its going forth	the sun	will be dark	their light	they will flash forth
אוֹרוֹ:	יַגִּיהַ	לֹא־	וְיָרֵחַ	
its light.	will shine	not	and moon	

Notice that the Hebrew text and the NASBU translation refer to the sun rising or going forth. The text says that when the sun goes forth, or rises, it will be dark. Hanegraaff conveniently leaves out this detail, and

11. Ibid., 232.
12. Ibid.

he asserts, "Surely no one supposes that the stars went into supernova when Isaiah pronounced judgment on Babylon in 539 BC."[13] Again, like so many times before, Hanegraaff engages in argument from innuendo and inflammatory rhetoric, attempting to persuade his reader to accept his conclusion by using words to mislead, or imply, or suggest a conclusion but not directly asserting the conclusion. By omitting the detail of the sun rising and by using the misleading description of the stars going supernova, Hanegraaff has diverted the attention of the reader from the real issue, and he has attempted to persuade the reader to accept his position without providing any real exegesis. But, whoever said that the stars will go supernova? Even if LaHaye or someone else claimed this, it is not a necessary part of a dispensationalist or premillennial perspective. For Hanegraaff to use this kind of language is disingenuous and is designed by Hanegraaff to make his opponents look bad in order to avoid having to deal with the real issue.

It is not necessary to suppose that the stars will supernova for them not to show their light. There are a myriad of possibilities that could cause this to happen, not to mention the supernatural power of God. Besides, the detail that Hanegraaff omitted indicates that the sun will not "supernova" or cease to exist. The text indicates that the sun will actually continue in its normal course, but that it will be dark. Once again there are other possible explanations. The point, however, is not to delineate the possible answers but, once again, to show Hanegraaff's tactics. The sun, moon, and stars could have actually and literally not given their light, and this could have happened by the miraculous power of God. This would be similar to God causing the sun to "stand still in the sky" in order to give Joshua and Israel time to complete the battle with the Amorites (Josh 10:12ff). It is not necessary to take this description as a metaphor, and to take it literally is not to engage in literalistic interpretation. So also, Jesus could be referring to actual, literal, physical events in Matt 24:29 that are accomplished by the power of God.

Also, just because there is a similarity of language between Isaiah and Matthew does not mean that Matthew is "quoting the prophet Isaiah" as Hanegraaff assumes. First of all, the text does not say anything about quoting the prophet Isaiah. There is a pattern in Matthew's Gospel that when he quotes from the OT he usually indicates this by some formula:

13. Ibid., 233.

"to fulfill what was spoken through Isaiah the prophet" (Matt 4:14) is an example of this pattern. There is no such indication in this passage. This is not a decisive argument, but it means, if someone were actually doing "faithful exegesis," he would need to explain why this could be a quote from Isaiah and yet without Matthew's formula. Of course, Hanegraaff is not doing "faithful exegesis." A similarity of wording would not be sufficient to prove Hanegraaff's claim.

In fact, when one looks at the two passages side by side (or over and under as in Table 10), it becomes clear that there are some significant differences that may indicate that Jesus may not be quoting from Isaiah at all.

Table 10: Comparison of Matthew and Isaiah

Matthew 24:29	But immediately after the tribulation of those days the sun will be darkened, and the moon will not give its light, and the stars will fall from the sky, and the powers of the heavens will be shaken.
Isaiah 13:9–10	Behold, the day of the Lord is coming, cruel, with fury and burning anger, to make the land a desolation; And He will exterminate its sinners from it. For the stars of heaven and their constellations will not flash forth their light; The sun will be dark when it rises and the moon will not shed its light.

First of all, Jesus doesn't say anything about the day of the Lord nor about the exterminating of sinners. Isaiah doesn't say anything about the stars falling from the sky or the powers of the heavens being shaken. Once again this may not convince anyone, but it shows, once again, that Hanegraaff has to do more than simply make claims. At some point he is going to have to present some actual evidence to support his claims.

Hanegraaff simply assumes that the Isaiah passage is talking about the judgment upon Babylon in 539 BC, but he has not demonstrated that this is the case. In fact, since Isaiah makes reference to the day of the Lord, this may not be talking about 539 BC at all. Isaiah may be referring to the end of the age, in which case Jesus and Isaiah may be referring to the same event. Another possibility is that Isaiah is using the judgment on Babylon as a type of the coming day of the Lord when the destruction will be even more far reaching. Wasn't it Hanegraaff who argued that "Peter's prophecy [2 Pet 3:10–13] was fulfilled in the destruction of Jerusalem, the events of AD 70 and the cosmic language Peter used to describe them point forward to an even greater day of judgment when the problem of sin and Satan will be fully and finally resolved!"[14] Why couldn't that be what's going on in Isaiah? Why couldn't the "cosmic language" Isaiah used of Babylon "point forward to an even greater day of judgment," just like Hanegraaff claims about the words of Peter? Of course, it's OK for Hanegraaff to do it when it supports his view, but it's not OK for others to do it when it contradicts Hanegraaff's view. And yet again, Hanegraaff has not presented any "faithful exegesis" to support his assertions or to disqualify such objections. He just makes claims without evidence. If this is an example of Exegetical Eschatology, or scriptural synergy then it can be used by anyone to say anything without having to support their claims, and it turns out not to be a help to train students of the Bible actually to study it and be the judge.

Also, Hanegraaff assumes that just because passages in Revelation use Old Testament terminology and images that these passages must therefore necessarily be talking about the same person or entity to which these Old Testament passages refer. But this does not follow. Just because Revelation uses terms like "Babylon" and "harlot" does not mean that these are necessarily references to Old Testament entities. Hanegraaff declares, "Anyone who has read the Bible even once must surely have flashbacks to the graphic images of apostate Israel when they first encounter the great prostitute of Revelation."[15] But "flashbacks" are hardly the basis for "faithful exegesis." People who read the Gospel of John must certainly have "flashbacks" to the graphic images of manna appearing on the ground, but I doubt that Jesus is referring to the actual manna of the Old Testament when He referred these images to Himself. To claim that the terms and images of Revelation are taken from the Old Testament does not demonstrate that Old Testament persons or entities are what these images in Revelation are meant to convey. Again, Hanegraaff has missed the point by not being familiar with the distinction between sense and reference.

Substance or Shadow

Hanegraaff declares, "Perhaps the most egregious error dispensationalists commit by failing to appropriately consider the import of scriptural syn-

14. Ibid., 135.
15. Ibid., 235.

ergy is to revert to Old Testament types that have been gloriously fulfilled in Jesus Christ."[16] This "egregious error," according to Hanegraaff, is the claim that "during the Millennium the Messiah will preside over animal sacrifices in yet another temple."[17] The aversion that Hanegraaff has to this position is that LaHaye apparently teaches "that these temple sacrifices are not merely memorial but are absolutely necessary for the atonement of sins, such as ceremonial uncleanness."[18] According to Hanegraaff, this is inconsistent with what the New Testament teaches: "The writer to the Hebrews explicitly counters all such contentions by writing that in Christ, the old covenant order, including temple sacrifices, are 'obsolete' and would 'soon disappear' (Hebrews 8:13)."[19]

But, once again Hanegraaff has actually misrepresented what the text says. Heb 8:13 says, "When He said, 'A new,' He has made the first obsolete. But whatever is becoming obsolete and growing old is ready to disappear."[20] The problem with Hanegraaff's complaint is that he confuses the sacrificial system with the covenant. Certainly the sacrificial system was part of the covenant, but it was a part, not the whole. In fact, what we know as the ten commandments—although they are never referred to as the ten "commandments"; rather, they are referred to as the ten "words" (עֲשֶׂרֶת הַדְּבָרִים, mîṯabdah teresᵃᶜ)—are just as much a part of the Old Covenant, and yet they were all reaffirmed in the New Testament.[21]

When the writer to the Hebrews is talking about the Old Covenant becoming obsolete, he is not necessarily referring to any particular part of that covenant, but that the Old Covenant has become obsolete as a way of maintaining a right relationship with God. Although salvation has

---

16. Ibid.

17. Ibid.

18. Ibid.

19. Ibid.

20. ἐν τῷ λέγειν καινὴν πεπαλαίωκεν τὴν πρώτην· τὸ δὲ παλαιούμενον καὶ γηράσκον ἐγγὺς ἀφανισμοῦ (Heb 8:13).

21. Many exegetes claim that only nine of the ten commandments have been reinstituted in the NT, omitting Sabbath keeping. However, this is actually a misunderstanding of the significance of Sabbath keeping. This is not the place to present a full explanation of this issue, but, briefly, since the principle of Sabbath keeping was ceasing from one's own works and resting in the completed work of God, Sabbath keeping was actually a picture of salvation by grace through faith—ceasing from our works and resting in the work that God has done for us. So, Sabbath keeping, in the sense of ceasing from our works, is also continued in the NT.

always been by grace through faith, even in the OT, the Old Covenant was instituted as a way for redeemed Israel to maintain a right relationship with God in the promised land. However, they failed in this endeavor, which was designed to demonstrate that a person's relationship with God cannot be based on a law written in stone and imposed from the outside. The law, as Paul put it, "has become our tutor to Christ, so that we may be justified by faith" (Gal 3:24).[22] But, even though the Law has become our tutor to lead us to Christ, the law has not been abolished, but fulfilled. Nevertheless, the Law still instructs us about the holiness of God, and as Christians we endeavor to live in a way that conforms to the righteousness of God, yet we know that our conformity, or lack thereof, is not the basis of our relationship with God.

So, the Old Covenant has become obsolete, but that does not necessarily mean that everything that was a part of the Old Covenant has also "passed away," just like the Law, which was a part of the Old Covenant has not "passed away." In fact, in Rom 3:31 Paul says, "Do we then nullify the Law through faith? May it never be! On the contrary, we establish the Law."[23] If the Law has not passed away even though it was a part of the Old Covenant, why must we think that the sacrificial system has passed away even though it was a part of the Old Covenant. Just as the Law serves a different function now that the New Covenant is in force, so the sacrificial system could serve a different function during the Millennial kingdom. Hanegraaff cannot simply quote verses and makes assertions. What he needs to do is to show that the sacrificial system, which was a part of the Old Covenant, can never be reinstituted for any reason whatsoever. He may be right, but he must show this by "faithful exegesis," not by bare declaration and verse citation. Even the Jehovah's Witnesses use this tactic, and it doesn't work for them either, as Hanegraaff has shown in an abundance of instances.

Besides, LaHaye's teaching, if in fact this is what LaHaye teaches, and we have no reason to doubt Hanegraaff's faithfulness in reporting this, that the temple sacrifices are necessary for the atonement of sins is not a necessary part of dispensationalist teaching. Dwight Pentecost declares, the sacrifices "will not be expiatory for it is nowhere stated that they are

22. ὥστε ὁ νόος παιδαγωγὸς ἡμῶν γέγονεν εἰς Χριστόν, ἵνα ἐκ πίστεως δικαιωθῶμεν (Gal 3:24).

23. νόμον οὖν καταργοῦμεν διὰ τῆς πίστεως; μὴ γένοιτο· ἀλλὰ νόμον ἰστά νομεν (Rom 3:31).

offered with a view to salvation from sin," and, "the sacrifices *will be memorial* in character."[24] Quoting Nathaniel West, Walvoord's treatment says the same thing: "How [*sic*] interpret these Chapters [in Ezekiel]? Do they belong to the 1,000 years of John? Are these also a Millennial picture? We answer, Yes. They cannot be literalized into the times of the Restoration under Zerubbabel, nor spiritualized into the times of the New Testament Church, nor celestialized into the heavenly state, nor allegorized into the final New Heaven and Earth, nor idealized into an oriental phantasmagorial abstraction. Whatever difficulties attend the interpretation which regards them simply as the expansion of Chapter xxxviith, a picture of Israel's dwelling safely in their own land glorified, with the temple shining on exalted Zion, as the prophets have predicted it, more and great difficulties attend any other exposition."[25]

Now, you may not agree with these explanations, but they show that LaHaye's interpretation is not a necessary part of dispensationalism. Hanegraaff's charge of an "egregious error" is not a charge against dispensationalism, but against LaHaye only. And, since there are proponents of dispensationalism who have offered exegetical reasons for their position—although we have not presented this exegesis here—Hanegraaff needs to do more than simply make charges and cite verses. If this is an "egregious error," then Hanegraaff needs to show his reader why he thinks this is such. Simply pointing to the New Testament and making claims about types and shadows is insufficient. Just because Hanegraaff thinks that the first and second temples are types and shadows does not demonstrate that they are.

Hanegraaff claims, "Jesus made his topological relationship to the temple explicit when he pronounced, 'One greater than the temple is here' (Matthew 12:6)."[26] Let us grant that this is a topological relationship, it still does not demonstrate why a Millennial temple cannot be a literal thing in the Millennial kingdom. But Hanegraaff goes on to declare, "All old covenant types and shadows including the Holy Land, the Holy City,

---

24. J. Dwight Pentecost, *Things to Come* (Grand Rapids: Zondervan Publishing House, 1958), 524, 525.

25. Nathaniel West, *The Thousand Years in Both Testaments* (New York: Fleming H. Revell, 1880), 424–26; quoted in John F. Walvoord, *The Millennial Kingdom* (Grand Rapids: Zondervan Publishing House, 1959), 313.

26. TAC, 236.

and the holy temple have been fulfilled in the holy Christ."[27] But, this bare, unsupported assertion does not prove that, "There is no need or room for a rebuilt temple with reinstituted temple sacrifices."[28] Why not? Then how does Hanegraaff deal with the claims in Ezekiel? He completely avoids the exegetical issues and makes accusations and declarations, and draws conclusions without providing any "faithful exegesis" to support any of it.

Hanegraaff claims, "Failure to interpret Scripture in light of Scripture creates a genuine conundrum for Christian Zionists."[29] However, failure to do any "faithful exegesis" to support his claim that LaHaye, or anyone else, has actually failed "to interpret Scripture in light of Scripture" creates an empty accusation. If anyone can establish a point by simply saying it and pointing to other verses, then Hanegraaff has no basis upon which to conduct his campaign against cults and aberrant religious movements—a very successful and much needed campaign I might add. The Christian Church needs Hanegraaff on the front lines combating the cults and false religions. But he needs to present the same kind of diligent research and argumentation that he uses against cults in his opposition to contrary eschatological views. A tirade against Tim LaHaye does not measure up to the "faithful exegesis" that Hanegraaff marshals against cults and false religions.

Sacrificing Traditions

Evangelicals certainly need to "recommit themselves to *faithful exegesis*— to mining what the Spirit has breathed into the Scriptures as opposed to superimposing our models onto the Scriptures."[30] Unfortunately for his readers, Hanegraaff has not demonstrated this in his invectives against Tim LaHaye. He promised at the beginning of this book that he would not attempt to "entice you to embrace a particular model of eschatology."[31] Rather, he promised to arm his readers "with the principles embodied in Exegetical Eschatology, you will be the judge."[32] However, throughout this excoriation of LaHaye, Hanegraaff has not presented any "faithful

27. Ibid.
28. Ibid.
29. Ibid.
30. Ibid. (emphasis in original).
31. Ibid., 3.
32. Ibid., 4.

exegesis," nor has he armed his readers with any exegetical tools. Rather, he has attempted, over and over by *ad hominem abusive*, argument from innuendo, selective reporting, poisoning the well, guilt by association, inflammatory rhetoric, and a host of other fallacies and tactics to persuade and entice his readers to accept his eschatological model—exactly what he said he would not do.

Hanegraaff concludes his book, "When eschatological models are imposed on the text, the tapestry is undone and the loose ends dangle ignominiously."[33] Similarly, when an eschatological model is advocated without "faithful exegesis," or when an eschatological model is promoted under the pretense of arming the reader with tools so that he might "be the judge" when all the while, though the reader was promised that this would not be done, the reader is shamelessly enticed to imbibe this particular eschatological, this is ignominious.

33. Ibid., 237.

8

Conclusion

IN LITERALLY A MULTITUDE of instances I have pointed out that Hanegraaff has failed to do any faithful exegesis, or any exegesis at all. It will probably be helpful to explain what I mean by exegesis so that you can see why I keep saying Hanegraaff is not doing it. There are many good books out on doing exegesis, but two very helpful and useful texts are, Gordon D. Fee, *New Testament Exegesis: A Handbook for Students and Pastors*,[1] and Douglas Stuart, *Old Testament Exegesis: A Primer for Students and Pastors*.[2] Both of these books give helpful and useful outlines of the exegetical process.

Of course it would not be possible to reproduce either one of these texts here, but I can show the basic outline of exegesis from one of the texts. Since most of what Hanegraaff has written focuses on the New Testament, I will show you the outline of exegesis from Fee's text:

Step 1. Survey the historical context in general.

Step 2. Confirm the limits of the passage.

Step 3. Establish the text [this would involve textual criticism].

Step 4. Make a provisional translation.

Step 5. Analyze sentence structures and syntactical relationships.

Step 6. Analyze the grammar.

Step 7. Analyze significant words.

Step 8. Research the historical-cultural background.

1. Gordon D. Fee, *New Testament Exegesis* (Philadelphia: The Westminster Press, 1983).

2. Douglas Stuart, *Old Testament Exegesis* (Philadelphia: The Westminster Press, 1984).

Step 9.   Determine the formal character of the [literature according to its genre].

Step 10.   Examine the historical context in particular.

Step 11.   Determine the literary context.

Step 12.   Consider the broader Biblical and theological contexts.

Step 13.   Accumulate a bibliography of secondary sources and read widely.

Step 14.   Provide a finished translation.[3]

This is only a bare outline of the exegetical process as Fee has constructed it. Aspects like interacting with the arguments of other exegetes and theologians, a point that is not specifically stated in the above outline, are part of steps 12 and 13. Although this is a bare outline, it is enough to show that Hanegraaff has not even come close to engaging in exegesis. His LIGHTS acronym is a fair approximation of the exegetical process, but although Hanegraaff dedicates a chapter to each point, he fails to show how the individual principles ought to the used. He talks about each principle and even gives some definitions. But then he simply declares his interpretations of various passages without showing the reader how he applied his principle in that instance.

At the beginning of his book Hanegraaff said he was going to give the reader the tools to be the judge concerning the issues of eschatology with which the book is concerned. Yet from the outset he engages in rhetoric, several different kinds of logical fallacies, inflammatory speech, innuendo, guilt-by-association, and instead of giving his readers the tools so that they can be the judges for themselves, he prejudices the reader by these and other tactics, and even though he said he was not going to entice the reader to a particular point of view, his tactics are deliberately calculated to do just that. And yet he completely fails to demonstrate his claims, and he presents little or no supporting evidence for his assertions. His lack of facility in the original languages of the Bible lead him to incorrect conclusions, and his fanciful flights of imagination serve to bring upon him his own criticisms.

Hank Hanegraaff is probably one of the best defenders of orthodox Christianity against the ever increasing threat of cults and isms. His

---

3. Fee, *New Testament Exegesis*, 15–17.

books, articles, and his radio program and journal provide Christians with invaluable help, instruction, and ammunition in the struggle against the ever growing multitude of aberrant religious claims. However, this book falls significantly short of the kind of scholarship that we all know he is capable of. The tone of the book sounds more like a rant than an instruction manual. And his persistent vilification of those who disagree with him, in particular Tim LaHaye, serves only to make the book and Hanegraaff's position distasteful and reinforce the view of unbelievers that Christians can't get along any better than natural men. This book is not even a good example of the theological position Hanegraaff is advocating, and it serves to put his own eschatological position in an undeserved bad light.

Bibliography

Aland, Barbara, et. al., ed. *The Greek New Testament, 4th ed.* Stuttgart: Deutsche Biblegesellschaft, 1993.

Aquinas, St. Thomas. *Summa Contra Gentiles.* Translated by Anton C. Pegis. Notre Dame: University of Notre Dame Press, 1975.

Aquinatis, S. Thomæ. *Summa Contra Gentiles.* Taurini, Italia: Marietta, 1850.

Bauer, Walter, Frederick William Danker, W. F. Arndt, and F. W. Gingrich. *A Greek-English Lexicon of the New Testament and Other Early Christian Literature*, 3d ed. Chicago: The University of Chicago Press, 2000.

Ben-Sasson, H. H., ed. *A History of the Jewish People.* Cambridge: Harvard University Press, 1976.

Brenton, Sir Lancelot Charles Lee. *The Septuagint Version of the Old Testament According to the Vatican Text Translated into English.* London: Samuel Bagster and Sons, 1844.

Brümmer, Vincent. *Theology and Philosophical Inquiry: An Introduction.* Philadelphia: The Westminster Press, 1982.

Buckley, Michael J. *At the Origins of Modern Atheism.* New Haven: Yale University Press, 1987.

Buswell, J. Oliver. *A Systematic Theology of the Christian Religion.* Zondervan Publishing House, 1962.

Caird, G. B. *The Language and Imagery of the Bible.* London: Gerald Duckworth & Company, 1980. Reprint, Grand Rapids: William B. Eerdmans Publishing Company, 1997.

Corley, Bruce, Steve Leme, and Grant Lovejoy. *Biblical Hermeneutics: A Comprehensive Introduction to Interpreting Scripture.* Nashville: Broadman & Holman Publishers, 1996.

Currid, John D. *Exodus 19–40.* Vol. 2, *A Study Commentary on Exodus.* Darlington, England: Evangelical Press, 2001.

Darby, J. N. *The Collected Writings of J. N. Darby.* Edited by William Kelly. London: G. Morrish, 1867–1900.

Davis, John J. *Biblical Numerology: A Basic Study of the Use of Numbers in the Bible.* Grand Rapids: Baker Book House, 1968.

DeMar, Gary. "Norman Geisler, 'You,' & 'Zechariah the Son of Berechiah,'" http://www .preteristarchive.com/PartialPreterism/demar-gary_07_01.html.

Dungan, David Laird. *A History of the Synoptic Problem: The Canon, the Text, the Composition, and the Interpretation of the Gospels.* New York: Doubleday, 1999.

Elliger, K., and W. Rudolph, ed. *Biblio Hebraica Stuttgartensia.* Stuttgart: Deutsche Bibelstiftung, 1977.

Gentry, Kenneth L., Jr. *The Beast of Revelation.* Tyler, Texas: Institute for Christian Economics, 1994.

———. *Before Jerusalem Fell: Dating the Book of Revelation.* Atlanta: American Visions, 1998.

Glare, P. G. W., ed. *Oxford Latin Dictionary.* Oxford: At The Clarendon Press, 2005.

González, Justo L. *The Early Church to the Dawn of the Reformation.* Vol. 1, *The Story of Christianity.* San Francisco: Harper & Row, Publishers, 1984.

Goodman, Martin. *Rome and Jerusalem: The Clash of Ancient Civilizations.* New York: Alfred A. Knopf, 2007.

Hale, Bob, and Crispin Wright. *A Companion to the Philosophy of Language,* ed. London: Blackwell Publishers, 1997.

Hanegraaff, Hank. *The Apocalypse Code: Find Out What the Bible REALLY Says About the End Times . . . and Why It Matters Today.* Nashville: Thomas Nelson, 2007.

Howe, Thomas A. "Does Genre Determine Meaning." *Christian Apologetics Journal* 6 (Spring 2007): 1–20.

Kohler, Ludwig, and Walter Baumgartner. *The Hebrew and Aramaic Lexicon of the Old Testament.* Translated by M. E. J. Richardson. Leiden: Brill, 2001.

Latourette, Kenneth Scott. *A History of Christianity.* New York: Harper & Brothers, Publishers, 1953.

Lewis, Charlton T., and Charles Short. *A Latin Dictionary.* Oxford: At The Clarendon Press, 1966.

Liddell, Henry George, and Robert Scott, ed. *A Greek-English Lexicon.* Oxford: Clarendon Press, 1996.

Louw, Johannes P., and Eugene A. Nida, ed. *Greek-English Lexicon of the New Testament Based on Semantic Domains,* 2d ed. New York: United Bible Societies, 1989.

Mathison, Keith A., ed. *When Shall These Things Be?* (Phillipsburg, New Jersey: P&R Publishing, 2004.

Matyszak, Philip. *Chronicle of the Roman Republic.* London: Thames & Hudson, 2003.

McKechnie, Jean L., ed. *Webster's New Twentieth Century Dictionary of the English Language,* 2d ed. New York: William Collins and World Publishing Company, 1977.

Metzger, Bruce M. *The Text of the New Testament,* 3d ed. New York: Oxford University Press, 1992.

Moulton, James Hope, and George Milligan. *The Vocabulary of the Greek Testament Illustrated from the Papyri and Other Non-Literary Sources.* Grand Rapids: William B. Eerdmans Publishing Company, 1976.

Murray, John. *The Epistle to the Romans.* Grand Rapids: Wm. B. Eerdmans Publishing Co., 1977.

O'Leary, Don. *Roman Catholicism and Modern Science: A History.* New York: The Continuum International Publishing Group, 2006.

Osborne, Grant R. *The Hermeneutical Spiral.* Downers Grove, Illinois: InterVarsity Press, 1991.

Oswalt, John N. *The Book of Isaiah: Chapters 40–66.* Grand Rapids: William B. Eerdmans Publishing Company, 1998.

Pentecost, J. Dwight. *Things to Come.* Grand Rapids: Zondervan Publishing House, 1958.

Schäfer, Peter. *The History of the Jews in the Greco-Roman World.* London: Routledge, 2003.

Sproul, R. C. *Knowing Scripture.* Downers Grove, Illinois: InterVarsity Press, 1977.

Terry, Milton S. *Biblical Hermeneutics: A Treatise on the Interpretation of the Old and New Testaments.* Vol. 2, *Library of Biblical and Theological Literature,* ed. George R. Crooks and John F. Hurst. New York: Phillips & Hunt, 1883.

Bibliography

Walker, Williston, et. al. *A History of the Christian Church*, 4th ed. New York: Charles Scriber's Sons, 1985.

Wallace, Daniel B. *Greek Grammar Beyond the Basics.* Grand Rapids: Zondervan Publishing House, 1996.

Waltke, Bruce K., and M. O'Connor. *An Introduction to Biblical Hebrew Syntax.* Winona Lake, Indiana: Eisenbrauns, 1990.

Walvoord, John F. *The Millennial Kingdom*, Grand Rapids: Zondervan Publishing House, 1959.

———, and Roy B. Zuck, ed. *The Bible Knowledge Commentary: Old Testament.* Wheaton, Illinois: Victor Books, 1985.

West, John G. *Darwin Day in America: How Our Politics and Culture Have Been Dehumanized in the Name of Science.* Wilmington, Delaware: ISI Books, 2007.

Index of Names

Index of Scripture